The world turned upside down?

B+T OCT 21 2002 $23.08 02-239

MANCHESTER
UNIVERSITY PRESS

With thanks to Stephanie
for her constant support and assistance

The world turned upside down?

Globalization and
the future of the state

R.J. Barry Jones

Manchester University Press
Manchester and New York

distributed exclusively in the USA by St. Martin's Press

Copyright © R.J. Barry Jones 2000

The right of R.J. Barry Jones to be identified as the author of this work has been asserted by him in accordance with the Copyright, Designs and Patents Act 1988.

Published by Manchester University Press
Oxford Road, Manchester M13 9NR, UK
and Room 400, 175 Fifth Avenue, New York, NY 10010, USA
http://www.man.ac.uk/mup

Distributed exclusively in the USA by
St. Martin's Press, Inc., 175 Fifth Avenue, New York,
NY 10010, USA

Distributed exclusively in Canada by
UBC Press, University of British Columbia, 6344 Memorial Road,
Vancouver, BC, Canada V6T 1Z2

British Library Cataloguing-in-Publication Data
A catalogue record for this book is available from the British Library

Library of Congress Cataloging-in-Publication Data
Jones, R.J. Barry,
    The world turned upside down? : globalization and the future of the
state / R.J. Barry Jones.
        p. cm.
    Includes bibliographical references and index.
    ISBN 0-7190-5100-2 (hc.) — ISBN 0-7190-5101-0 (pbk.)
    1. International economic relations. 2. International trade. 3. Technological
innovations. 4. Industrial policy. 5. Competition, International. 6. State,
The I. Title. II. Title: Globalization and the future of the state.
HF1359.J66 2000
337 21—dc21

ISBN   0 7190 5100 2 hardback
       0 7190 5101 0 paperback

First published 2000

06 05 04 03 02 01 00   10 9 8 7 6 5 4 3 2 1

$$337$$
$$JON$$

Typeset in Sabon
by Graphicraft Limited, Hong Kong
Printed in Great Britain
by Bell & Bain Ltd, Glasgow

Contents

List of tables

List of figures

I

Globalization – concepts, precedents, origins and implications

1

Introduction: the problem of globalization

This book is a study of the fate of one of the most dramatic and dynamic institutions of the modern world – the nation state. Nation states, or more properly states that have succeeded in securing the attachments of territorially identified populations, have defined the contemporary political universe. In combination with the other, and related, forces of industrialism and capitalism, states have also driven the transformation of the human condition between the late medieval age and today.

A thoroughgoing review of the contemporary role and effectiveness of states is prompted by the challenges that appear to have been posed to the traditional states by the progress of globalization. A central paradox informs contemporary concerns: that, on the one hand, the state seems to be under threat from economic, technical and cultural developments, while, on the other hand, the military capabilities of states have never been greater and the concentration of state military strength – in the hands of the United States of America – has never been exceeded. By one view, therefore, the government of the USA is faced with the progressive erosion of policy effectiveness across a wide range of central issues; by another view, the government of the USA possesses an unprecedented capacity to intervene among, exercise coercive force over, and ultimately annihilate peoples in all quarters of the globe.

Both of the alternative visions of the current realities are, however, far too simple. Globalization remains a contested[1] interpretation of the contemporary global condition. Moreover, any advance of globalization is far from complete and highly uneven in its form and impact.[2] Most significantly for this discussion, globalization is far from being an autonomous phenomenon – a pattern of developments driven purely by economic forces and technological imperatives. Many other factors both drive and check globalization. Most particularly, the actions of governments of established states have created many of the basic conditions within which movement towards greater globalization has taken place.[3] Moreover, many of those same states retain the most powerful capacities for restraining, and even reversing, the further development of globalization. The governments of states continue, furthermore, to exert a profound influence upon the practical impact of globalization upon individual societies.

It is the purpose of this discussion to explore the contemporary and future role of states in a world in which those developments that are commonly associated with the idea of globalization have been unleashed.

The modern state: rhetorics and realities

The contemporary world has been forged by the combined effects of a number of powerful, composite forces: the market economy; the accelerating advance of science and technology; the progress of foundational ideas about the human condition; and, by no means least, the pressures of political and military competition and conflict. At the intersection of these forces has been the modern state. The state has been a major influence upon the development of many of these forces, which have, in turn, moulded its own development.

The pivotal role of the modern state has not, however, excluded it from controversy and contestation. The definitive claim of the modern state is to unchallenged domestic sovereignty, or absolute legitimate jurisdiction over all peoples inhabiting its established territory and over all issues arising therein. Such a claim to sovereignty has long been challenged by its many practical qualifications throughout history, many of which now appear to be increasing under the seemingly remorseless advance of globalization.

The practical limitations of state sovereignty may not always have been obvious to the citizens of the relatively small number of states that have enjoyed leading positions within the system of states and high levels of domestic order and economic comfort. Such states have, however, never constituted more than a small minority within the world 'community'. The inhabitants of smaller, or more fragile, states and societies have long confronted the substantial limitations to practical sovereignty that existed even within the most settled periods in the history of the system of states.[4] Many were colonized by the leading states during the seventeenth, eighteenth and early nineteenth centuries. Many of those that were not formal colonies fell under the influence of the leading states, with consequential limitations upon their practical freedom of manoeuvre and domestic sovereignty, their status as independent states remaining little more than a legal fiction.

Practical limitations upon effective sovereignty have not been the only impediment to statism. There have also been profound political and philosophical challenges. Indeed, the very emergence of the modern state prompted its rejection. In the emergent monarchical state of France, centralizing tendencies were opposed through popular uprisings from the regions, while the secular statist project was challenged, fundamentally, by the Gnostics of the Albigensian heresy.[5]

Religious opposition to the crystallization of the strong, secular state was equally evident in many of the popular movements that emerged within the Parliamentary arm – Levellers, Fifth Monarchists, and the like – as the English Civil War progressed towards the emergence of the new Cromwellian Commonwealth.[6]

Concepts of the modern state thus vary considerably on the role and contribution of the institution; the proper functions that ought to be performed for, and within, its constituent society; and on its very naturalness. Early advocates of the strong state, including Jean Bodin[7] in France and Thomas Hobbes[8] in post-Civil War England, saw it as an essential source and guarantor of peace and stability within domestic society. Recent history demonstrated for both Bodin and Hobbes that a strong and viable state was by no means guaranteed; it was something to be preferred and promoted, rather than assumed as inevitable in the face of anarchical tendencies.

However, a problem of consistency confronted advocates of the modern state who sought its justification in the preservation of internal peace yet had to acknowledge its role in international conflict. Such tensions could most readily be resolved through the invocation of communitarian principles, in which actual or imagined communities formed the 'natural' bases of social existence and, hence, 'international' life. Such referents became increasingly important as the power of religious beliefs and warrants began to wane. In an increasingly secular age, it thus became increasingly difficult to deploy the 'divine right' of sovereigns as the basis for legitimacy or to invoke some 'god-given' aggressiveness of mankind as the reason for violent inter-societal conflict. Legitimacy now had to rest upon the relations of mutual obligation between sovereigns and subjects within a 'natural' community,[9] with inter-societal conflict justified by supposed differences of substance between the members of distinct societies.

The perceived pressures of external competition and threat appeared to reinforce domestic requirements for an effective state. A seemingly ceaseless struggle for power and resources amongst state sovereigns thus came to parallel, and frequently complement, the intensifying competition amongst commercial interests for trade routes, overseas resources and, increasingly, colonial acquisitions. The mercantilist state of the early modern period thus sought the dual objectives of domestic control and external primacy, in addition to the prosecution of commercial aims.[10] The growing range of interests that were reflected in the purposes and policies of mercantilist states had, however, the effect of diluting the primacy of the interests of the sovereign. Commercial interests were keen not only to recruit the state to support their foreign aspirations but also to ensure that the state did not, in turn, seek to restrain their activities unduly or undermine their rights to the property that they had accumulated.

The notion of the limited state thus enjoyed increasing advocacy throughout the modern era. Such a state contrasts with that of the authoritative (and often authoritarian) Leviathan of the earlier theorists of the state like Bodin and Hobbes. It is also distinct from the aggressive mercantilist European state of the seventeenth and eighteenth centuries, in its limited range of legitimate purposes and practices. The liberal state is one such limited state, in which the state is prescribed a role as a guarantor of supposedly pre-existing individual rights and freedoms, including that of freedom of economic endeavour and exchange.[11]

Limited states are not, however, confined to the liberal variant. A tradition of 'Republican', or constitutional, states also exists that emphasizes the constructive role of the political institutions of the modern state[12] in forming a civic culture, supportive of a politics of tolerant association, reasoned compromise and harmony amongst peoples of diverse interests and preferences. Such a republican or constitutional polity echoes the Aristotelian prescription of politics as the foundation of the good life[13] and, while not inevitably modest and pacific in all its doings, does afford the prospect of reasoned and restrained behaviour towards its citizens and towards other societies.

However, states, in whatever variant, have not met with universal acclaim or acceptance. A strong anti-statist sentiment has, as was suggested earlier, been evident from the earliest days of the emergence of the modern state. Modern anti-statism was, however, to flourish with full force only after the dramas of the French Revolution and the era of Napoleonic rule.

Napoleon Bonaparte's conversion of the French revolutionary republic into an expansionary empire had a profound impact upon critical views of the modern state. Radical thought within France and much of the rest of Europe became transfixed by the apparent betrayal of the equalitarian ideals of the French revolution and by the spectre of 'Bonapartism'.[14] Most sections of the First International agreed upon the diagnosis of what had gone wrong, while disagreeing vociferously, and sometimes violently, about how to avoid its repetition in future revolutionary ventures. From such debates and disputes emerged, eventually, an identifiable anarchist critique of, and programme for action against, the modern state.[15]

Modern anarchism poses profound practical and ethical challenges to the state. Practically, anarchist critics highlight the central, if often disguised, role of violence within the modern state. They argue that the state maintains itself in a society that is characterized by vast inequalities of wealth, status, influence and effective power only by its monopolization, and potential deployment, of considerable levels of coercive force.[16] Force is thus internalized within, and integral to, the modern state.[17] The relations among such states are, therefore, also founded upon force. Indeed, the 'myth' of external threat is often the nominal excuse for the preservation of extensive armed forces, which are thence available for internal repression when necessary. The contemporary state thus exhibits a Janus-like character, with the complexion of both faces coloured and distorted by the means, and disposition, to violence.

The moral challenge posed by anarchists to the contemporary state derives from their diagnosis of its essentially violent character. Inequality and exploitation within societies are maintained through such inherent violence. War and destruction amongst societies are occasioned and sustained by the institutionalized violence of the state. Only when the state and its attendant culture of institutionalized violence is abolished will, in the view of anarchists, humanity be free to realize its potential for peace, harmony, general well-being and personal fulfilment. Karl Marx and his immediate followers adopted a similar view of the state, its ill effects and its desirable abolition, differing only (but highly significantly) over the means by which this end might best be achieved. Contemporary 'critical' theorists also echo, often unconsciously, the earlier anarchist critique of the state, identifying its essentially constructed character and its divisive and repressive effects upon humanity.[18]

Disputes over the desirable form, and even the desirability of the existence, of the state are further complicated by the question of the appropriate membership of the state. The progressive secularization of political authority within the modern era generated a need, as has been seen, for new forms of legitimation for the state and its rulers. The primary answer to this problem was that of the 'nation state'. The idea that the state encompassed, and represented the interests of, the 'nation' had been gradually emerging during the sixteenth and seventeenth centuries. It was, however, to be crystallized in the era of the French Revolution and the subsequent Revolutionary, and then Napoleonic, Wars. The armies of the new France were no longer fighting merely for their sovereign, no longer as mercenaries in the service of commercial interests, but were now the 'nation in arms', fighting the foreign enemies of their new society. The state was now nationalized; and, with it, so was war.

The notion of the nation state has, however, continued to raise difficulties. The simplest formula embraces a clearly differentiable, pre-existing national grouping for which the state comes to act. Unfortunately, few coherent definitions of a national grouping fit the population of virtually any modern state, and the notion that any such national groupings clearly pre-existed the emergence of their corresponding states is highly contentious.[19] Rather than being created to serve the needs of the pre-existing 'nation', the crystallization of the modern, and particularly the secular, state is closely connected to the emergence of the notion of a 'nation' and to its practical definition. Indeed, in the extreme cases of populations of considerable ethnic, cultural, or linguistic diversity, the notion of a nation-state has been replaced by that of a state-nation: that is, a 'nationality' that has been defined by, and formed through, participation in the institutions and practices of a state that embraces, or is created to embrace, such a diverse constituency. The modern state is thus a highly variable and much debated institution. It has, however, marked the culture and functioning of the modern world system profoundly. It has been highly variable in its forms and effectiveness. States, it is argued by political geographers, have dictated and dominated the territorial configuration of global space.[20] Political sociologists have viewed the modern state as a container of political and military power and of society.[21] It has certainly imposed itself upon the political landscape as one of the most powerful institutions, with considerable powers of self-justification and capacities for self-preservation.

The desirable character of the state has also been much debated within political theory and has remained open to the most profound of practical and moral challenges. Such diversity in practice and principle significantly complicates any discussion of the effects upon 'the state' of contemporary globalization.

Globalization: fact or fiction

If the contemporary state is a complex and contested institution, the phenomenon of globalization is elusiveness itself. The key problems here are those of definition in principle and those of identification in practice. Definitions of globalization are generally imprecise in content and impressionistic in referent. They highlight some of the more dramatic features of contemporary economic, social and political life and then proceed to presume transformational implications for the human condition, or at least the condition of a large part of humanity. The concept does, however, command considerable attention and therefore requires further careful consideration.

The meaning of globalization
Most discussions of globalization focus initially upon contemporary changes in the economic realm. Two such changes stand out: the rapid advance of cross-border integration in a number of areas of economic activity, particularly financial and manufacturing; and the related application of ever more powerful technologies for the gathering, processing and transmission of information. The

combined effects of these two changes is then witnessed in the steady acceleration of the rate at which human beings experience changes in their economic lives and an apparent reduction in the spaces that separate them from their fellows, both within established societies and, most significantly, across traditional territorial frontiers: such space–time compression being thus distinctive and definitive of contemporary globalization, in the view of some influential observers.[22]

The practical manifestations of such profound changes are many. Competitive pressures impact with greater force and speed upon firms and workers than they did historically. New technologies become available more rapidly than in the past and demand more speedy application in the defence of competitiveness. People are able to travel internationally with far greater ease and at lower financial cost than previously. World-wide electronic communications are also possible with a speed, lack of restriction, and cheapness that is unprecedented.[23] Such new conditions create the possibilities of new global networks in all areas of life, of global tastes for consumer products, of new global social and political movements and, in the ultimate, a new global society with a new global culture.[24]

Three interrelated questions immediately arise about such a notion of globalization. The first question is whether the identified sources of globalization have, or will come to have, the effects anticipated by globalization theorists and, if so, how far matters have advanced to date. The second is whether the supposed sources of globalization are actually that new: if not, then doubts might be raised about the novelty of the resultant condition. The third concerns the current condition of the world: whether globalization is an established fact or merely a state of affairs that will (or might) emerge from processes and developments that are currently in train. Many of these complex questions can be unravelled by comparing a condition of globalization with that of increased internationalization within the world system. They will be further elaborated in the next chapter, when a brief historical comparison is made between contemporary conditions and those existing a century or so ago.

Such issues lie behind the emergence of four broad positions that can be identified within the 'globalization debate'. The first identifies globalization with increasing homogenization within the global system. The second – the 'strong globalization' view[25] – contends that homogeneity remains highly unlikely within the global system, but that a range of qualitative and quantitative changes have combined to introduce a new condition, or set of processes, into world affairs that warrant the novel term 'globalization'. The third position – the 'weak globalization' perspective – maintains that many of the undoubtedly important developments of recent decades signal a significant increase in internationalization within the international political economy that has complex but variable consequences for politics, economics and society, but that has not ushered in a distinctively new era in human affairs. The final – rejectionist – position defends the view that nothing of any great or irreversible significance has taken place in the latter half of the twentieth century and that the world continues with 'business as usual', with states retaining full sovereignty and peoples continuing to be divided by culture, language and attachments of nationality.

The prospects of global homogeneity are dismissed by all but the most utopian (or dystopian) of observers. The rejectionists' view of a world of no substantial change also flies in the face of far too many pressing features of the contemporary world to bear close examination. However, the debate between the globalization of the 'strong globalizationists' and the internationalization of the 'weak globalizationists' remains central to the analysis of recent developments.

The world has experienced considerable variation in levels of 'international' trade and financial flows, cross-border social interactions and communications, and migration from one country to another. Internationalization has been the term traditionally ascribed to increases in such inter-societal flows in the past: internationalization of finance, trade, social patterns and human mobility. Moreover increased internationalization, and the growth of benign interdependencies, has often been heralded as the coming of new dawn in the past: the emergence of a new, more prosperous and more peaceful era for humanity, as will be seen subsequently. A central issue, therefore, remains that of differentiating between the mere advance of internationalization and the grander notion of globalization: an exercise that requires both a direct comparison of the two concepts and an interrogation of the ultimate significance of globalization itself.

Globalization versus Internationalization

A central debate for most students of contemporary developments thus concerns the differentiation of globalization from internationalization. This is a demanding task, for many authoritative uses of the term internationalization also embrace conditions that are emphasized by globalization theorists. Thus Robert Keohane and Helen Milner, while discussing internationalization, declare that: 'Internationalization . . . refers to the processes generated by underlying shifts in transaction costs that produce observable flows of goods, services and capital.'[26] Such processes suggest, in these observers' view, the following propositions: 'As internationalization progresses, the tradables sector will expand and the economy will become more sensitive to world market price trends and shocks. The likelihood of major domestic policy and institutional reforms will grow as internationalization makes the economy more vulnerable to externally generated economic shocks' and 'Internationalization will undermine the autonomy and efficacy of government macroeconomic policy. It will more seriously constrain the behavior of left-wing governments than of right-wing governments. Capital mobility will have more far-reaching consequences than trade openness.'[27] Two important corollaries also follow from such core propositions: 'Internationalization should affect even countries whose economies are not open' and 'Internationally mobile capital will gain political power, relative to labor and political officials, as internationalization proceeds.'[28]

The growth of international financial integration and of international trade are both highlighted in Keohane and Milner's view of internationalization, with heaviest emphasis being placed upon the enhanced flows of capital and finance. Moreover, the shift in effective power from labour and politicians to those in control of capital is also signalled. Internationalization thus shares common core characteristics with the more ambitious notion of globalization, and it is this element of commonality that complicates the differentiation of the two terms.

The difficulty of distinguishing between globalization and internationalization thus requires the characterization of an extreme – or 'strong' – form of globalization, which can then be compared systematically with the conditions characteristic of the looser notion of internationalization. Table 1.1 thus offers a 'strong' outline of globalization and its systematic comparison with the less demanding notion of internationalization.

Table 1.1 Globalization or internationalization?

Issues	Internationalization	Globalization
Space–time compression	'Distant' events and developments impact unevenly upon 'local life', including economic life, depending upon context and issue.	'Distant' events and developments impact powerfully and rapidly upon many aspects of 'local life', especially economic life.
Finance	Shares are readily traded between 'national' markets.	Investment, borrowing and lending take place with no regard to national borders.
	Flows of finance and capital are growing substantially.	There is a seamless global market for capital and finance, with 24-hour trading and no barriers between the markets of different countries.
	The maintenance of currency values by national governments grows more difficult in the face of the pressures of international financial flows.	Currency values cannot be controlled without the surrender of control of 'national' monetary policy.
	Fiscal policies remain under the control of state governments but are subject to some growing external pressures and constraints.	Fiscal policy is wholly dictated by 'external' factors and forces, as mobile capital, management and skilled labour are able to relocate to areas with more favourable tax regimes.
Trade and business activities	Exports increase as a proportion of GDP.	All goods and services are exported, save for those that have to be supplied and consumed locally.
	Increasing levels of transnationally integrated production.	Transnationally integrated production is the norm.

Table 1.1   (*cont'd*)

Issues	Internationalization	Globalization
	FDI increase, but remain less significant, proportionally, than 'domestic' and/or 'regional' levels.	FDI levels exceed 'domestic' levels of investment and show no territorial biases proportionally.
	More manufacturing is undertaken within the home country or region proportionally.	Manufacturing activity is evenly distributed worldwide, with no territorial bias proportionally.
	Increasing levels of R&D are undertaken 'overseas', but remain lower proportionally than 'domestic' and/or 'regional' levels.	R&D is fully distributed around the world and shows no territorial biases proportionally.
	Non-domestic sales increase, but remain lower proportionally than 'domestic' and/or 'regional' sales.	Firms' sales are now world-wide and show no territorial biases proportionally.
	Firms' earnings from foreign activities are growing, but remain lower proportionally than 'domestic' and/or 'regional' earnings.	Firms' earnings are now world-wide and show no territorial biases proportionally.
	Senior management of the leading TNCs is increasingly multinational, but foreign recruits remain lower proportionally than 'domestic' and/or 'regional' recruitment.	Firms' senior management is recruited proportionally world-wide and shows no territorial biases.
Society and culture	International travel increases, but remains far lower than the levels of 'domestic' travel.	There are no territorial, or societal, biases in patterns of interpersonal interaction and association.

Table 1.1 (*cont'd*)

Issues	*Internationalization*	*Globalization*
	There is increasing cross-border contact and trans-societal transmission of cultural products and cultural values, but the products and values of some cultures are more prominent than others.	Culture is homogenous and world-wide, with all areas of the world contributing equally (or proportionally) to the new global culture.
Major effects	Increasing internationalization provides opportunities for economies and societies, but complicates the task, and prospects, of public governance. States are challenged, especially in areas of macro-economic policy, but retain substantial capabilities. Effective international public governance is likely to lie in reinforced inter-governmentalism and regime construction and/or regionalization of the world political economy.	*Benign:* There is a new era of global opportunity and prosperity. A new global society emerges and new forms of genuinely global public governance are created. *Malign:* There is intensified global exploitation, economic and social disruption and resulting disorder. Effective public governance is compromised at all levels. The state, in particular, has lost effective control of economic developments. The path forward from general disorder is uncertain and hazardous, with a considerable danger of revivalist nationalisms and other divisive-isms.

Table 1.1 *(cont'd)*

Issues	Internationalization	Globalization
Theoretical implications	The international system is to be viewed as complex and uneven, with varying patterns of unilateral, bilateral and multilateral developments in different domains.	Holistic tendencies are evident in the world system.
•	The approach is essentially non-deterministic (merely possibilistic, or no more than probabilistic) about future developments.	A small number of basic factors or forces (or even one) are pushing the world, irresistibly and irreversibly, in one overall direction towards a transformed human condition.

Note: GDP: Gross Domestic Product; FDI: Foreign Direct Investment; R&D: Research and Development; TNCs: Transnational Corporations.

Such a comparison of globalization with internationalization raises a wide range of critical issues, many of which will be addressed at later stages in this discussion. Some, however, require immediate comment, however brief.

An initial observation, which will be taken up again later in the discussion, is that of the general unevenness of developments in different arenas of the global economy, social system and political system. Global integration has thus proceeded further in the financial arena than in most others. Within the various arenas, there is also considerable variation in the level of global integration, with variations between different sectors of activity and amongst different actors within each sector.

Globalization, it will be recalled, is not necessarily synonymous with global homogenization, however. Many factors and influences will continue to sustain differences amongst societies. However, highly advanced globalization should narrow, substantially, many of the traditional differences that have characterized distinct states and societies in the past and that often persist into the present.

However, an advanced level of globalization might still be indicated by the ending of all territorial differentiation in markets and production systems, save for those dictated by such unavoidable geographical constraints as the location of physical reserves like oil or minerals or by physical conditions, such as decisive differences in climate. A fully globalized company should thus market identical goods in all markets, produce those goods wherever locational advantages dictate, and secure geographical proportions of global sales in direct proportion to the relative size of each market within the overall world market.

Such observations do not, however, overwhelm the more subtle arguments about the current, or emergent, condition of globalization. Levels of international economic integration that fall short of the criteria of full globalization that have been outlined in Table 1.1 could be compatible with the operation of those processes and forces, such as the progressive compression of time and space, that some globalization theorists identify with the phenomenon.[29] The core analytical problem of quantity versus quality thus confronts the 'globalization debate' and complicates all references to empirical 'evidence'.

If evidence about current conditions in any aspect of economic, social or political developments can support either the proposition that globalization has arrived, or is soon to arrive, or the alternative argument that we are witnessing no more that the enhancement of internationalization, with ultimately limited and even reversible implications for states and their constituent societies, then conclusive deliberations are rendered difficult if not impossible.

In practice, a 'weak globalization' perspective may be far more compatible with a world in which increased internationalization coexists with the persistence of many differences amongst societies, and other actors upon the global stage, than would be true for the 'strong globalization' view.

Any orderly discussion of the contending views about globalization and its implications does, thus, require some examination of the empirical evidence – of contemporary trends and their comparison with past conditions – and a careful evaluation of the varying arguments about the sources and likely effects of the further advance of globalization in the future and of potential obstacles to such developments. A condition, or set of processes, that had no identifiable, or comprehensible, effects upon important conditions or developments would be so lacking in substance as to command little interest or analytical attention.

The state of globalization: contrasting evidence and contending arguments

The current state of globalization will be the subject of the bulk of the next chapter. A brief initial survey of the contrasting evidence will, however, help to set the scene for much of the subsequent discussion.

Globalization theorists, of the 'strong' and sometimes of the 'weak' varieties, usually blend two elements into their arguments about the arrival of this new condition. Qualitative arguments are developed about the probable, and sometimes inevitable, effects of recent developments like the integration of world financial markets or the introduction of new technologies of information gathering, processing and transmission. The globalization argument is then supported by quantitative evidence pointing to the high, and growing, levels of global financial transactions; cross-border business mergers and acquisitions; internationalized production; globalized branding and marketing of products; the international movement of peoples; and the rapid growth in the levels of, and media for, inter-societal communications.

Trade is one clear indicator of increasing internationalization and possible globalization. Jonathan Perraton and his associates point to the rapid rise in the ratio of exports to national wealth creation in recent decades (Table 1.2) and the equally impressive rise in imports as a proportion of domestic wealth creation (Table 1.3). Increasing cross-border financial transactions are a further indicator in these directions. Lowell Bryan and Diana Farrell highlight the massive recent expansion of transactions in the international currency markets (Table 1.4) and of cross-border sales and purchases of stocks and shares (Table 1.5).

Table 1.2 Exports to Gross Domestic Product ratios for all Advanced Industrial Countries in constant prices (percentages)

	1913	*1951*	*1973*	*1985*
Exports–GDP %	11.2	8.3	18.0	23.1

Source: Table 3 of J. Perraton, D. Goldblatt, D. Held and A. McGrew, 'The Globalization of Economic Activity', *New Political Economy*, vol. 2, no. 2, p. 262.

Table 1.3 Imports to Gross Domestic Product ratios for Developed Countries in constant prices (percentages)

	1880–1900	1901–13	1959–72	1973–87
Imports–GDP %	12.4	13.3	15.4	21.7

Source: Table 3 of J. Perraton, D. Goldblatt, D. Held and A. McGrew, 'The Globalization of Economic Activity', *New Political Economy*, vol. 2, no. 2, p. 262.

Table 1.4 Daily trading in international currency markets ($US billion)

1986	1989	1992	1995
207	620	880	1,100

Source: L. Bryan and D. Farrell, *Market Unbound: Unleashing Global Capitalism* (New York: John Wiley and Sons, 1996), p. 26.

Table 1.5 Cross-border sales and purchases of stocks and shares ($US billion)

1980	1982	1984	1986	1988	1990	1992	1994
93	96	155	378	517	616	789	1,523

Source: L. Bryan and D. Farrell, *Market Unbound: Unleashing Global Capitalism* (New York: John Wiley and Sons, 1996), p. 34.

However, the extent and impact of such advances in international economic integration are both questioned by other observers. Some argue that the pace of growth in international trade has been more modest and has, most significantly, only recently risen above the levels achieved in the years immediately before the outbreak of the First World War (Table 1.6). Again, while global financial integration has advanced substantially in recent years, it has, for a wide variety of reasons, yet to eliminate all state-based divisions within the world's financial system. Thus, while overnight interest rates in different major economies continue to show some signs of correlated movement, they continue to diverge significantly in

Table 1.6   Ratio of merchandise trade to Gross Domestic Product at current prices (exports and imports combined)

	1913	1950	1973	1993
France	35.4	21.2	29.0	32.6
Germany	35.1	20.1	35.2	38.1
Japan	31.4	16.9	18.3	14.3
Netherlands	103.6	70.2	80.1	85.9
UK	44.7	36.0	39.3	47.2
USA	11.2	7.0	10.5	17.0

Sources: P. Hirst and G. Thompson, *Globalization in Question* (Cambridge: Polity Press, 1996), Table 2.5 for 1913, 1950 and 1973; and *World Development Report, 1995* (Oxford University Press for the World Bank), Tables 13 and 3 for 1993 figures.

Figure 1.1   Overnight interest rates – UK, USA and Japan, 1984–95

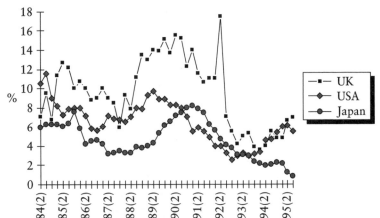

Datum points: end of second quarter of each year.
Data sources: various.

levels and direction of movement at critical moments as they come under the influence of a variety of such factors as local economic and monetary policies, market expectations about exchange rates and future inflation rates (Figure 1.1).

Globalization and the state

Controversy over globalization, its existence, nature and extent, also extends to its implications for individuals, businesses, economies, societies and, most particularly, the contemporary state. Indeed, the more extreme statements of the 'strong' theory of globalization anticipate the imminent demise of the state as an instrument of economic governance.

Much of the subsequent discussion will be devoted to the challenges posed by growing globalization, or indeed internationalization, to the contemporary state. The argument that the state is declining as an economic agency rests upon many of the definitive features emphasized in the earlier discussion of the meaning of the term globalization: internationalization of finance and production; accelerating applications of transformational technologies; and the growing interconnections among the peoples of the world. In consequence, much of economic and social life is believed to be escaping from the effective control of established states at the same time that the range and complexity of the problems facing such states are becoming overwhelming.

Such a vision prompts two central sets of questions. The first set concerns the empirical veracity of the vision itself: does it do justice to the role of states, individually and collectively, in the developments that have driven growing internationalization, and possible globalization; is it an accurate description of the current situation with regard to the roles and capacities of states; and, by no means least, does it capture the entire range of possibilities facing states, the global system and their interrelationship?

The second set of questions stimulated by the 'strong' globalization view of the faltering state focuses upon the consequences of such a development: what functions will still have to be performed for the peoples of the world as a whole, and/or as differentiable societies; what will be the prospects that such functions will be performed effectively if the effective states dissolve; and, what will be the consequences if such needs cease to be met within the global system?

The discussion in later chapters will explore each of these issues and questions in detail. It will be argued that the 'strong' globalization thesis neglects the central role that states have played and continue to play in the movement towards greater internationalization;

overstates, substantially, the current weaknesses of states; and, most significantly, is dangerously monotonic in its vision of the further dilution of the role and influence of states, or at least of some states. The discussion will also review the wide range of requirements that states have traditionally fulfilled for their peoples, differentiating, as carefully as possible, those requirements that will tend to diminish, and even disappear, in the face of increasing internationalization and globalization, and those that will persist, and even grow, as such developments continue upon their course.

This detailed review of the problems of possible state dissolution will require a reconsideration of the functions that justify the existence and operation of states, or their functional equivalents. This discussion will, it is important to emphasize, explicitly abjure functionalist teleology: it will be consistently argued that the mere existence of a need amongst any portion of humanity is not a guarantee of its satisfaction, through individual behaviour, collective action, the emergence of 'appropriate' institutions or the adoption of effective policies by responsible authorities. Moreover, it is not intended to convey the impression that such requirements can be met effectively only by the kinds of states that are the dominant formal political institutions on the world political stage. Indeed, a plethora of alternative political arrangements might be deemed desirable on a wide range of considerations. This discussion will, however, focus on the prevailing 'reality' of a system of states that exerts a profound influence upon political, economic and social affairs; upon the challenges that are posed to states by the growth of internationalization and/or globalization; and the continuing role that states will play in the further development of an international system beset by the pressures of increasing internationalization and/or globalization.

Notes

1 Paul Hirst and Grahame Thompson, *Globalization in Question* (Cambridge: Polity Press, 1995).

2 R.J. Barry Jones, *Globalisation and Interdependence in the International Political Economy: Rhetoric and Reality* (London: Pinter Publishers, 1995).

3 On the financial sector see: Susan Strange, *States and Markets: An Introduction to International Political Economy* (London: Pinter Publishers, 1988).

4 On the limitations of small and micro states see: Robert L. Rothstein, *The Weak in the World of the Strong* (New York: Columbia University Press, 1977); and M. Handel, *Weak States in the International System* (London: Frank Cass, 1991).

5 M.D. Costen, *The Cathars and the Albigensian Crusade* (Manchester, Manchester University Press, 1997).

6 G.H. Sabine, *A History of Political Theory* (London: Harrap, 3rd edn, 1937), Ch. 24.

7 Sabine, *A History of Political Theory*, esp. Ch. 20.

8 Sheldon S. Wolin, *Politics and Vision: Continuity and Innovation in Western Political Thought* (London: George Allen and Unwin, 1961), Ch. 8.

9 J. Hampton, *Hobbes and the Social Contract Tradition* (Cambridge: Cambridge University Press, 1986).

10 W.E. Minchinson (ed.), *Mercantilism: System or Expediency* (Lexington, MA: D.C. Heath, 1969).

11 Especially Herbert Spencer, *The Man versus The State* (first published 1884), Penguin books edition with an introduction by Donald Macrae (Harmondsworth: Penguin Books, 1969).

12 On Montesquieu's see: Sabine, *A History of Political Theory*, pp. 553–4.

13 Aristotle, *Politics*, Bk I Ch. 2, Penguin edn, trans. T.A. Sinclair (Harmondsworth: Penguin), pp. 26–9.

14 George Lichtheim, *The Origins of Socialism* (New York: Praeger, 1968), esp. Part 1.

15 On anarchist political theory see: George Woodcock, *Anarchism* (Harmondsworth: Penguin Books, 1963); and April Carter, *The Political Theory of Anarchism* (London; Routledge and Kegan Paul, 1971).

16 Especially Michael Bakunin, *Statism and Anarchy* (1873), reprinted in Marshall S. Shatz (ed.), *The Essential Works of Anarchism* (New York: Bantam Books, 1971), pp. 155–83.

17 See Leo Tolstoy, *The Kingdom of God is Within You* (1893), reprinted in Shatz, *The Essential Works of Anarchism*, pp. 231–65.

18 R.J. Barry Jones, *Anti-Statism as a Critical Disposition in International Relations* (Reading: Reading Papers in Politics, 1991).

19 Anthony Smith, *The Ethnic Origins of Nations* (Oxford: Blackwell, 1986).

20 J.A. Agnew and S. Corbridge, *Mastering Space: Hegemony, Territory and International Political Economy* (London: Routledge, 1995).

21 Michael Mann, *The Sources of Social Power*, Vol. 1 (Cambridge: Cambridge University Press, 1986).

22 David Harvey, *The Condition of Postmodernity* (Oxford; Basil Blackwell, 1989).

23 Manuel Castells, *The Informational City: Information Technology, Economic Restructuring, and the Urban-Regional Process* (Oxford: Basil Blackwell, 1989).

24 Martin Shaw, *Global Society and International Relations* (Cambridge: Polity Press, 1994); and Martin Albrow, *The Global Age* (Cambridge: Polity Press 1996).

25 Hirst and Thompson, *Globalization in Question.*

26 Robert O. Keohane and Helen V. Milner, *Internationalization and Domestic Politics* (Cambridge: Cambridge University Press, 1996), p. 4.

27 *Ibid.*, p. 18.

28 *Ibid.*, p. 19.

29 Harvey, *The Condition of Postmodernity.*

2

Then and now – continuity and discontinuity in the international political economy

Much of the debate about the nature and reality of contemporary globalization turns upon the issue of novelty. Advocates of the 'strong globalization' view contend that the world is now entering a new, and qualitatively unique, phase of its development. More sceptical observers argue, in contrast, that recent developments reveal merely the further internationalization of a number of admittedly important areas of economic, social and political life; that levels of internationalization have fluctuated in the past; and that the current phase of internationalization is neither unique nor irreversible.

A comparison with past circumstances is thus an important part of evaluating the nature and significance of contemporary conditions and developments. It is easy for such a comparative exercise to assume the appearance of a party game in which sets of conditions are listed and the respondent is invited to say whether the time being described is the late twentieth century or the late nineteenth century. Such an exercise, pursued with care and caution, however, can prove illuminating. Commonalities across a century allow the identification of significant patterns of continuity or repetition within the modern international political economy. Establishing such a baseline of such regularity then throws discontinuities and novelties into far sharper relief, allowing attention to those contemporary developments that might indicate a genuinely new condition within human affairs.

Features that have been emphasized particularly by advocates of the 'strong globalization' view provide a schedule for comparative review. Contemporary globalization rests, according to such a view, upon transformational technologies of transport and communication and rapid innovation and diffusion of new productive technologies. The effects of these central features are manifest, in turn, in the increasing speed and intensity of world-wide economic integration, particularly financial; the rapid emergence of, and intensification of economic competition from, a number of newly industrialized economies; and massive increases in international travel, transnational human contacts and migration. For the more optimistic of 'globalizationists', the aggregate effect of such causes and consequences is to place the market in the driving seat of human developments, progressively to reduce the role and potency of national governments, and to herald a world of enduring peace and general prosperity. The years of the late nineteenth century and early twentieth century can be inspected for resonances of just such conditions and then compared directly with the contemporary scene.

Transformational technologies

The world at the end of the twentieth century is characterized by the pervasive influence of electricity, the internal combustion engine, and, most significantly, the microprocessor and its allied technologies of information processing and transmission.

Electricity was already making an impact, albeit limited in scale and scope, by the end of the nineteenth century. The great electrification of home and workplace had to wait upon the twentieth century. However, electricity had already transformed global communications with the introduction, and widespread deployment, of the telegraph; the news agency Reuters having, by the 1890s, established a world-wide network of agencies linked by the telegraph.[1] The electrically-driven telephone was also beginning to make a hesitant appearance.[2] Significantly, the arrival of the early cinema allowed the Second Boer War of 1899–1902 to be the first major conflict to be displayed in moving images to the general public.

The internal combustion engine, however, had been perfected only in 1885, and the diesel engine had to wait until 1897 for its full development. The era of the internal combustion engine, and the development of effective aircraft, thus had to await the full flowering of the twentieth century. The second half of the nineteenth century did have its transformational technology of transportation, however, in the form of the ever more complex and efficient steam engine. From its origins in mine pumping and factory power, the steam engine had been refined in form, and often reduced in size, sufficiently to allow its employment in moving vehicles: first on land in steam-driven locomotives and then at sea as a replacement for wind-power in the propulsion of ocean-going vessels.[3]

The significance of the steam engine for the second half of the nineteenth century was quite as great as that of the internal combustion engine, or of electricity, for the twentieth. Manufacturing on a large scale at a distance from rivers became a possibility. Railways allowed the rapid and reliable transportation of bulky items over long distances, in a manner that had previously been impossible. Steam-driven vessels allowed the international shipment of cargoes and passengers on a scale and at a speed that had formerly been unimaginable and with a steady fall in transport costs. Steam power spearheaded the growing mechanization of production; a process that the advent of electricity reinforced and further extended. The innovation of mass production within the United States of America marked the logical, and all but inevitable, outcome of such a process of progressive mechanization.[4]

The steady advance of railway construction throughout the more developed sections of the world was remarkable during the later years of the nineteenth century, as Table 2.1 demonstrates. No less impressive was the growth in the numbers and size of steam-driven ships. The 3,270 tons of the then revolutionary *SS Great*

Table 2.1   The growth of railway mileage in the nineteenth and early twentieth centuries

	Austria-Hungary	France	Germany	Britain	Italy	Russia
1850	1,579	2,915	5,856	9,797	620	501
1860	4,543	9,167	11,089	14,603	2,404	1,626
1870	9,589	15,544	18,876	21,558	6,710	13,641
1880	18,507	23,089	33,838	25,060	9,290	22,865
1890	26,519	33,280	42,869	27,827	13,629	30,596
1900	36,330	38,109	51,678	30,079	16,429	53,234
1910	43,280	40,484	61,209	32,184	18,090	66,581

Source: B.R. Mitchell, Statistical appendix, in C.M. Cipolla (ed.), *The Fontana Economic History of Europe: The Emergence of Industrial Societies – Part 2* (London: Fontana Books, 1973), Table 1, p. 789.

Figure 2.1 Growth of railways 1850–1910 (kilometres of open lines)

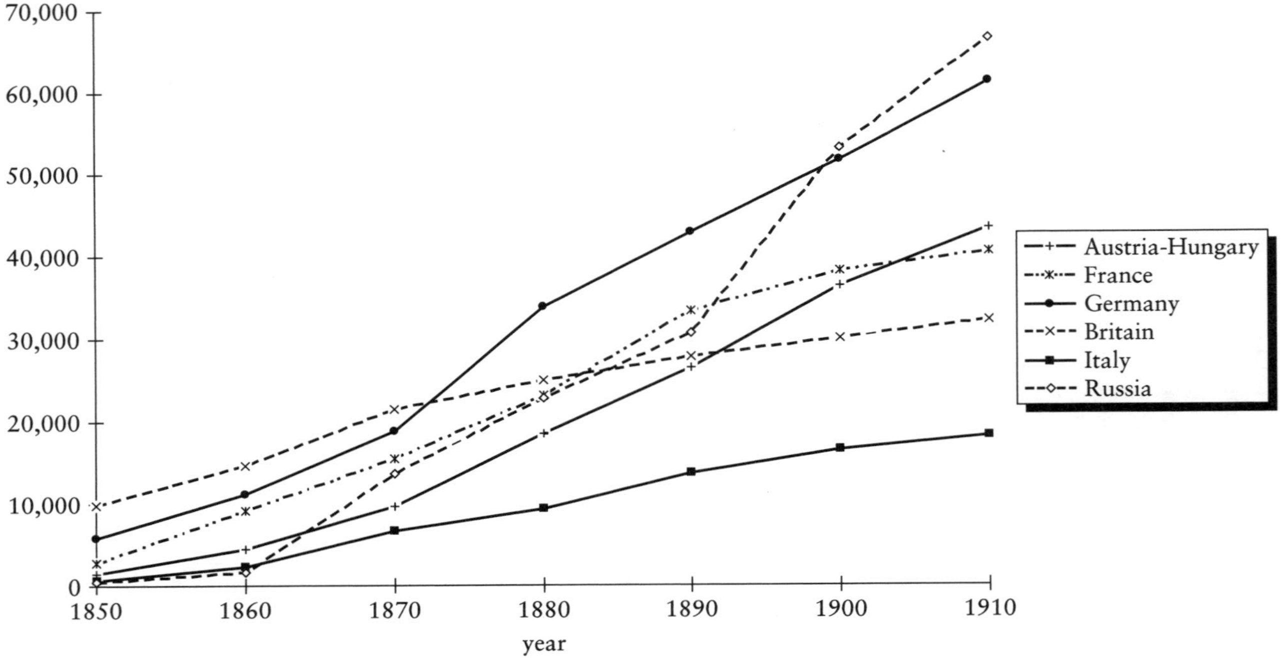

Source: B.R. Mitchell, Statistical appendix, in C.M. Cipolla (ed.), *The Fontana Economic History of Europe: The Emergence of Industrial Societies – Part 2* (London: Fontana, 1973), Table 1, p. 789.

Britain, launched in 1843 had, by the 1890s, been dwarfed by the 10,000 tons plus of the Inman Line's *City of New York* and *City of Paris*. By the turn of the century these massive ships had been dwarfed in their turn by the 17,272 tons of the White Star Line's *Oceanic*.[5]

The innovation and diffusion of production

Just as at the end of the twentieth century, the late nineteenth century was also an era in which the rate of technical innovation and international diffusion also continued to accelerate and achieve near feverish rates.[6] The forces of competition and emulation fuelled both innovation and diffusion. Within private industry, the speed and intensity of transnational competition grew steadily. Exposure to intensified competition was partly a product of governmental policies. Free trade had become an increasingly popular political programme within Great Britain earlier in the nineteenth century and resulted in the freeing of agricultural trade with the repeal of the Corn Laws in 1846. Such, often hesitant, moves towards greater free trade merely reinforced the need to adopt the latest technologies to meet ever-growing competitive pressures within the international market. Moreover, the flow of international investment facilitated an unprecedented speed and range of international technological diffusion.[7]

Market competition was not the only, or even the primary, force for technical innovation and diffusion during the later nineteenth century, however: political and military competition amongst the leading powers were also intensifying remorselessly. The governments of both ambitious and apprehensive countries were equally concerned to build ever-greater military strength upon the foundations of strong and technically innovative industrial societies. Indeed, military concerns were central to the programmes of industrialization in the later nineteenth century of such emergent economic forces as Germany[8] and Japan.[9] The resultant pattern of industrialization was thus a form of militaristic mercantilism, rather than a purely market-driven phenomenon. As such, it entailed extensive and intensive governmental involvement in the construction of a suitable infrastructure, both human and physical; the guidance of the industrialization process; and the modulation of purely market influences. It also reflected, and encouraged, the rapid growth of the state's capacity for the efficient monitoring and management of its internal affairs.[10] The acquisition of new techniques and technologies thus acquired a strategic significance of central interest to state authorities.

The rapid build-up of military capabilities, particularly those resting upon an industrial base, was one of the clear products of the new era of militarily orientated technical and industrial competition. Between 1890 and 1910 the naval tonnage of Great Britain rose by some 330 per cent; that of Germany by 507 per cent; that of the USA by 345 per cent; and that of Japan by no less than 1210 per cent.[11] The picture during the later nineteenth century was thus one of a complex, and ultimately precarious, balance between the rapid growth of productive capabilities and the equally rapid growth of destructive forces.

Rapid economic growth and the development of the international economy

Technical innovation, the expansion of the world market and widespread build-up of industrial capacity combined to generate rapid economic growth and the steady expansion of the world economy. Output of the basic source of energy – coal – rose dramatically during the latter half of the nineteenth century and the early years of the twentieth, as Table 2.2 demonstrates. By the turn of the century, steel was also beginning to play a more central role in high-quality manufactures and munitions,[12] and its output was also increasing at a dramatic rate, as Table 2.3 indicates.

Table 2.2 Coal output 1850–1910 (annual averages in millions of metric tons)

	1850–54	1860–64	1870–74	1880–84	1890–94	1900–4	1910–13
Austria	1.2	3.6	9.2	15.9	25.7	33.5	41.1
France	5.3	10.0	15.4	20.2	26.3	33.0	39.9
Germany	9.2	20.8	41.4	65.7	94.0	157.3	247.5
Russia	—	0.4	1.0	3.7	7.1	17.3	30.2
UK	50.2	86.3	123.2	158.9	183.2	230.4	275.4

Source: B.R. Mitchell, Statistical appendix, in C.M. Cipolla (ed.), *The Fontana Economic History of Europe: The Emergence of Industrial Societies – Part 2* (London: Fontana Books, 1973), Industry Table 2, p. 770.

Table 2.3   The growth of steel output, 1880–1910 (annual averages in millions of metric tons)

	1880–84	1890–94	1900–4	1910–13
Austria-Hungary	0	0.55	1.16	2.45
France	0.46	0.77	1.70	4.09
Germany	0.99	2.89	7.71	16.24
Russia	0.25	0.54	2.35	4.20
UK	1.82	3.20	5.04	6.93

Source: B.R. Mitchell, Statistical appendix, in C.M. Cipolla (ed.), *The Fontana Economic History of Europe: The Emergence of Industrial Societies – Part 2* (London: Fontana Books, 1973), Industry Table 5, p. 775.

The general level of industrial activity within the world's leading economies, much of its based upon advanced sciences,[13] was thus advancing at a considerable rate towards the turn of the century, as Figure 2.2 demonstrates. International trade was expanding substantially as both a cause and consequence of the general growth of production, reflected in the rising levels of exports of the major European powers, detailed in Table 2.4. Colonial control also drew many parts of the world into close economic ties with the industrialized, metropolitan societies.[14] Japan, too, had begun to emerge as a major force upon the world's industrial scene by the end of the nineteenth century, as it has, again, at the end of the twentieth.

The growth of trade in general also included the incorporation of a wider range of societies into the international market. The rapid change of the United Kingdom from being a major exporter to being a leading importer of basic commodities and foodstuffs both reflected and stimulated the greater spread and complexity of the international economy by the late nineteenth century. The United Kingdom's major sources of supply of a number of important commodities had already changed substantially. Thus 86 per cent of the United Kingdom's imports of grains had been drawn from European sources in 1831, but by 1900 Europe was supplying only 10 per cent of her import requirements in this area, with 58 per cent coming from the USA, 8 per cent from Canada and 19 per cent from Argentina.[15]

The result of the combined processes of industrial growth and advance of the world market was the achievement, by the eve of

Figure 2.2 Indices of growth of industrial output 1855–1904 (1905–13 = 100)

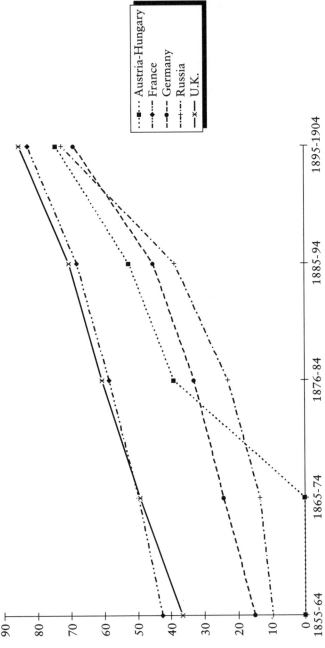

Legend:
..■.. Austria-Hungary
—◆— France
——●—— Germany
—+—+— Russia
—✕— U.K.

Source: B.R. Mitchell, Statistical appendix, in C.M. Cipolla (ed.), *The Fontana Economic History of Europe: The Emergence of Industrial Societies – Part 2* (London: Fontana, 1973), Industry Table 1, pp. 768–9.

Table 2.4 Growth of value of exports, 1850–1910

	1850	*1860*	*1870*	*1880*	*1890*	*1900*	*1910*
Austria-Hungary (million Kronen)	252.0	610.0	791.0	1352.0	1543.0	1942.0	2419.0
France (million Francs)	1068.0	2277.0	2802.0	3468.0	3753.0	4109.0	6234.0
Germany (million Marks)	—	—	—	2923.0	3327.0	4611.0	7475.0
Russia (million Roubles)	98.1	181.4	360.0	498.7	692.2	716.2	1449.1
UK[a] (million Pounds)	83.4	164.5	244.1	286.5	328.2	354.4	534.2

Source: B.R. Mitchell, Statistical appendix, in C.M. Cipolla (ed.), *The Fontana Economic History of Europe: The Emergence of Industrial Societies – Part 2* (London: Fontana Books, 1973), Overseas Trade Table 1, pp. 797–800.
[a] UK figures are exports plus re-exports.

Table 2.5 Ratio of merchandise trade to Gross Domestic Product at current prices (exports and imports combined)

	1913	*1950*	*1973*	*1993*
France	35.4	21.2	29.0	32.6
Germany	35.1	20.1	35.2	38.1
Japan	31.4	16.9	18.3	14.3
Netherlands	103.6	70.2	80.1	85.9
UK	44.7	36.0	39.3	47.2
USA	11.2	7.0	10.5	17.0

Sources: P. Hirst and G. Thompson, *Globalization in Question* (Cambridge: Polity Press, 1996), Table 2.5 for 1913, 1950 and 1973; and World Bank, *World Development Report, 1995* (Oxford: Oxford University Press, 1995), Tables 13 and 3 for 1993 figures.

the First World War, of a level of international trade that many of the leading economies were not to experience again until the 1970s. Table 2.5 gives the ratios of external trade to Gross Domestic Products for a number of such economies over the period 1913 to 1993.

Figure 2.3   Population growth in high-income, middle-income and low-income countries 1980–95 (millions)

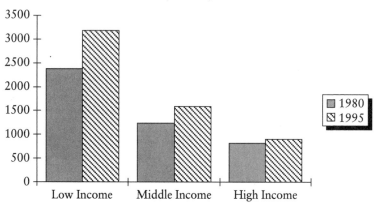

Source: World Bank, *World Development Report 1997* (New York: Oxford University Press, 1997), Table 4, pp. 3220–1.

Population growth and the rise of mass migration

Rapid population growth and rising pressures of mass migration are often held to be a peculiar feature, and problem, of the latter half of the twentieth century. The populations of many Less Developed Countries (LDCs) have grown substantially during the latter decades of the century, as Figure 2.3 indicates. A combination of poverty, greater economic opportunities elsewhere and a range of political upheavals has also stimulated substantial movements of populations both within LDCs and across their borders, and towards safer and more prosperous havens in one Advanced Industrial Country or another.

The late nineteenth century also exhibited dramatic population growth and mass migration. The populations in question, however, were primarily those of today's Advanced Industrial Countries. Table 2.6 provides evidence on the growth of population of a number of more industrialized European countries between 1870–71 and 1990–91. Table 2.7 indicates the scale of the migrations and the origins of the migrants of the later nineteenth century, as imperial territories and the territories of the Americas were opened to new settlement by European migrants. Such voluntary movements of people followed the earlier, forced transatlantic shipments

Table 2.6 Population growth of selected industrialized European countries 1870–1900 (millions)

	1870/1	*1880/1*	*1890/1*	*1900/1*
Belgium	4.8	5.3	6.1	6.6
France	36.1	37.7	38.3	39.0
Germany	40.8	45.2	49.4	56.4
Great Britain	26.1	29.7	33.1	37.0
Italy	26.8	28.5	30.3	32.5
Russia	84.5	97.7	117.8	132.9

Source: B.R. Mitchell, Statistical appendix, in C.M. Cipolla (ed.), *The Fontana Economic History of Europe: The Emergence of Industrial Societies – Part 2* (London: Fontana Books, 1973), Population Table 1, p. 747.

Table 2.7 Emigration from selected industrialized European economies, 1870–1910 (thousands)

	1871–80	*1881–90*	*1891–1900*	*1901–10*
Belgium	2	21	16	30
France	66	119	51	53
Germany	626	1,342	527	274
Italy	168	992	1,580	3,615
Russia	58	288	481	911
United Kingdom	1,849[a]	3,259	2,149	3,150

Source: B.R. Mitchell, Statistical appendix, in C.M. Cipolla (ed.), *The Fontana Economic History of Europe: The Emergence of Industrial Societies – Part 2* (London: Fontana Books, 1973), Population Table 3, p. 751.
[a] Excluding Irish ports.

of many millions of slaves during the sixteenth, seventeenth and early eighteenth centuries.

Migratory pressures would thus appear to be common to periods of rapid change in economic and political conditions, particularly when allied to rapid population growth. At the end of the twentieth century there were, however, substantial obstacles to the free movement of migrating peoples, particularly into the more prosperous societies. In marked contrast, migrants in the late nineteenth century were confronted by far lower hurdles, once they had met the costs of transport, usually by ship. Formal obstacles were singularly lacking in the late nineteenth century, as is indicated by the introduction of passports for all its citizens by the United Kingdom as late as 1915.

Financial integration in the world economy

One of the most prominent features of contemporary globalization is the high, and increasing, level of financial integration within, and across, the international economy. Financial integration is, indeed, a prominent feature of the new, globalized economy. Levels of financial transactions have risen dramatically during the past two to three decades. There are many possible measures of global financial integration, ranging from volumes of foreign exchange dealings on international money markets as national currencies are bought and sold, through to the level of cross-border borrowing. Figure 2.4 illustrates the dramatic increase of foreign exchange dealings between the mid-1980s and the mid-1990s. Figure 2.5 indicates something of the rapid rise of international borrowing and lending between the mid-1970s and the mid-1980s.

Figure 2.4   Foreign exchange volumes 1986–95 ($US billion)

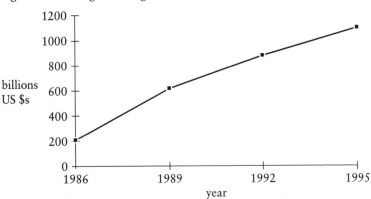

Source: Exhibit 2.2, in L. Bryan and D. Farrell, *Market Unbound* (New York: John Wiley and Sons, 1996), p. 26.

Figure 2.5   Total borrowings on international capital markets 1976–93 ($US billion)

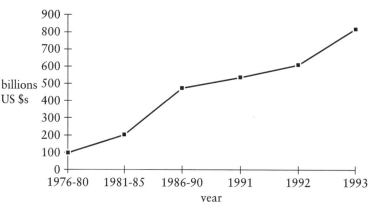

Source: P. Hirst and G. Thompson, *Globalization in Question* (Cambridge: Polity Press, 1996), Table 2.9, p. 40.

A number of crises within the international financial system during the last quarter of the twentieth century have also reinforced the impression of marked, and unprecedented, financial integration. General concern about the 'debt crisis' of a number of leading Less Developed debtor states from 1982 onwards indicated growing international financial connections and sensitivities. The worldwide anxiety precipitated by the widespread stock market crashes of 'Black Monday', on 19 October 1987, demonstrated both the intimate practical and perceptual interconnections now existing among previously separate financial markets. The economic and financial crisis that erupted in Asia in late 1997 further evidenced the level of practical and psychological interconnections within the world's financial system, as will be seen in Chapter 11. The international transmission of economic and financial crisis is far from novel, however, as Charles Kindleberger's magisterial survey of the subject demonstrates.[16]

Global financial integration is, however, far from complete. Statistical data suggest that a wide variety of financial developments continue to be influenced by primarily local, or regional, factors.[17] National policies and practices continue to obstruct the complete openness of national equity markets to foreign-based firms, particularly in the area of issues of new stocks and shares.[18] Pension funds in the Advanced Industrial Countries continue to retain the bulk of their investments within the countries in which they are based.[19] Even the most enthusiastic heralds of a brave new globalized world thus admit that financial integration remains far from perfect.[20]

The picture of global financial integration presented by such evidence is, however, primarily a private market phenomena. Indeed, the great part of contemporary financial globalization is a matter of the actions and interactions of private financial enterprises. The activities of private businesses are not the whole story of contemporary international financial interaction, however. Global financial integration has also been served substantially by the post-war institutions of international financial support and regulation.

Two factors combined to prompt the creation of authoritative international financial institutions after the end of the Second World War: the clear need for massive post-war economic reconstruction; and critical reflection upon the manifest failures of international financial management in the late 1920s and 1930s that had contributed so substantially to the Great Depression of the 1930s and the subsequent political upheavals. The product of such concerns had been the twin institutions of the International Bank for Reconstruction and Development (the World Bank) and the International Monetary Fund (IMF), founded at the Bretton Woods Conference in 1944. The post-war role, and contribution, of these institutions was to orchestrate the financing of the immediate recovery of the war-torn industrial economies and to oversee the gradual establishment of a system of fixed exchange rates and relatively free currency convertibility amongst the industrialized economies, which endured until 1971. In such endeavours they were assisted by such surviving pre-war institutions as the Basle-based Bank for International Settlements and the emergence of new, more informal international associations like the Trilateral Commission and the Davos Conferences.

The existence and operation of the World Bank and the IMF in the post-war international system have reflected the level of concern for the general functioning of the economic and financial system among the governments of its leading members. In combination with the General Agreement on Tariffs and Trade, these institutions supported and directed the general, if sometimes slow, move towards liberalization and openness within the system. However, their general strategic role was diluted in a gradual shift in focus away from the recovering industrialized countries to the problems and needs of the Less Developed or Newly Industrialized Economies.

The initial capacity for international financial and economic control by the World Bank and the IMF rested largely upon the dominant economic and strategic position of their major sponsor, the United States of America. However, when a range of developments, from the re-emergence of serious industrial competitors to the financial strains of the Vietnam War, began to weaken the relative position of the USA, the effectiveness of that underwriting role was undermined. The fixed exchange rate system collapsed finally in 1971. International financial and economic management thus became increasingly a matter of multilateral negotiations and co-ordination among the governments of the world's leading industrial economies. However, the nature and extent of the USA's decline from effective hegemony within the world economy has often been exaggerated, as its decisive role in underwriting and encouraging the IMF-based rescue mission in the Asian economic and financial crisis of 1997–98[21] and the continuation of the US dollar as the world's 'top currency'[22] have both demonstrated.

The extent of global financial integration in the private sphere is thus not matched by integration in the arrangements for, and institutions of, public international regulation and control, where the picture is far more mixed, muddy and uneven in impact and effectiveness. The attention of international institutions varies in focus and intensity. Their effectiveness is significantly influenced by their current levels of financial resources and the current attitudes and concerns of their major patrons, and by prevalent fashions in economic and financial thinking. Such characteristics are amply illustrated by the past, and continuing, management of the LDCs' 'debt crisis'.

The procedures and arrangements adopted to deal with the LDCs' 'debt crisis' since its crystallization in 1982, with the threat of a default on its international financial obligations by Mexico, involved a complex mix of public and private institutions. Nominally, the debt that LDCs owed to public authorities – governments of individual creditor countries or the multilateral agencies of discretionary finance – was managed through the Paris Club. The commercial debt, incurred primarily by the larger and richer 'Less Developed Countries', that was owed to the large private international financial institutions was managed through the London Clubs of consortia of businesses with loans outstanding to one or other of the indebted LDCs.[23]

Such a simple division between public authorities and private interests does insufficient justice to the complexity of the actual situation, however, particularly in the case of the commercial debts of the larger LDCs and some of the Newly Industrialized Countries (NICs). The International Monetary Fund undertook detailed reviews of the economic conditions and policies within many of those debtor countries that were falling into difficulties, negotiated 'structural adjustment' policy packages, provided financial support and, through the combination of such actions, gave implicit approval to the rescheduling agreements that were being negotiated simultaneously between debtors and private creditors. Moreover, national governments reinforced the gate-keeping and legitimizing role of the IMF by using a range of domestic policy instruments, or the threat of their use, to secure discipline among the creditor institutions and deter any unilateral actions that might have precipitated the premature calling in of various countries' debts and, thereby, the probable formal default of the countries in question.[24]

The mixed-actor arrangements for dealing with the acute LDC 'debt crisis' of 1982 to 1986 provided numerous indications of the growing integration of the world's financial system. The concern that underlay the intense web of activity surrounding the London Clubs, the IMF and the governments of the home countries of the major lending institutions reflected an acute concern about the consequences of default by any major debtor countries. Such a default in a highly integrated financial world, it was feared, might precipitate a chain-reaction of failures amongst leading financial institutions that would, in turn, plunge both the industrialized countries and the wider world economy into deep and highly damaging recession. Moreover, the 'success' of these arrangements in staving off any full-blown defaults by debtor countries until the creditor institutions had been able to build up sufficient reserves to insulate them against the worse consequences of major defaults illustrated the relative intimacy and cohesiveness of the leading private and public financial institutions within the contemporary international economy. The limits of this set of arrangements for regulating the world financial system equitably and efficiently were, however, revealed by two significant, but often neglected, aspects of the 'debt crisis' of the early 1980s: the apparent paradox that the 'resolution' of the crisis actually left many of the major debtor countries with higher levels of commercial debt by the end of the process in 1987 than they had accumulated at its 'start' in 1982;[25] and the anomaly that the official debts of the world's poorest LDCs were largely neglected by the process.[26]

The picture of the emerging world financial system over the last two decades of the twentieth century is strongly suggestive of advancing globalization, in one arena at least. Many of the features of the financial situation at the end of the twentieth century had, however, strong parallels a century before. While formal inter-governmental institutions like the International Monetary Fund, the World Bank and the Bank for International Settlements were missing from the later nineteenth-century scene, a set of less formal 'institutions' suggested a considerable level of international financial integration: the Gold Standard, which was maintained for the national currencies of many countries; the complex[27] but predominant role of the City of London within the world's financial system, with the Gold Sovereign as the 'top currency';[28] and a widespread, and often intimate, network of private financial interests that contributed considerably to international financial flows and *de facto* co-ordination – the *haute finance* of radical demonology.[29] Moreover, 'abstract money' – credits rather than physical cash or bullion – had already been fully developed and extensively applied throughout the commercially active part of the world economy of the late nineteenth century.[30]

Such institutional arrangements complemented the financial consequences of rapid economic growth and the development of the international market economy. Overseas lending and investment grew steadily during the latter years of the nineteenth century, with overseas investments accounting for more than 50 per cent of the net investment of the United Kingdom in 1890.[31] The bulk of international financial transfers assumed the form of direct loans by commercial lenders, or portfolio investments (acquisitions of stocks and shares) and direct investments in extractive industries or agricultural facilities by private investors, although German manufacturers were beginning to acquire manufacturing facilities in both Russia and France during this period.[32] The most marked contrast between the late nineteenth century and the late twentieth century, then, lies in the significance of direct overseas investment in manufacturing facilities and, increasingly, in service industry facilities, in

Table 2.8   Foreign assets of the world's top 100 TNCs by industrial sector in 1995

Industrial sector	% of overall assets
Petroleum and Mining	18
Food and Beverages	8
Construction	2
Metals	2
Chemicals and Pharmaceuticals	13
Automotive	21
Electronics	16

Source: United Nations Conference on Trade and Development, *World Investment Report 1997: Transnational Corporations, Market Structure and Competition Policy* (New York: United Nations Publications, 1997), Table 1.12, p. 35.

the latter case. Table 2.8 indicates the proportion of the overseas investments of the leading transnational corporations by industry and sector in 1995.

Divergence and instability in a 'global economy'

The internationalization or globalization of the world economy is no guarantee of identical experiences for all its members. Unevenness of effect is as characteristic of global economic developments in the late twentieth century as it was in the late nineteenth.

By the late twentieth century, the world revealed a markedly uneven picture with regard to economic inequalities, as Figure 2.6 indicates, with massive inequalities also persisting within societies of all types. In the late nineteenth century, growth had been extensive and substantial, and the general condition of the working classes within the more industrialized societies was improving to a marked extent.[33] However, the combination of technological change and the opening of economies to new competitive challenges always has varying effects upon the economic prospects of different groupings within society. The latter half of the nineteenth century experienced a 'Great Depression' as new competitive pressures impacted unfavourably upon the agricultural sectors of many European countries, particularly that of Great Britain.[34]

Figure 2.6 GDP growth 1965–89 ($US billion)

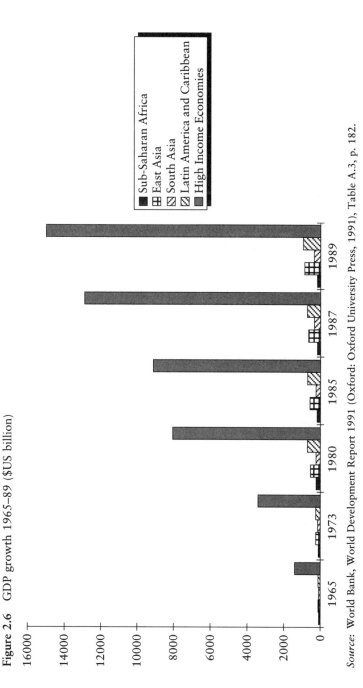

Source: World Bank, World Development Report 1991 (Oxford: Oxford University Press, 1991), Table A.3, p. 182.

Stimuli to growth and serious economic disturbances are also transmitted more readily around an internationalized or globalized economy than within a relatively fragmented system. The combination of the rapid diffusion of technology, the stimulus of inward investment and the opportunities of the expanding international market combined to generate dramatic economic changes amongst the 'developing' economies of the late nineteenth century.[35] However, once the boom of the later 1890s came to an end, newly industrializing economies like Russia and Italy experienced serious reduction in demand, prices and output of industrial commodities,[36] with consequential increases of industrial unrest, moves towards industrial consolidation and calls for governmental action.[37]

For Karl Polanyi,[38] and to a slightly less extent Joseph Schumpeter,[39] the creative waves of vigorous capitalism carried, and always do carry, a destructive influence. The destructive side of technological change combines its effects with the inherent disruptiveness of the cyclical patterns within dynamic free-market systems. The longer-term effects of such processes upon social structures, popular thinking and, ultimately, political developments were, in Polanyi's view in particular, to be seen in the massive disruptions and disorders of the first half of the twentieth century. However, the late nineteenth century was similar to the late twentieth in the existence of vocal advocates of the primacy of the market and the need to disregard its more disruptive effects upon the weaker groups within society.[40] Equally, however, growing pressures from the international economy, at the end of both the nineteenth and the twentieth centuries, prompted protectionist currents of opinion, first within many of the established industrial societies[41] and then in the United States of America.[42] Such responses have, however, been but one example of a wide backlash against advancing globalization at the end of both centuries,[43] another being early experiments with the welfare state, particularly within Bismarck's Germany.[44]

One of the clear consequences of the destabilizing impact of rapid economic change during the late nineteenth century was the growth of industrial unrest and the formation of political parties founded upon the working classes of the industrialized societies. Such were the omens of internal division within many of the leading industrialized societies that some, like Cecil Rhodes, believed that reinvigorated imperialism offered the only path to future social peace and stability for Great Britain.[45]

The experiences of the late twentieth century thus echo many features of the end of the nineteenth. A combination of rapid technological change and intensifying international economic competition has placed many of the more mature industrial societies under pressures unprecedented in the post-Second World War era. The substantial growth of unemployment in some mature industrial societies and the spread of part-time and temporary employment in others are all partial reflections of the new world economic conditions of the end of the century and partial echoes of the dramatic economic developments of the late nineteenth century.

The boom and bust experiences of the East and South-East Asian economies during the late 1990s also echo the problems experienced by the more recently industrializing economies in the later nineteenth century and the transmissive features of the increasingly interconnected world economy of that time.

The varying economic experiences of different groups of societies are thus common to both the late nineteenth and the late twentieth Centuries. Such differences both reflect and underlie another marked similarity between the two eras: the marked, and often awesome, disparities in the general strength, wealth and capabilities of societies and their state institutions; and, curiously, a remarkable similarity in the identities of the world's ten richest societies. Thus the international systems of both the late nineteenth and the late twentieth centuries were marked by the preponderant (although far from omnipotent) position of one superpower. In the later nineteenth century, the economic, financial and imperial strength of Great Britain underpinned her overwhelming naval strength[46] and her capacity, with time and some effort, to mobilize, and project around the world, a major military presence. In the aftermath of the collapse of the Soviet Union, the leading economic, financial and military position of the United States of America has allowed her to play a broadly comparable role at the end of the late twentieth century.

Superpowers do not necessarily retain hegemonic positions indefinitely. They are subject to challenges from outside and to weakening developments within. The United Kingdom's position at the end of the nineteenth century was to be progressively eroded by the combined, and ultimately interrelated, effects of debilitating confrontations with repeated challenges in Europe from Germany, the hesitant rise to global prominence of the United States of

America and the gradual change in the bases of economic and military power. Many observers throughout the last two decades of the twentieth century have identified multifaceted roots of an impending loss of dominance by the United States of America:[47] a fate that may, however, be postponed for the foreseeable future in the absence of an identifiable hegemonic challenger in the military sphere and by the serious set-back experienced by the economies of East and South-East Asia during the late 1990s.

Many states that are not superpowers do, however, retain the ability for effective, and even decisive, action within their own geographical regions of operation or on specific issues over which they retain wider potential influence. The nineteenth century revealed numerous powers in the rank just below that of superpower: from such second-rank imperial powers as France, to rising international challengers like Germany, and emergent regional hegemons like the United States of America.[48] At the end of the twentieth century, considerable regional politico-military influence is exerted by states like China; massive economic influence regionally and globally is exercised by states with modest military capabilities like Japan; and former major powers like France and Great Britain still continue to enjoy a discernible level of influence within the world economy, whilst retaining the ability to project modest levels of armed force well beyond their home regions.

Below the middle-rank powers, with their combinations of economic weight, military strength and relative domestic cohesion, a large number of states in both the late nineteenth and late twentieth centuries continued, and continue, to enjoy a combination of internal effectiveness and of influence in their bilateral relationships, particularly with immediate neighbours. The most obvious difference between the two eras, however, is the entry into the club of states of societies that were still under the control of imperial powers in the late nineteenth century. The death of the imperial impulse is one of the two most dramatic contrasts between the world of the 1890s and that of the 1990s. It has resulted in the ending of a distinctive, but historically quite common, type of relationship between otherwise quite disparate societies and has brought into the lists of 'nation states' many new members who lacked such an identity previously or had suffered its suppression for many decades, if not centuries.

The character of the international system in the latter half of the twentieth century, with its absence of formal imperialism and relative stability under the influence of a structurally conservative hegemon – the United States of America – has encouraged the emergence and survival of a considerable number of micro-states, with very small populations and territories. Such micro-states were relatively rare at the end of nineteenth century, and were often threatened, or actually absorbed, by larger neighbours at time of wider tension within the system. By the late twentieth century, however, micro-states, particularly island-based, have emerged and flourished within the Mediterranean – Malta and Cyprus; the Pacific Sea – Vanuatu, Western Samoa; and the North Atlantic – Iceland. Such examples signal possibilities for relatively small ethnic and cultural groups that are currently located within larger polities but that aspire to political independence.

Not all societies, however, are blessed with cohesion and functional effectiveness. Political disintegration can be visited upon societies of all shapes and sizes. The Control of the Dowager Empress over China was beginning to falter in the late nineteenth century under the interrelated strains of internal dissolution and pressures from incursive foreign powers. The Boxer Rebellion of 1898–1900 was directed nominally against foreign influences, but confronted and defeated imperial Chinese forces in its course. A protracted period of discontent and instability within China led, eventually, to the nationalistic, but Western-looking, revolution of 1911, which brought to an end both the Qing Dynasty and the millennia of imperial rule over China.

China at the end of the twentieth century is also experiencing a period of rapid and profound change. The tension between Western-orientated market industrialization and a 'conservative' political establishment is strongly reminiscent of the fault line running through China in the late nineteenth century. Then, as now, Russia was also experiencing substantial change and upheaval in most areas of life.

China and Russia are not the only societies with profound internal problems, however, for a number other states have experienced near-total internal collapse during the last two to three decades of the twentieth century. Manic ideology plunged Cambodia into genocidal self-destruction for many years. Ideologically based insurgency and counter-insurgency plagued many states in Latin America during the 1970s, 1980s and early 1990s, ushering in decades of brutal approximations to civil wars. Inter-tribal loathings unleashed chaos and genocide in Rwanda and Burundi in the middle to late 1990s. Complex combinations of ambition and tribal rivalry destroyed balance, cohesion and ultimately economic normality in Sierra Leone, Somalia and Ghana.

Any simple comparison between a stable and cohesive imperial world of the late nineteenth century and the turbulence of the post-imperial era of the late twentieth century does not however do full justice to the complexity of the earlier period. The late nineteenth century was witness to the gradual, but troublesome, collapse of the Ottoman Empire in the Middle East and the Balkans. The assertion of new, or rediscovered, national identities was one of the manifest consequences of this process of imperial dissolution. The first blow for Balkan nationalism had been struck by Greece in its successful war of independence against Turkey between 1821 and 1829. A widespread uprising against Turkish (Ottoman) rule in 1875–6 precipitated the Russo-Turkish war of 1877–8, securing the independence of Romania, Serbia and Montenegro at the Congress of Berlin in 1878. However, in a move that was to prove all too fateful during the early twentieth century, Bosnia and Herzegovina fell under the control of Austria. Bulgaria, moreover, was not to secure full independence from Turkey until 1908. In terms of the Balkans, then, what the weakening of imperial control produced in the late nineteenth and early twentieth centuries, the ending of the Cold War and the dissolution of the Yugoslavian state spawned in the late twentieth century.

Sentiments at centuries' end: optimism and pessimism in times of rapid change

Periods of rapid change in economics, technology, society and politics exert profound influences upon the outlook and expectations of the affected populations. The prevalence of novelty is a common sentiment during both the late nineteenth and the late twentieth centuries. In Asa Briggs's account: 'By 1894 the word "new" was being applied, sometimes enthusiastically, sometimes pejoratively, to almost everything from gender to morality, from objects ... to ideas, from fiction to art ...'.[49] Views of a contemporary world transformed by new technologies and the globalization of economies parallel such a psychology of novelty.

The late nineteenth century differed somewhat from the late twentieth, however, in the wider sense of optimism during the former.[50] Technological advance, enhanced prosperity, the steady growth of the world market and the absence of major international conflicts combined to create a belief that humanity was moving into a new era of enlightenment and well-being.[51] Such thinking found its highest expression in Norman Angell's *The Great Illusion,* which contended that the growth of the world market and of a new international division of labour would make it undesirable in principle, and virtually impossible in practice, for states to engage in major conflicts with one another.[52] Ironically, Angell's study was published in 1913, just as such optimistic expectations were about to be swept away so brutally by the cataclysm of the First World War. Moreover, general confidence within the contemporary hegemon – Great Britain – had already been dented at the turn of the century by the messy and demoralizing experience of the Boer War.[53]

The end of the twentieth century, in contrast to that of the nineteenth, has been characterized by far deeper divisions of opinion about the future of humanity, economic prospects and, indeed, the very fate of the planet and its natural ecology. Optimists there certainly have been, who believe in the triumph of the market, the coming of global prosperity, the ending of ideological divisions, with the triumph of democratic liberalism, the banishment of major military conflicts[54] and the application of new technologies to the solution of humanity's environmental and resource problems. Such optimistic expectations have, however, been countered by many who fear that an unrestrained market system will trample upon the majority of humanity and/or precipitate its own eventual collapse; that inequalities of income and wealth will increase rapidly, with disastrous social and ethical consequences; that unrestrained economic growth will inflict profound, and possibly irreversible, damage upon the ecological system; that the current 'triumph' of liberal democracy will be shallow and short-lived, with ideologically-based tensions erupting at many times and places; and that serious political and military conflicts will eventually emerge from such varied tensions and troubles, however 'irrational' such conflicts might ultimately be in their methods and motives.[55]

Given the complexities and inherent uncertainties involved in developments within the human condition and the natural environment, simple and reliable judgements about the future are rarely, if ever, possible. The ending of centuries does, however, seem to prompt intensified speculation upon the future and increased apprehensions about its shape. One feature of the end of the twentieth century is, however, unique historically. The speed, character and ubiquity of the 'computer revolution' has endowed humanity with one potential problem that is unprecedented. The peculiarities of microprocessor design and software design, particularly in the 1980s and very early 1990s, have created a problem of considerable potential danger – the notorious 'millennium time-bomb', in which computers that are central to a range of vital functions within modern societies may fail at the arrival of the year 2000 as the new date proves indigestible and unmanageable to programs that cannot recognize dates other than those of the twentieth century.[56] Moreover, concern was rising that the growing dependence upon complex, interconnected computer systems of a range of vital services in at least the more advanced industrial societies had created a vulnerability to a novel form of cyber-warfare, in which hostile computer specialists might 'hack into' critical systems and disable them, with catastrophic consequences.

Overview

There are thus many similarities between the late nineteenth and late twentieth centuries, but also some differences of substance. Rapid economic change, technological innovation, an expanding and intensifying international market have been common to both periods. So too has been a tension between advancing liberalization in the world economy and the fluttering of projectionist impulses as reactions arise against the pressures of internationalization/globalization. A high level of financial interconnectedness, or even integration, is also common to both eras. The Gold Standard, the City of London, *haute finance* and the telegraph were central to financial integration in the late nineteenth century; the dollar, US financial institutions, the International Monetary Fund and the World Bank, and world-wide computer networks pivotal in the latter era. Mass migrations of peoples also developed during the two periods: from industrializing countries to areas of new opportunity in the former; from LDCs to other LDCs or richer neighbours in the latter. Restraints upon migration, other than financial, were, however, far less severe in the late nineteenth century.

Some of the critical differences between the late nineteenth and the late twentieth centuries are evident. The internal combustion engine has transformed human travel, particularly in its aerial applications. The microprocessor, and a complex of associated technologies, have transformed the gathering, processing and transmission of information, particularly the latter two functions. The microprocessor has, however, also become increasingly pervasive in a wide range of everyday products and in their design, manufacture and distribution. The advent of electricity was probably the closest analogue of the microprocessor in the later nineteenth century, and then with a rather more delayed general impact. The world of the late twentieth century is, finally, enmeshed within a network of international organizations and transnational associations of a far greater density and scope than could have been imagined, or sustained, at the end of the nineteenth century.

Politico-military tensions were increasing among a number of the leading powers at the end of the nineteenth century, with arms races on the verge of eruption – a clear difference from the situation at the end of the twentieth. Moreover, imperialism was in full flood during the former period, while it has been relegated to an increasingly distant, though no less contentious, memory in the latter.

The combination of a growing and intensifying world market with the advent of a micro-computing revolution lies at the heart of the developments that many believe to herald the emergence of a new era. The argument is that a set of changes, each of which may be incremental in its effects in isolation, may, in combination, usher in qualitatively new conditions. The notion of 'space and time' compression[57] captures many of these features and signals the sense of uncontrolled and uncontrollable acceleration in the pace and scale of change that confronts the inhabitants of the globalizing world. Whether such 'space and time' compression does constitute a qualitatively different, and ultimately irreversible, condition within the world system is, however, an issue that requires debate, partly in theoretical terms, and partly on the basis of the tangible consequences that such a new condition must have if it is to be more than a mere rhetorical construct. Such issues will be at the heart of much of the subsequent discussion.

Notes

1 See: Asa Briggs, 'The 1890s past, present and future in headlines', pp. 157–95 in Asa Briggs and Daniel Snowman, *Fins De Siècle: How Centuries End 1400–2000* (New Haven and London: Yale University Press, 1996), p. 158.

2 Briggs, 'The 1890s past, present and future in headlines', p. 158.

3 William Woodruff, 'Emergence of an international economy 1700–1914', in C.M. Cipolla (ed.), *The Fontana Economic History of Europe, Vol. 4*, Section 11 (London: Fontana Books, 1971), esp. p. 689.

4 N. Stone, *Europe Transformed 1878–1919* (London: Fontana, 1983), pp. 79–84.

5 R. McAuley, *The Liners* (London: Boxtree, 1997), p. 154.

6 Stone, *Europe Transformed 1878–1919*, pp. 13–15.

7 *Ibid.*, p. 87.

8 Knurt Borchards, 'The Industrial Revolution in Germany 1700–1914', in C.M. Cipolla, *The Fontana Economic History of Europe: The Emergence of Industrial Societies – 1* (London: Fontana Books, 1973), pp. 76–160.

9 Gautam Sen, *The Military Origins of Industrialisation and International Trade Rivalry* (London: Pinter, 1984), esp. pp. 125–35.

10 Stone, *Europe Transformed 1878–1919*, pp. 129–43.

11 See: Paul Kennedy, *The Rise and Fall of the Great Powers: Economic Change and Military Conflict from 1500 to 2000* (London: Fontana Books, 1989), Table 20, p. 261.

12 William Woodruff, 'The emergence of an international economy 1700–1914', *The Fontana Economic History of Europe, Vol. 4*, section 11, p. 674.

13 *Ibid.*, p. 685.

14 *Ibid.*, p. 66.

15 *Ibid.*, Table 1, pp. 718–19.

16 C.P. Kindleberger, *Manias, Panics and Crashes: A History of Financial Crisis* (New York: Wiley, 3rd edn, 1996).

17 R.J. Barry Jones, *Globalisation and Interdependence in the International Political Economy: Rhetoric and Reality* (London: Pinter, 1995), esp. pp. 105–11; and see also: P. Hirst and G. Thompson, *Globalization in Question* (Cambridge: Polity Press, 1996), pp. 40–9.

18 With such anomalies as the greater ease of circulation within the European Union of equities issued by non-EU companies than for EU-based enterprises. See: 'Single market for equities', *Financial Times*, 26 January 1998.

19 'Stay-at-home shareholders', *The Economist*, 17 February 1996, p. 91.

20 L. Bryan and D. Farrell, *Market Unbound* (New York: John Wiley and Sons, 1996), esp. Chs 2, 3 and 4.

21 'Steam taken out of revitalised agenda', *Financial Times*, 26 January 1998, p. 4.

22 Prior to the arrival of the Euro.

23 For a critical discussion see: S. George, *A Fate Worse than Debt* (Harmondsworth: Pelican Books, 1987).

24 *Ibid.*, Chapter 3.

25 Up from $88.2 billion to $114.5 billion in the case of Brazil; from $38 billion to $49.4 billion for Argentina; and from $82 billion to $105 billion for Mexico. Source: World Bank, *World Development Reports*, various editions (Oxford: Oxford University Press).

26 For contemporary accounts see: Marko Milivojevic, *The Debt Rescheduling Process* (London: Pinter, 1985); and H. Lever and C. Huhne, *Debt and Danger: The World Financial Crisis* (Harmondsworth: Penguin Books, 1985).

27 Stone, *Europe Transformed 1878–1919*, p. 40.

28 Briggs, 'The 1890s past, present and future in headlines', p. 187.

29 A. Walter, *World Power and World Money: The Role of Hegemony and International Monetary Order* (Hemel Hempstead: Harvester/Wheatsheaf, 1991); also: Karl Polanyi, *The Great Transformation: The Political and Economic Origins of Our Time* (Boston: Beacon Press, 1957).

30 Stone, *Europe Transformed 1878–1919*, p. 38.

31 'The century the earth stood still: 1897 and 1992', pp. 77–9 in *The Economist*, 20 December 1997, p. 79.

32 Stone, *Europe Transformed 1878–1919*, p. 88.

33 *Ibid.*, p. 144.

34 *Ibid.*, especially pp. 20–8.

35 *Ibid.*, p. 87.

36 *Ibid.*, p. 100.

37 *Ibid.*, pp. 110–28.

38 Polanyi, *The Great Transformation*.

39 J.A. Schumpeter, *Capitalism, Socialism and Democracy*, 5th edn (London: George Allen and Unwin, 1976) (first published in the UK in 1943), esp. Ch. 12.

40 Stone, *Europe Transformed 1878–1919*, p. 116.

41 *Ibid.*, pp. 62, 105.

42 Briggs, 'The 1890s past, present and future in headlines', pp. 183–4.

43 'The century the earth stood still: 1897 and 1992', pp. 77–9 in *The Economist*, 20 December 1997, p. 79.

44 See Stone, *Europe Transformed 1878–1919,* pp. 116–17.

45 *Ibid.*, p. 101.

46 Which, during the late nineteenth century, was based upon the 'Two Power Standard' – a policy of ensuring the Britain had the same number of battleships and cruisers as those of the largest two other European maritime powers combined.

47 See, for example, Paul Kennedy, *The Rise and Decline of the Great Powers* (New York: Random House; and London: Unwin Hyman, 1988), especially, Ch. 8.

48 For an interesting discussion of the USA's assertive role within the American continent in the late nineteenth century see: 'Forget the *Maine*: the war of 1898', *The Economist*, 3 January 1998, pp. 42–4.

49 Briggs, 'The 1890s: past, present and future in headlines', p. 175.

50 Stone, *Europe Transformed 1878–1919*, p. 15.

51 Briggs, 'The 1890s past, present and future in headlines', p. 162.

52 Norman Angell, *The Great Illusion: A Study of the Relation of Military Power in Nations to their Economic and Social Advantage* (London: Weidenfeld and Nicolson and New York: Putnam, 1909); and see, also, Briggs, 'The 1890s past, present and future in headlines', p. 171.

53 Briggs, 'The 1890s past, present and future in headlines', pp. 166–7.

54 Elements of which view are to be found in Francis Fukuyama's *The End of History and the Last Man* (London: Hamish Hamilton, 1992).

55 Vincent Cable, *The World's New Fissures: Identities in Crisis* (London: Demos, 1994); Samuel P. Huntington, *The Clash of Civilizations and the Remaking of the World Order* (New York: Simon and Schuster, 1996); James Goldsmith, *The Trap* (London: Macmillan, 1994). For a survey of some of the problems generated by contemporary globalization see the set of essays in the special edition of *New Political Economy*, vol. 2, no. 1 (March, 1997), edited by Barry K. Gills; and the special edition of *New Left Review – Confronting Globalization*, Number 225 (September/October 1997).

56 Alan Case, 'Bomb without boundaries', *Financial Times*, 2 February 1998, p. 16.

57 David Harvey, *The Condition of Postmodernity* (Oxford: Basil Blackwell, 1989).

3

The roots of globalization

The term 'globalization' is often used in a way that suggests a simple, one-dimensional phenomenon. To the extent that the contemporary world is characterized by increased internationalization or globalization, such a condition is actually highly complex and multidimensional in its sources, manifestations and implications. Moreover, many of the possible sources of globalization may, in a sense, also be taken to be symptoms of the condition. The subject of this chapter will thus be a review of the many sources of contemporary tendencies towards greater internationalization and globalization, their varied character and diverse implications for future developments.

States and the construction of the post-war international political economy

The essence of 'political economy' is the investigation of the problematical relationship between the 'political' and the 'economic' in life, both past and present. The dominant political institution of the modern era has been the state. The relationship between the modern state and economic developments, both domestic and 'international', is thus central to contemporary political economy.

Many accounts of the nature and origins of the contemporary advance of economic internationalization and globalization neglect the contributory role of states, preferring, in contrast, to emphasize the forces of technological innovation, market processes, or the influence of such powerful private economic interests as transnational corporations, in both the recent and the more distant past.

However, the state played a central role in the restoration of the international market after the dislocations and devastations of the Second World War, and, through various acts of commission and omission, did much to create the conditions for the progressive liberalization of the international economic system, particularly from the late 1960s onward.

Considerable confusion, and much discussion, has resulted from the unwarranted conflation of the formal status of all states in the modern inter-state system and the massive differences of practical capability that exist among contemporary states. Much of the legal and institutional framework of the contemporary inter-state system rests upon the principle of formal equality. Votes in the General Assembly of the United Nations are not weighted by size, wealth or any other measure of differential strength and capability. Many central contemporary 'international' institutions, however, do recognize the disparities amongst sovereign states and reflect such practical inequalities in their institutional arrangements. The United Nations thus enshrines the position of the world's leading military powers in permanent membership of the Security Council. The councils of the International Monetary Fund and the World Bank allocate voting strength to individual state members in direct proportion to their financial contributions to the organizations, which, in turn, reflect their 'national' wealth.

The informal organization of the contemporary inter-state system, moreover, clearly reflects, and has always reflected, the disproportionate influence of those states that are, and have been, able to deploy the greatest military force and economic strength in their relations with their fellows – whether intentional or unintentional.[1] It is unsurprising, therefore, that the general framework, institutional pattern and path of development of the post-war inter-state system owes most to its leading members, particularly the United States of America. The Bretton Woods Conference of 1944 was established with the explicit purpose of creating a new, and more durable, institutional framework for the management of the anticipated post-war international financial system, based upon the free convertibility of national currencies at relatively fixed exchange rates. It was a system that reflected the views and desiderata of the United States of America, with some influence from the United Kingdom,[2] and it was these interests that oversaw the system from its progressive emergence until its final breakdown in 1971.[3]

The shape of the post-war international trade system was equally dominated by the views of the United States of America. A clear commitment by the USA to the reconstruction of a free trade system underlay the Havana Charter of 1947 to introduce a new International Trade Organization (ITO). The ITO was, however, destroyed by opposition within the Congress of the USA, leaving the US Administration with no option but that of using a general declaration in favour of a free-trade system that had been signed by participants at the Havana conference – the General Agreement on Tariffs and Trade (GATT) – as the basis for constructing such a system.[4]

The dominant influence of the USA in the immediate post-war international economic system was again witnessed in its extraordinary contribution to the recovery of the war-damaged industrialized economies of Europe and Asia through the Marshall Aid Programme, through which some \$17 billion of direct financial aid was provided to support both former friends and foes.[5] Toleration for very slow progress towards currency convertibility, and genuinely free trade, by the recovering economies was at the discretion of the USA and its government. Growing pressure on the remaining imperial powers within Europe to divest themselves of their colonial possessions was equally in the power of the USA: a power that was deployed dramatically against the British currency during the post-imperial spasm of the Suez invasion in 1956.

The state and contemporary internationalization and globalization

The United States of America was thus overwhelmingly the richest and most influential actor upon the immediate post-war economic scene. In parallel with the decisive influence of the USA in favour of the progressive liberalization of the international trade system, the larger of the USA's corporations also embarked upon a revived programme of international expansion. Foreign investments and acquisitions by such companies were aided by the high value of the widely desired US dollar and positively encouraged by US governments, which saw the active participation of US businesses as a positive contribution to the recovery of war-damaged economies around the world. The foundations of an open world economy, and of the extensive activities of Transnational Corporations (TNCs), were thus laid early in the post-war era.

The gradual evolution of the international economy in a more open and integrated direction was substantially reinforced by developments from the 1960s onwards. The first critical development was the maturation of the recovery process of those industrial economies that had been most damaged by the Second World War. As France, Germany and Japan revived and reasserted themselves within the world economy, as Great Britain completed its conversion from war-time mobilization to peace-time production, and as formerly semi-industrialized countries like Italy achieved a measure of industrial maturity, the United States encountered the intensification of competition in international markets. Moreover, a set of decisions and non-decisions, mainly by US governments, sowed the seeds of the rapid growth of offshore finance and, in due course, the emergence of an integrated international financial system.

Susan Strange has provided one of the most effective surveys of the earlier roots of contemporary financial globalization. She highlights five key background 'non-decisions' that led to the financial turbulence of the 1970s onwards. These critical 'non-decisions' came against a background of a number of management failures within the international political economy since the 1950s: the failure of NATO allies to accept a proportionate burden of European defence costs in the early 1950s, thereby facing the USA with a disproportionate financial burden and a major cause of a sustained deficit in her balance of payments;[6] a collective failure to devise a standard procedure for handling bad international debts;[7] the proliferation of export subsidies, in the form of tied aid and export credits and guarantees;[8] a failure to create effective institutional restraints upon the expanding transnational corporations of the USA and other leading industrial powers;[9] and, finally, the fateful decision to reopen London commodity markets for international trading and, hence, the restoration of London as a centre of international financial operations.[10] Many of these 'non-decisions' continued to exert an influence throughout the remaining decades of the twentieth century.

Five further critical 'non-decisions' were to have dramatic consequences against such a background. First among these 'non-decisions' was the inability to restore effective authority over the foreign exchange markets after the failure of the Smithsonian Agreement on monetary stabilization of 1971.[11] The second non-decision was the failure to return, in due course, to a modified form of gold-exchange standard for major currencies and, hence, an inability to develop new rules for international economic and financial adjustment, holdings of monetary reserves and general exchange rate management.[12] The third and fourth non-decisions were the failure to establish a new *modus vivendi* between the major oil-importing and the major oil-producing countries, or to take seriously the plight visited upon the non-oil-producing Less Developed Countries, during the period of dramatic oil price rises in the 1970s.[13] The final international 'non-decision' was the inability to establish an effective new 'lender of last resort' for the international 'community'.[14] Again, developments during the later decades of the twentieth century merely compounded the character and consequences of these further key 'non-decisions'.

Such critical 'non-decisions' reinforced the effects of the earlier domestic policy decisions of the governments of some of the leading member states of the international financial system. The decision to allow British banks to accept deposits and make loans in dollars in 1958 had opened the door to the emergence of the eurodollar market from the early 1960s onwards. This was reinforced by the US government's permissive attitudes towards overseas branches of US banks that engaged in dollar deposit-taking and lending; restrictive policies on bank lending within the USA; tax support for US banks competing in overseas financial markets; and a generally relaxed attitude towards the emergence of the eurodollar market, and its wider international financial effects.[15]

The scale and speed of international financial transactions were substantially enhanced by the combined effect of such a series of 'non-decisions', permissive policies and other contributory conditions, with the ratio of financial transactions in the London Eurodollar market to the value of annual world trade increasing from 6:1 in 1979 to 25:1 by 1986.[16] International financial volatility was, in turn, substantially increased by such developments, with increased vulnerability of national currencies to speculative pressures, and expanded availability of funds for (ultimately risky) loans to Developing Countries. Many of the roots of the Less Developed Countries' 'debt crisis' of the early 1980s, the dramatic stock market gyrations of October 1987, and the tribulations of the European Exchange Rate Mechanism (ERM) during 1992 and 1993, can thus be identified in a series of political decisions and 'non-decisions' made in, and by, the major economies during the preceding decades.

The condition of, and policy choices within, the United States of America thus remained central to many of the key decisions and non-decisions that shaped the emergence of an increasingly integrated international financial system in the 1960s and 1970s. Such factors were also central to the USA's role in promoting the increased openness of the trade system. Confronted with increased competition in international markets, the USA could have placed major obstacles in the path of further international economic liberalization by resorting to outright protectionism. However, a combination of 'liberal' economic ideology and the considerable influence of economic interests within the USA that were committed to international and transnational trade, and exchange, sustained the country's commitment to the broad principles and general practices of a free trade system. Governments of the USA thus maintained support for the progressive liberalization of international trade under the auspices of the General Agreement on Tariffs and Trade and its successive rounds of trade-liberalization negotiations.[17] Successive GATT agreements, in turn, did much to establish the broad framework within which the expansion of international trade and changing patterns of specialization and locations of competitive advantage could take place.

The extent of the USA's commitment to liberal economic principles and free market trade practices was not, however, unqualified. The ability of the USA to sustain the competitive pressures unleashed within an ever-freer international economy rested, in part at least, upon the persistence of a range of neo-mercantilist policies and practices, ranging from massive support for aerospace and armaments industries, via state-funded Research and Development and extensive procurement programmes,[18] to widespread financial subsidies for major segments of the country's agricultural industry.[19] Indeed, many of the industrial areas within which the USA has retained an edge in international competition – civilian aircraft; computer hardware and software; a range of high-technology products; and foodstuffs of many types – owe something to such structures of direct and indirect support.

However, the USA has maintained a general disposition in favour of trade liberalization and the major institutions of an open trade system – the GATT and its successor the World Trade Organization (WTO) – and abjured, thus far, wholesale retreat into extensive protectionism. Such a persisting USA commitment to an open international economy has encouraged similar dispositions amongst other major actors upon the world economic stage. The European Union, and its major member states, eventually acceded to the concluding agreement of the GATT's Uruguay Round and the formation of the WTO. Japan has responded to steady pressure – bilateral from the USA and multilateral via the GATT and WTO – to open itself to competitive imports. China, too, has shown some signs of beginning to accept a range of measures to liberalize its trade relations and open up its domestic economy as a *quid pro quo* for its eventual membership of the WTO.[20]

The fruits of the mechanisms and measures of enhanced liberalization within the international economy have been varied. Formal tariffs and quotas were the target of the early rounds of GATT negotiations. As such restraints upon free trade were progressively reduced, however, many states resorted to less visible means of protection of, and support for, domestic producers. Non-tariff Barriers (NTBs) became increasingly common during the post-war era and attracted the increasing attention of those states and multinational authorities that were committed to liberalization. Moreover, earlier rounds of GATT negotiations excluded some critical areas of economic activity, particularly agriculture, trade in services and intellectual property rights (and, thereby, trade in intellectual property).

Action to eliminate NTBs and to extend the GATT's area of coverage was undertaken on both a bilateral and a multilateral basis. Bilateral pressures to reduce informal barriers against imports were often exerted by the more industrialized countries against more protectionist industrialized countries and against Less Developed Countries that were seeking to cushion their fragile, emergent industries. However, the purity of the richer countries' opposition to NTBs was frequently limited by the need – perceived or actual – to dampen the speed and extent of competitive pressures from new entrants to the world market.[21] The Multi-Fibre Arrangement for Developing Country exporters of textiles and cheap clothing had been introduced in 1973 to facilitate the orderly expansion of market opportunities within the Advanced Industrial Countries for exports from the Less Developed Countries. However, the Arrangement incorporated protective clauses against rapidly rising levels of imports that might threaten stability, and employment prospects, within the textile and clothing industries of the importing countries. Such clauses were deployed extensively during the 1970s and 1980s to constrain the volumes of textile and clothing imports being shipped to a number of AICs from LDCs that had begun to specialize in the production and exportation of such products.[22]

Bilateral 'arrangements' between AIC importers and competitive exporters have also been concluded in a number of industrial areas where the established AICs feared a substantial threat in domestic markets from new international competitors: particularly automobiles and steel. Japan was the first major target of such 'arrangements', with many importing countries inducing Japan to undertake 'voluntary' agreements to limit volumes of exports directed towards the importing AIC concerned. Successive industrializing economies of East and South-East Asia have been subject to similar 'voluntary' restraints as their competitive capabilities have developed and begun to pose a potential threat to producers within the AICs.[23]

Multilateral initiatives have, in contrast to the mixed record of bilateral efforts, made a more even contribution to the liberalization of international trade in recent decades. The Uruguay Round extended the principles of the GATT to agricultural trade and secured agreements, in principle, to extend coverage to trade in services and intellectual property rights. The success of the Uruguay Round on the agricultural front, while qualified in many respects, was notable given the centrality of regulated agricultural trade to the Common Agricultural Policy of the European Community and the large role played by Federal regulation and subsidy policies in the agricultural industry of the USA.[24] Disputes between the European Community and the United States of America over the terms of the agricultural agreement threatened, at one stage, to sabotage the entire Uruguay Round of negotiations. However, agreement and the conclusion of the Round provided both for the formal extension of coverage to agriculture, with the promise of the progressive elimination of barriers against, and subsidies for, agricultural trade and for the establishment of a new World Trade Organization with responsibility for overseeing fair and free trading within the international economy and for securing future agreements on trade in services[25] and intellectual property rights.

It is important to recall, however, that the Uruguay Round negotiations were undertaken by the representatives of states (or of the European Union collectively in the case of its member states); that the agreement was signed by state representatives; and that the component members of the World Trade Organization are states (and the EU). States bring actions over disputed trade issues to the WTO and have the responsibility for implementing (or not implementing as the case may be) the judgements of the WTO. States, individually or severally, remain the only agencies that can, through their actions, give life to the WTO and its rulings and regulations or destroy it through non-compliance.

Negotiations to develop new rules and regulative agencies for international multilateral investment have also remained firmly in the hands of states and their representatives. The terms of a Multilateral Investment Agreement were established by early 1998, after two years of intense inter-state negotiations, but were placed under threat by the growing reluctance of the government of the United States of America to endorse what it saw as an agreement that would be unbalanced and prejudicial to US interests.[26]

It is also states that have been the prime agents of deregulation and liberalization. The Reagan administration in the USA and the Thatcher governments in the UK in the early 1980s provided examples of progressive deregulation of their domestic economies. Mrs Thatcher's government also abolished exchange controls for the British economy, with major consequences for the outward flow of capital and the further development of an integrated world financial system.

The initiatives of the Reagan administration and the Thatcher governments thus heralded a new orthodoxy of economic management that became the global shibboleth of the late 1980s and early 1990s. All manner of economic difficulties, from the continuing underdevelopment of many African economies, through the rising unemployment of many European countries, to the economic and financial crisis of East and South-East Asia in 1997–98[27] have attracted broadly similar prescriptions involving the elimination of regulations, the abolition of trade controls, the liberalization of the financial sector and, in many cases, the privatization of large tranches of state-owned or state-controlled economic assets.[28]

Liberalization, and hence the foundational conditions of advancing internationalization and globalization, have thus been primarily a function of the policies and commitments undertaken by the leading states within the international economy during the last three decades of the twentieth century. The critical role of states in stimulating developments in one direction does not, however, imply that those same states are, or will be, equally able to reverse any departures that may prove to be untenable or undesirable. This asymmetry in state power and subsequent process is one of the critical complexities of the contemporary international political economy, and one to which the discussion will return at various points.

The technological roots of contemporary internationalization and globalization

Technology looms large in many accounts of contemporary trends towards greater internationalization and globalization, the key technologies being those of information processing, communications and transport. Indeed, so central has been the role of such technologies in some interpretations of contemporary developments as to constitute a form of technological determinism, in which all developments of importance are seen to be driven exclusively and irresistibly by a relatively small number of technological innovations and their effects. For observers like Manuel Castells the advent of micro-electronics-based communications networks is so central and significant as to have introduced a qualitatively new kind of human society – the information society – which is now able to operate on a global scale.[29]

The arrival of the internal combustion engine, particularly in its aeronautical applications, and of the microprocessor have certainly wrought profound changes in many aspects of the lives of a substantial proportion of the population. The steam engine and the telegraph had already done much to transform transport and communications in the nineteenth century, as was demonstrated in Chapter 2. The internal combustion engine, however, was the invention that facilitated powered flight and its transformational implications for human transport and the conduct of warfare. Massive advances in aeronautics were made, it is important to note, under the pressures of the two world wars of the twentieth century and massive state-funded programmes of research and development, airfield construction and aircraft procurement. Governments have also done much to promote the civilian applications of air transport, with grants of monopolies for the aerial transportation of mail; support for the development of ever more opulent airports; and, in many cases, succour for state-owned airlines. The regulation of movement within air-lanes and control of access to airport landing rights also remain under the close control of state or delegated authorities. State involvement with local aircraft manufacturers through military–industrial linkages and direct support for research and development also remain high, as the cases of the USA and Boeing and the European Union and Airbus Industries amply demonstrate.[30]

Governments may thus have played a central role in many economic and industrial developments. The wider economic effects have, however, often been less under the direction of states and their governments. Business travel by air has expanded massively; airborne package tour holiday-making has exploded in scale and scope; and the aerial shipment of high-value goods has progressed substantially, with many electronic 'chips' moving from places of production to points of final assembly by air.

The evolution of the aircraft industry, and of its wider impact upon the world economy and society, is a particularly complicated tale. Governments have continued to play an interested and active role in the fundamentals of industrial organization and performance within the sector, have remained intensely involved in its military aspects, and have facilitated much of the broader infrastructure that is essential for the functioning of the commercial side of the industry. Much of the commercial development of the air transport industry has also involved a complex relationship between states and commercial operators of various kinds. As in all dynamic markets, however, many of the more significant developments within the world's air-transport industry have been undirected by governments, whether or not they were expected or desired.

The advent of the microprocessor and the micro-electronics revolution reflect a similar tale of state support, state direction and commercial dynamism to that of the twentieth-century aeronautical revolution. The earliest electronic computers were nurtured by small groups of university professors. The ever more complex requirements of code-breaking during the Second World War, however, brought governments firmly into the picture and ensured a substantial acceleration of computing know-how and capability. Post-war advances towards the development of electronic transistors, in enterprises such as the British Post Office and the USA's Bell laboratories,[31] were then overtaken by, and subsumed into, the demand of the military and space authorities of the United States of America for miniaturized control and communications equipment for ballistic rocketry and battlefield communications, in the aftermath of the shock of the launch of the Soviet Union's Sputnik satellite.[32]

The rapid emergence of a new military–industrial complex in the micro-electronics sphere within the United States of America ensured that the major breakthrough in the design and manufacture of integrated circuits – electronic 'chips' – and their subsequent commercial exploitation, took place in that country. Indeed, the size of the US market for micro-electronics-based goods, combined with the substantial head-start gained by its industries, has sustained an innovative edge for US companies in most micro-electronics-based goods during subsequent decades.

The deep interrelationship between state and commercial institutions in the foundation of the US micro-electronics and computing industries, and the clear centrality of these industries to the world economy, prompted state-level emulatory programmes in many other countries. Japan's Ministry of International Trade and Industry (MITI) moved from a watching brief into a highly active programme to support the collaborative development of random access memory chips in the mid-1970s,[33] including the use of non-tariff barriers to protect domestic producers.[34] By the early 1980s, the Japanese government had committed some $500 million to a somewhat ill-fated programme of support for the development of 'Fifth Generation' computers.[35]

Britain individually, and the European Union collectively, have also pursued policies of support for 'national champions', and extensive programmes of financial support for research and development and technical innovation, ranging from Britain's Alvey Programme of the early 1980s to the continuing EU Esprit programme.[36]

The United States of America again played the decisive role in the development of the transformational computer-communication network – the internet. The network was initially established to link US military facilities through a multi-routed network that would be less vulnerable to disruption in time of war than conventional 'hub and spoke' telephone systems. The network was then expanded to accommodate a range of universities and similar research institutions, most of which were government-funded, to a greater or lesser extent. Once, however, the internet expanded beyond its military and university origins, its take-up, scale and scope of utilization, and potential impact upon world society, exploded in an apparently uncontrollable manner. Even here, however, states can continue to play a moderating role, as illustrated by the Chinese government's regulation of access to and of acceptable content for the internet within its jurisdiction.[37]

As in the case of the air-transport industry, the micro-electronics and internet industries demonstrate the crucial initial role of states and state-linked institutions, a subsequent commercial dynamic, and the continuing role of the state in providing support where needed and regulation where required. Thus, the government of the United States of America, faced with the unanticipated emergence of a potential monopolist in computer software – Microsoft – initiated determined anti-trust actions through the law courts.[38] Such a complex pattern of state involvement is widespread and enduring in many of the critical areas of industrial and economic development that lie at the heart of growing internationalization and globalization.

Transformational technologies have thus been brought forth, and accelerated, by a range of past state actions, often motivated by strategic considerations.[39] Moreover, any supposed 'imperative' of technological developments is thus both muted and modulated by states acting individually and collectively. The future impact of any given technological innovation will thus be as much a function of the political, economic and social context within which it appears as it will be a result of any self-evident features of that innovation itself.

Economic processes and the advance of internationalization and globalization

Increasing internationalization and globalization are primarily an economic phenomenon. It is common, therefore, to emphasize the economic sources of this central contemporary development. Such an emphasis upon the economic can, however, lead to a simplistic, if not a deterministic, view of the roots of core processes and developments in the human condition.

Deterministic approaches seek to explain central developments in terms of the invariable and irresistible effects of one basic force, or factor, or, at most, a small number of such forces or factors. Classical Marxism-Leninism was couched in explicitly deterministic terms, with the edifice of political and social life being determined by the identifiable (and predictable) development of the economic infrastructure of human existence.[40] In the extreme versions, the entire pattern of human history, past, present and future, could be adduced from an analysis of the successive, and inevitable, stages in the development of the economic mode of production, from primitive subsistence production, through serfdom and capitalism, and on to the future nirvana of socialism. History, however, has proved too complex and unaccommodating to provide convincing support for such analytical visions.

A wider, though more diffuse, form of (non-Marxist) economic determinism also infuses much of the contemporary discussion of increasing internationalization and/or globalization. Here a few prominent features of contemporary economic developments are emphasized and held to have irresistible (at least at acceptable costs) consequences for the further development of the global political economy. The further advance of financial integration; the further internationalization of production; the continued erosion of the economic power of states; and the further homogenization of world-wide consumer tastes and goods are all held to be inevitable given the patterns and processes that now characterize the contemporary world economy. Free markets, allied to contemporary technologies, thus render further internationalization, and ultimate globalization, an inevitable, and in some views a desirable, end-state for humanity.[41]

If there are any clear and inevitable patterns in human history they are far from simple or immediately accessible to the human intellect. The historical record, in practice, has exhibited dramatic shifts and reversals, as well-established trends have been suddenly, and often brutally, overturned. Indeed, few centuries have exhibited more dramatic reversals than the twentieth century, with its two catastrophic world wars that overwhelmed the naive expectations (and simple trend extrapolations) of a world of benign and peaceful economic interdependence as envisaged by such observers as Norman Angell.[42]

More promising perspectives upon developments within the international political economy are those that rest upon more possibilistic, or possibly probabilistic, foundations.[43] Such perspectives allow an emphasis upon sets of powerful influences that are likely to shape the general pattern of developments, but accommodate, explicitly, the range of other forces and factors that may deflect, or modify the effects of, even the strongest of potential influences.

The constraints and opportunities inherent within prevailing conditions may thus be credited with considerable influence; but accidents, mistakes, and unanticipated effects are also accorded their rightful analytical place. Within the international economy, a range of possibilities – new technologies, the market opportunities of an opening international market, advantages of scale of operation and new prospects for specialization – may all offer opportunities to firms and societies; they do not, however, guarantee that such opportunities will be seized fully or effectively, or that their exploitation will have predictable or predicted consequences.

From such a perspective, prevailing conditions and trajectories within the contemporary international political economy are thus the starting place for, and preponderant influence upon, future development. No single force or factor, nor any simple trend, will determine future developments. Current trajectories may be maintained, may be deflected in unexpected directions or, in the extreme, may even be reversed by the as yet unanticipated confluences of many factors and forces.

The immediate future may, however, witness the further advance of internationalization and/or globalization in many, if not all, aspects of the international political economy. Technological innovation and implementation will persist in many industrial areas. Financial integration will continue unless sundered by dramatic crises like the Asian economic and financial crash of late 1997 and early 1998. Levels of inter-state trade and foreign direct investment by transnational corporations are likely to grow. The international relocation of production will continue and continue to put pressure upon employers and employees in many Advanced Industrial Countries. None of these developments are, however, inevitable, and they could well have consequences that lead to their own reversal. Such possibilities will be the subject of much of the subsequent discussion.

Transnational corporations and internationalization and/or globalization

Many critical economic developments within the contemporary global economy do not have the impersonal character suggested by standard textbooks on economics. An increasing range of central elements – decisions on transnational investment; patterns of 'international' shipments; movements of funds between one currency and another – are actually made by a small group of identifiable human beings who occupy leading positions within a relatively small number of highly influential enterprises. The major transnational corporations are particularly prominent within the ranks of such influential actors in the contemporary international political economy.

The post-war growth of transnational corporations has been the object of considerable study. The USA's post-war dominance contributed considerably to the establishment of a general climate within which foreign investments could be made with confidence and operated with good effect. The strength of the US dollar in the immediate post-war decades also provided US-based companies with considerable financial advantages in establishing new operations overseas and/or in their acquisition of existing foreign assets.

Companies' motives for such international expansion are varied and have been much debated. Raymond Vernon's 'product cycle theory' highlighted the relationship between the maturation of a firm's technical and industrial innovations and its growing interest in extending its control to overseas suppliers of goods and services related to those innovations.[44] The innovating company can be relatively secure in its market advantages during the 'introductory phase' of the product or technique. As the product or technique enters its 'maturation phase', competition begins to confront the innovating company, which then starts to consider the establishment or acquisition of foreign subsidiaries as a means of retaining overseas sales. Finally, the product or technique becomes universally accessible during the 'standardization phase', and production advantages shift to low-skilled, low-wage economies, at which point the innovating company may seek to preserve its market position by relocating the bulk of its world-wide production to such economies, with re-imports back to its home country.[45] Such a response to the cycle of innovation – maturation – standardization of industrial innovations can be viewed in defensive or offensive lights: as a survival technique or as a means of dominating world markets and suppressing foreign competitors.

The diversity of experiences in different industries and among firms based in different countries, however, has prompted the search for an eclectic theory of international production, which is more sensitive to such diversity and abjures any one explanatory perspective. Such an eclectic approach is sensitive to the different economic and technical conditions affecting operating within different industrial sectors and arising within varying 'national' industrial cultures.[46] Whatever the motives and patterns of transnational investment, production and operation, such activity has grown substantially, if unevenly, during the post-Second World War era, and has come to involve companies based in many more countries than the United States of America.

Transnational investments; shipments of commodities, goods and services; cross-border flows of information; and the massive international flows of funds overseen by transnational corporations are the tangible substance of much of contemporary internationalization and globalization. However, to the extent that the activities of transnational corporations are the stuff of internationalization and globalization, the latter phenomena are far from impersonal or automatic, and remain firmly within the realms of human deliberation and choice.

Transnational financial actors and the integration of the global financial system

Financial enterprises are a special and highly significant type of actor within contemporary movements towards greater internationalization or globalization. Finance remains an essential lubricant of a complex economy, but can, as is suggested by a range of recent developments, become virtually an end in itself.[47] Modern technologies have, moreover, facilitated a scale and speed of communication that is unprecedented and that is ideally suited to communications and transfers amongst those whose business concentrates upon market-sensitive information; 'abstract' money, such as loans, credits, and payments settlements; and symbolic property in the form of stocks, shares and bonds.

A suitable framework of politics and policy has, however, been essential to the current condition of global financial integration, as was indicated earlier in this chapter. The effects of the specific decisions and non-decisions identified by Susan Strange,[48] however, also required a broader framework of political and economic stability within which international transactions and liaisons amongst financial interests could be developed with confidence. The *Pax Americana* was the foundation of such a supportive framework during the early post-war decades. A wider structure of political stability, sustained by the leading democratic/free-market societies, then complemented the initial role and contribution of the USA.

Within such a context of general stability, financial interests have been able to pursue transnational links with confidence and increasing enthusiasm. 'National' stock markets have been opened to participation by firms headquartered overseas. Major financial enterprises in many economies have been acquired by foreign firms and consolidated into ever-larger transnational financial companies, primarily in the wholesale and professional sectors thus far, but with increasing efforts devoted to the retail financial services sector in the late 1990s.[49] The scale and intensity of 'international' transactions in loans, currencies, stocks and shares, bonds, 'derivatives' of various kinds, and insurance and pension services have burgeoned during the 1980s and 1990s.

Representatives of the firms engaged in various financial sectors have been actively engaged in attempts to establish new, global performance standards and corresponding regulative agencies. These negotiations have often associated representatives of private interests, states and intergovernmental agencies, as in the case of the suggestions by the Joint Forum on Financial Conglomerates, in February 1998, for new common international standards for transnational operators in banking, insurance and securities industries.[50] Such activities mark both a response and a contribution to the steady advance of global financial integration, as further integration generates a need for new levels and modes of regulation and as, in turn, the establishment of new regulative capacities increases the stability of the global financial system and enhances general confidence.

Social and cultural sources of internationalization and globalization

A distinct, and growing, group of observers of the contemporary world claim to detect the emergence of a new form of global society.[51] Such a phenomenon would provide the internationalized or globalized world of high finance, transnational corporations, transformational technologies and intensifying economic competition with a social and cultural dimension that would otherwise be lacking. Moreover, the emergence of a global society might mute the more depersonalizing and frictional features of the other dimensions of internationalization and/or globalization, thereby promising humanity a more gentle and convivial future.

The sources, nature and consequences of any new global society are, however, tricky matters. Two general sources of a global society are commonly cited: the need for transnational popular association and joint action generated by the emergence, or intensification, of new problems confronting humanity on a world-wide scale; and the possibilities created by the new technologies of personal travel and communication to establish transnational relationships that are, at once, both closer and more extensive than was possible for the majority of humanity in the past.

The problems created by such visions are both analytical and empirical. The critical analytical issues concern the cohesiveness of any emergent global society and the relationship between the supposed sources of such a society and its emergence in practice. Cohesiveness has two dimensions. The first concerns the degree to which any emergent 'society' is one such society or a set of distinct, and more specialized, 'societies' that vary in the extent and intensity of their interlinkage. The latter, far from presaging one 'global society', might occasion the emergence of a multitude of partial 'societies', whose interactions might range from the mutual indifference (probably) of stamp collectors and boating enthusiasts to the intense mutual antagonism (presumably) of global networks of paedophiles and those of religious fundamentalists. A 'society' founded upon commonalities is a fundamentally different phenomenon from that encompassing sets of diverse and possibly antagonistic special interests.

The second dimension of cohesiveness relates to the problems of the homogeneity/heterogeneity of any emergent global society. A fully cohesive global society would have to transcend not only the sectional divisions (and possible antagonisms) of those whose interests differentiated them from others, but also the more 'traditional' differences based upon state membership, ethnicity, ideological adherence and/or religious affiliation. The advance of internationalization or globalization might merely compound rather than dissolve such potentially divisive differences.

Some of the possible sources of a new global society offer the promise of transcending 'traditional' differences and divisions. New global needs provide possible stimuli for future global common action, and possible community. Indeed, there is evidence of growing transnational communication and concerted action on issues of apparent common concern to humanity – particularly environmental issues. The widespread popular activity directed against the Shell petroleum company over its plans to sink the redundant Brent Spar oil platform in the Atlantic Ocean[52] is frequently quoted as an example of just such transnational communication, co-ordination and mobilization. Organizations like Greenpeace give institutional expression and substance to such functionally orientated global interest movements.

There are two problems with such a vision of a new functionally directed global society. The first is that functional requirements have never shaped humanity's responses in a consistent and reliable manner. Far too many logical requirements of, or solutions to, pressing problems have been ignored in the past to warrant confidence in the supposedly automatic influences of functional imperatives. Moreover, needs and interests often clash with other needs and interests. The success of one global movement on one issue is no guarantee, therefore, that another movement addressing some other issue will not encounter overwhelming opposition when confronting the needs and interests of more powerful groups. The weakness of functional imperatives, and the clash of competing needs and interests, thus challenges simplistic expectations about the likely force and effectiveness of global interest movements in shaping a new future and spawning a new global society.

A range of new technologies of transport and communication provide, in the view of many, new possibilities for transnational contact and communication, and the foundations of a new global society. The problems with this vision are, however, all too obvious. First, far too large a proportion of the world's population still lacks ready access to high-speed, long-distance transport or communications. Frequent air travel is affordable only to a minority, albeit a growing minority, of humanity. Access to the internet is only slightly less limited. Second, the patterns of contact and communication of those who do have ready access to transnational travel and/or communications are far from undifferentiated. Most travellers journey to a highly restricted number of destinations and limit themselves, on arrival, to a highly constrained set of holiday activities or to a restricted range of business contacts. Communications via the internet or other means of long-distance communication are equally focused and limited for the vast majority of users.

Such general qualifications to simple notions of a world of increasingly homogeneous and intense transnational contact and communication illustrate the difficulties inherent in the empirical identification of any emergent global society. Evidence of growing transnational activity does not, in itself, demonstrate the emergence of a new global society, or of a general response to any functional imperatives generated by an increasingly internationalized or globalized world economy. Quantitative measures of transnational contact and communication must be leavened with qualitative judgements about the kinds of contacts and communications that are being undertaken and their qualitative effects upon participants. Specialized activities, associations and networks may, in particular, provide little evidence of a new global society and may, indeed, indicate the emergence merely of new transnational levels of division and antagonism.

The necessary qualifications outlined above to postulating any simple and straightforward notion of a new global society apply with equal force to the associated notion of a new global culture. Such a global culture is of analytical significance in two ways. First, a genuine global society would require a minimal core of basic beliefs, values and behavioural expectations; the foundations of *Gemeinschaft*, rather than the looser sharing of a set of common interests – a global *Gesellschaft*. Second, a global culture is supposed, by some observers, to be the inevitable product of the continued advance of the global market, with common products and brands being sold world-wide to an increasingly homogeneous world of consumers.

The diversity of beliefs, values and behavioural expectations within the contemporary world is far too great to support any expectations of imminent global cultural homogeneity. The arrival of any global *Gemeinschaft* is thus likely to be both tortuous and slow. The pressures of the increasingly global market do, however, create interesting processes and possibilities that remain difficult to interpret with confidence.

At one level, contemporary economic internationalization or globalization appears to be creating an increasingly uniform world market. The breakfast cereals of a small number of Western-based transnational food companies appear on the shelves of shops around the world. Japanese consumer electronics products share shops world-wide with video recordings of Hollywood films and compact discs of popular music recorded primarily by British and American musicians.

Three crucial points have to be made about the apparent homogenization of the world's consumer market. First, the culture that is embedded in such products is that of the Advanced Industrial West: explicitly so in the case of video recordings and compact discs; implicitly in the electronics goods and clothing, which may be made in one of the countries of East or South-East Asia or Latin America, but which are 'Western' in their technological or cultural origins. Any contemporary cultural globalization is thus a product primarily of the expansionary impulses of commercial and cultural interests within a relatively small number of Advanced Industrial Countries, and mainly Western Advanced Industrial Countries, rather than of a genuine global cultural melting-pot.

The second point of salience is that even where such 'global' products and fashions are widely consumed, their homogenizing impact upon local cultures cannot be assumed. In some cases local cultures may be swamped by cultures embedded in imported goods, particularly where the 'goods' are cultural artefacts like films, television programmes, popular music or fashion. In other cases, however, there will be no more than a partial, or conditional, acceptance of the cultural implications of the imports: many traditional beliefs, values and behavioural expectations will be preserved. In extreme cases, a reaction to the embedded culture of imported goods may develop, or be encouraged by local leaders, and lead to a vigorous reassertion of some, or all, of the core elements of the traditional culture, as happened in Iran after the revolution against the pro-Western Shah, or has been happening more recently in the revival of traditional music within urban Greece.

The final pertinent point about global society and global culture is that of the limited penetration of global goods and 'culture' in many parts of the world, where televisions remain rare, films may be shown only rarely, and literacy levels remain low, and where, indeed, even electricity has yet to be provided.[53] No true global society or global culture can develop and flourish where a large proportion of the world's population is cut off from the main mechanisms for, and manifestations of, cultural homogenization.

Conclusions

The sources of the contemporary growth of internationalization or globalization are thus many and varied. Conventional accounts emphasize the role of new technologies of long-distance transportation and communication; the role of financial integration; the activities of transnational business enterprises; the development of new, world-wide problems; and the emergence of new popular transnational associations, themselves reflecting new world-wide problems and the facilitating influence of new technologies.

Each of the conventional sources of internationalization and globalization has a role in contemporary developments. The account is, however, seriously deficient if it neglects the critical role of states and their governments in shaping the post-Second World War political and economic order in general, and in establishing the framework within which the more recent advance of internationalization and globalization could take place. States and their governments have, through acts of commission and omission, exerted a fundamental influence upon central developments within the world economy of the late twentieth century and unleashed processes that have had, and are continuing to have, profound and often unanticipated consequences.

Notes

1 Robert W. Tucker, *The Inequality of Nations* (New York: Basic Books, 1977).
2 Barry Eichengreen and Peter B. Kenen, 'Managing the world economy under the Bretton Woods system: an overview', in Peter B. Kenen (ed.), *Managing the World Economy: Fifty Years After Bretton Woods* (Washington, DC: Institute for International Economics, 1994), pp. 3–57, esp. pp. 11–15.
3 Joan E. Spero and Jeffrey A. Hart, *The Politics of International Economic Relations*, 5th edn (London: Routledge, 1997), pp. 16–24.
4 Susan Strange, *Casino Capitalism* (Oxford: Basil Blackwell, 1986; and Manchester University Press, 1997), pp. 50–7.
5 *Ibid.*, pp. 12–13.
6 *Ibid.*, p. 31.
7 *Ibid.*, pp. 32–3.
8 *Ibid.*, pp. 33–6.

9 *Ibid.*, pp. 36–7.

10 *Ibid.*, pp. 37–8.

11 *Ibid.*, pp. 38–41.

12 *Ibid.*, pp. 41–3.

13 *Ibid.*, pp. 34–5.

14 *Ibid.*, pp. 45–6.

15 *Ibid.*, pp. 47–8.

16 Andrew Walter, *World Power and World Money: The Role of Hegemony and International Monetary Order* (Hemel Hempstead: Harvester/ Wheatsheaf, 1991), pp. 196–7.

17 On which see the survey article on world trade, 'Where next', *The Economist*, 3 October 1998 (after p. 88), p. 9.

18 On neo-mercantilist possibilities, see: R.J. Barry Jones, *Conflict and Control in the World Economy, Contemporary Economic Realism and Neo-Mercantilism* (Brighton: Harvester/Wheatsheaf, 1986), esp. Chs 6, 7 and 8.

19 On US agricultural support policies see: 'Of wheat and welfare', *The Economist*, 11 February 1995, pp. 55–9; and see also: 'Tobacco country fights back', *The Economist,* 21 March 1998, pp. 59–60.

20 See: 'Chinese traders at the door', *The Economist*, 11 October 1997, pp. 107–8.

21 Bernard Hoekman and Michel Kostecki, *The Political Economy of the World Trading System: From GATT to WTO* (Oxford: Oxford University Press, 1995), pp. 206–10; Robert Gilpin, *The Political Economy of International Relations* (Princeton, NJ: Princeton University Press, 1987), esp. pp. 205–8; and see also: Jones, *Conflict and Control*, pp. 159–60.

22 Carl. B. Hamilton, *Textiles Trade and the Developing Countries: Eliminating the Multifibre Arrangement in the 1990s* (Washington, DC: World Bank, 1990).

23 Jaime de Melo and L. Alan Winters, *Voluntary Export Restraints and Resource Allocation in Exporting Countries* (Washington, DC: World Bank, 1990).

24 'Of wheat and welfare'.

25 On the new telecommunications pact in 1997 see: 'Not quite magic', *The Economist*, 22 February 1997, pp. 79–83.

26 'US shies away from accord on investment', *Financial Times*, 14/15 February, 1998, p. 3.

27 'New illness, same old medicine', *The Economist*, 13 December 1997, pp. 95–6.

28 See: Osama J.A.R. Abu Shair, *Privatization and Development* (Hound-mills: Macmillan; and New York: St Martins, 1997).

29 Manuel, Castells, *The Informational City: Information Technology, Economic Restructuring and the Urban-Regional Process* (Oxford: Basil Blackwell, 1989).

30 'Peace in our time', *The Economist*, 26 July 1997, pp. 79–81.

31 E. Braun and S. MacDonald, *Revolution in Miniature: The History and Impact of Semiconductor Electronics* (Cambridge: Cambridge University Press, 1978).

32 *Ibid.*, esp. pp. 81–2 and 91–3.

33 M.J. Wolf, *The Japanese Conspiracy* (New York: Empire Books; and London: New English Library, 1983), Ch. 4.

34 *Ibid.*, pp. 77–8; 'All's not fair in the chip war', *The Guardian*, 21 April 1982, p. 15.

35 'Vaulting into the fifth generation: Japan goes for no. 1', *South* (September 1983), pp. 21–2; and 'Coming shortly – the world domination machine', *The Guardian*, 12 October 1983; and 'Computer drive', *The Guardian*, 15 April 1982, p. 14.

36 Jones, *Conflict and Control*, pp. 236–47.

37 'The Great Wall wired', *The Economist*, 7 February 1988, p. 89.

38 'Competing in cyberspace', *The Economist*, 19 November 1994, p. 98; and 'High noon for Billy the Kid?', *The Economist*, 24 June 1995, pp. 85–6.

39 On the military and strategic dimensions of industrialization see: Gautam Sen, *The Military Origins of Industrialisation and International Trade Rivalry* (London: Pinter, 1984).

40 F.M.C. Howard and J.E. King, *The Political Economy of Marx* (Harlow: Longman, 1975); and for the distinctive Leninist element see: V.I. Lenin, *Imperialism: The Highest Stage of Capitalism* (Petrograd, 1916 – various editions).

41 Kenichi Ohmae, *The End of the Nation State* (New York: Free Press, 1995); and Lowell Bryan and Diana Farrell, *Market Unbound: Unleashing Global Capitalism* (New York: John Wiley and Sons, 1996).

42 Norman Angell, *The Great Illusion: A Study of the Relation of Military Power in Nations to their Economic and Social Advantage* (1909, various editions, including London: Weidenfeld and Nicolson and New York: Putnam).

43 On possibilism and probabilism see: H. and M. Sprout, *The Ecological Perspective on Human Affairs with Special Reference to International Politics* (Princeton, NJ: Princeton University Press, 1965).

44 Raymond Vernon, *Sovereignty at Bay* (New York: Basic Books, 1971).

45 See: Robert Gilpin, *US Power and the Multinational Corporation: The Political Economy of Foreign Direct Investment* (New York: Macmillan, 1975), pp. 120–1.

46 John H. Dunning, *International Production and the Multinational Enterprise* (London: George Allen and Unwin, 1981), esp. Chs 2, 3 and 4.

47 Eric Helleiner, 'When finance was the servant: international capital movements in the Bretton Woods order', in P.G. Cerny (ed.), *Finance and World Politics: Markets, Regimes and States in the Post-hegemonic Era* (Aldershot: Edward Elgar Publishing Ltd., 1993), pp. 20–48.

48 Strange, *Casino Capitalism*, pp. 31–48.

49 'Peter Martin, What's in a name', *Financial Times*, 26 February 1998, p. 3.

50 'Global finance watchdog's new rules', *Financial Times*, 20 February 1998, p. 4.

51 Martin Shaw, *Global Society and International Relations: Sociological Concepts and Political Perspectives* (Cambridge: Polity Press, 1994).

52 'Greenpeace at sea', *The Economist*, 15 July 1995, p. 61.

53 However, the new generation of 'Freeplay', wind-up products may go some way to overcome this obstacle. See: 'A new generation of business', *Financial Times*, 21 December 1998, p. 12.

4

The ambiguous impact of globalization

The uneven advance of internationalization and/or globalization has potentially profound implications for humanity, and its impact will depend on both the nature and the extent of development in each particular field. Any tendencies towards greater internationalization and/or globalization will, however, be of significance and analytical concern.

Grand pronouncements about the implications of internationalization or globalization are legion. Charting the relationship between different forms of internationalization or globalization, and their varying levels within the contemporary world political economy, is, however, a matter that requires care and discrimination, for considerable complications, and contrary tendencies, are evident within many current developments. Such complications and contrary tendencies form the subject-matter of this chapter.

A new international division of labour?

Many of the mechanisms and processes commonly identified with increasing internationalization and/or globalization encourage, and reflect, a rapidly changing international division of labour. Early signs of this transformation within the international economy were signalled by expressions of concern in the 1970s at the 'deindustrialization' of many of the mature industrial economies: a process that reflected the combined effects of the increasing consumption of services, the growing internationalization of finance, and the transfer of some basic manufacturing to developing countries.[1] Subsequent developments have compounded the processes identified in, and reinforced the anxieties raised by, the early deindustrialization literature.

The most pessimistic of the deindustrializers envisaged the complete loss of manufacturing industry by the mature industrial societies. Economic policy in Great Britain during the early 1980s explicitly embraced the vision of a coming service-based economy, exporting advanced services of all kinds while importing required physical goods and commodities from whichever developing economies had taken up their production. Such a vision of the future was, however, unwarranted, for it ignored the implications of varying factor mixes in the production of a wide range of commodities, goods and services.

The extraction of commodities and the production of manufactured goods are rarely simple matters. Some productive activities are inherently complex, requiring high levels of skill and human involvement, and are likely to be retained within more advanced industrial societies. Employees engaged in such activities will, moreover, be relatively highly paid, irrespective of the country within which they live and work. The design of electronic micro-chips thus remains one area of productive activity in which firms based in mature industrial economies can compete on a relatively level footing with those based in Less Developed or Newly Industrialized Countries.[2]

Of equal significance to the persistence of decisive expertise within mature industrialized societies is the wider consideration that many areas of industry are open to considerable variations in the mix of physical capital and human labour, of skilled and unskilled human activity, that can be employed in the productive process. Thus the components of motor vehicles can be manufactured directly by human beings or mass-produced by machines. The body panels of Rolls Royce cars have traditionally been hand-beaten, while those of more popular vehicles are conventionally pressed by machine presses. Again, some motor cars are still welded together by individual workers, while others are welded automatically by computer-controlled lasers. Between the extremes of hand manufacture and total automation, a wide variety of combinations of man and machine is available in the production (and distribution) of many goods and commodities. Manufacturers in mature industrial economies that wished to remain active in areas of manufacture that have come under increasing competitive pressures from new producers in low-wage-cost developing economies have often had the option of designing, and/or investing in, more productive, labour-saving technologies that preserve price-competitiveness. This, coupled with the maintenance of high design quality in goods that are not yet entirely homogeneous globally, has allowed the survival within the mature industrial societies of manufacturers in a wide range of goods, from motor vehicles, to cruise ships, to textiles and clothing.

The preservation of substantial areas of manufacturing within the Advanced Industrial Countries does not, however, signify the absence of any tendencies for the relocation of manufacturing from Advanced Industrial Countries (AICs) to the Newly Industrialized Countries or the Less Developed Countries. Casual inspection of retailers' shelves reveals the range of goods now manufactured in, and imported from, formerly Less Developed Countries, particularly within East and South-East Asia. The statistical evidence supports this impression of the new role of East and South-East Asia in world manufacturing, as indicated by Table 4.1, in which it is clear that the bulk of the 'loss' of manufacturing share by the Developed Industrial Economies can be attributed to the increased share secured by South-East, and even more notably East, Asia.

Table 4.1 Regional shares of world manufacturing output, 1970–95 (percentages)

Country/Region	1970	1980	1990	1995
Industrialized Countries[a]	88.0	82.8	84.2	80.3
Developing Countries, of which:	12.0	17.2	15.8	19.7
Latin America	4.7	6.5	4.6	4.6
North Africa and West Asia	0.9	1.6	1.8	1.9
South Asia	1.2	1.3	1.3	1.5
East Asia[b]	4.2	6.8	7.4	11.1
Sub-Saharan Africa[c]	0.6	0.5	0.3	0.3

Source: UNCTAD, Trade and Development Report, 1997 (New York and Geneva: United Nations, 1997), Table 28, p. 82.

[a] Including the former socialist countries of Eastern Europe and also South Africa.

[b] Including China.

[c] Excluding South Africa.

The significant increase in the share of world manufacturing output secured by the East and South-East Asian economies during the last decades of the twentieth century does not, however, tell the whole story, for the world economy was not a zero-sum game during the period: expanding output from the East and South-East Asian economies occurred at the same time as rapid expansion in the world market for manufactured products, particularly within the East and South-East Asian economies themselves, with their share of Global Gross Domestic Product rising from approximately 4 per cent in 1980 to some 7 per cent by 1995.[3] Thus, growth within the domestic economies of East and South-East Asia provided markets for some of their additional output and intra-regional exports. The effect of such increased domestic demand was to dampen slightly the impact upon home markets in the Advanced Industrial World of the surge of production from the Newly Industrialized Economies and to provide continued export opportunities for producers based within the older industrial societies: trade creation rather than pure trade displacement.

Fortunately, the advent of the Newly Industrialized manufacturers of East and South-East Asia coincided with a period of general growth in the world economy. Markets within the Advanced Industrial Economies were also expanding during the last decades of the twentieth century, and this expansion further helped the absorption of some of the growth of output from East and South-East Asia and the increase of productivity within many of the AICs themselves. The impact of new international centres of competition in the markets for many well-established goods was further dampened by the emergence of a wide range of new goods and services, often introduced by, and manufactured within, the older industrial societies (including, for these purposes, Japan). Notable examples of such novel products have been mobile phones for personal communication and Global Positioning Systems for world-wide navigational purposes.

Internationalization and/or globalization: world-wide prosperity or intensified exploitation and inequality?

Advanced goods and technologically advanced manufacturing techniques may have combined their effects with that of general growth within the world economy and the markets of both the Advanced

Table 4.2 Growth of Gross Domestic Product of the high-income economies 1980–94

	1980	*1995*
A. High-income economies	7,758,074	22,485,548
B. World	10,768,090	27,846,241
A as % of B =	72%	81%

Source: World Bank, *World Development Report, 1997* (New York: World Bank, 1997), Table 12, pp. 236–7.

Industrial Countries and the Newly Industrialized Economies to reduce the disruptive consequences of global economic developments during the late twentieth century. Such factors have not, however, overcome all problems or eliminated all sources of tension, as reactions to the Asian crisis of 1997–98 demonstrated.

Rhetoric and reality often diverge in discussions of the effects of growing internationalization and/or globalization upon inequalities within and amongst societies and, hence, on the possibilities of intensifying local or international 'exploitation'. It remains true that the mature industrial societies continue to generate and enjoy the overwhelming proportion of the world's wealth, as Table 4.2 demonstrates. However, the distribution of income within many of the world's economies, as measured by the proportions of income enjoyed by the top 20 per cent and the bottom 20 per cent of households, has not changed dramatically since the late 1970s and has shown only a slight levelling out of wealth consumption within the emerging industrial economies, as is indicated by Table 4.3. A combination of local economic conditions and the policies adopted by governments remains the most significant factor in patterns of equality/inequality, as indicated by the steady growth of inequality within the United Kingdom between 1979 and 1997 when compared with the modest equalization of incomes within Japan and the United States of America and the variable record of France.

Internationally, too, experiences of the developing world economy have varied markedly.[4] Again, local conditions and policies have had a profound effect. The rapid growth in the share of world production achieved by the East and South-East Asian economies was the success story of the internationalizing and globalizing world

Table 4.3   Income distribution 1979–97, selected economies (percentage of shares of household incomes)

Country	1979		1993		1997	
	lowest 20%	highest 20%	lowest 20%	highest 20%	lowest 20%	highest 20%
India	6.7	48.9	8.8	41.3	8.5	42.6
Philippines	3.7	53.9	6.5	47.8	6.5	47.8
Kenya	—	—	2.7	60.9	3.4	62.1
S. Korea	5.7	45.3	—	—	7.4*	42.2*
Malaysia	3.3	56.6	4.6	53.7	4.6	53.7
Mexico	2.9	54.5	4.1	55.9	4.1	55.3
Japan	7.9	41.0	8.7	37.5	8.7	37.5
France	4.3	46.9	6.3	40.8	5.6	41.9
UK	6.3	38.8	5.8	39.5	4.6	44.3
USA	4.5	42.8	4.7	41.9	4.7	41.9

Source: *World Development Reports* (New York: World Bank) for: 1979 –
Table 24, pp. 172–3; 1993 – Table 30, pp. 296–7; 1997 – Table 5, pp. 222–3.
* 1975 figure.

economy of the 1980s and 1990s; the increasing marginalization of a number of African economies was its less desirable face. The decline of sub-Saharan Africa's share of world manufacturing output from 0.6 per cent in 1970 to 0.3 per cent by 1995, as detailed in Table 4.1, is one facet of this process of economic marginalization. Further, no less serious, indicators of economic troubles are the statistics for the 'growth' of wealth production (Gross Domestic Product or GDP) between 1990 and 1995 and per capita wealth creation (Gross National Product (GNP) per capita) between 1985 and 1995, as indicated in Table 4.4. The scatter plot in Figure 4.1 provides further illustration of the variable, but often seriously poor, performance of many sub-Saharan economies since 1985.

Again, local conditions and local policies have played a vital role in the variation of experience in the sub-Saharan economies during the last decades of the twentieth century, rather than any common experience of past colonial control or contemporary internationalization and/or globalization. Thus the poor performance

Table 4.4   Wealth creation in sub-Saharan Africa 1985–95[a]

Country	Annual average GNP per capita growth 1985–95[b]	Annual average GDP growth 1990–95[c]
Mozambique	3.6	7.1
Tanzania	1.0	3.2
Burundi	−1.3	−2.3
Malawi	−0.7	0.7
Chad	0.6	1.9
Rwanda	−5.4	−12.8
Sierra Leone	−3.6	−4.2
Niger	—	0.5
Burkina Faso	−0.2	2.6
Uganda	2.7	6.6
Guinea-Bissau	2.0	3.5
Mali	0.8	2.5
Nigeria	1.2	1.6
Kenya	0.1	1.4
Togo	−2.7	−3.4
The Gambia	—	1.6
Central African Republic	−2.4	1.0
Benin	−0.3	4.1
Ghana	1.4	4.3
Zambia	−0.8	−0.2
Angola	−6.1	−4.1
Mauritania	0.5	4.0
Zimbabwe	−0.6	1.0
Guinea	1.4	3.8
Senegal	—	1.9
Cameroon	−6.6	−1.8
Côte d'Ivoire	—	0.7
Congo	−3.2	−0.6
Lesotho	1.2	7.5
Namibia	2.9	3.8
Botswana	6.1	4.2
Gabon	−8.2	−2.5

Source: World Bank, *World Development Report*, 1997 (New York: World Bank, 1997), Table 1, pp. 214–15 and Table 11, pp. 234–5.
[a] Excluding South Africa.
[b] GNP: Gross National Product.
[c] GDP: Gross Domestic Product.

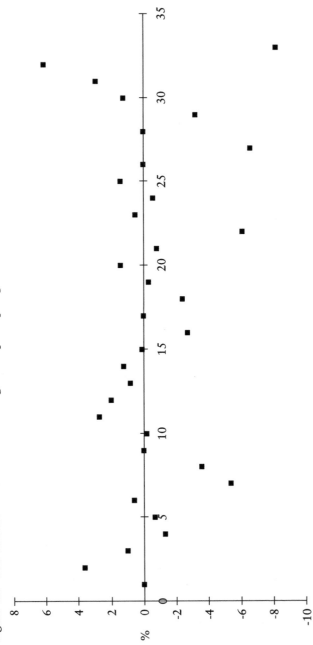

Figure 4.1 Sub-Saharan Africa – annual average GNP per capita growth rates 1985–95

of some sub-Saharan economies can be attributed to poor management of the economy, as in Tanzania, to predatory local regimes, like that of Mobutu's Zaire (now Congo) or to the eruption of destructive armed conflicts, as in Ghana and Sierra Leone. Such clear qualifications apart, it is clear that the advance of internationalization and/or globalization is redefining the wider economic context within which developing African economies have to operate, providing some new market opportunities on the one hand, while intensifying competitive pressures on the other.

The wider debate about the impact of internationalization and/or globalization concerns the issues of the subordination of employees, and the constraints imposed on 'national economies', world-wide. A paradox has arisen during recent decades: that of the growth of feelings of insecurity amongst the working populations of many mature industrial societies[5] at a time of rising real incomes and sustained security of employment. Thus recent economic developments have fostered a widespread sense of personal insecurity that, thus far at least, seems to exceed the prevailing reality. Studies have thus revealed a pattern of long-term employment amongst those male members of the work forces of most Advanced Industrial Countries that is as durable as it was in past decades.[6] The perception of growing insecurity, rather, has been a product of the growth of performance pressures upon those in full-time, longer-term employment, coupled with the rapid increase of both contract employment and part-time jobs, particularly for women.[7] Moreover, arguments for more flexible labour markets in the 1980s and 1990 reinforced such popular anxieties and have often reflected, and been identified explicitly as responses to, the supposed pressures resulting from increased internationalization and/or globalization.

Responses to the economic and financial crisis of East and South-East Asia in 1997–98 also included prescriptions for greater labour market flexibility, particularly in countries with extensive legal protections for the workforce, such as South Korea.[8] The popularity of such doctrines of labour market flexibility underlies the emergence of an atmosphere of apprehension that has, in turn, encouraged a new politics of 'resistance' to internationalization and/or globalization, with local and transnational union activity; the formation of groups to oppose undesired developments; and the emergence of a corresponding academic literature.[9] The problems for such politics of resistance, apart from preserving coherence, are, however, those of successfully differentiating between the effects of internationalization and/or globalization *per se* and those of the consequences of technological change and/or local policies.

Globalization and social, economic and political destabilization

The record on economic inequality both within and amongst contemporary economies is mixed. Moreover, many of the pressures experienced by those in work, and those seeking gainful employment, are often a product of technological changes or the policies adopted by state governments, as much as a consequence of growing internationalization and/or globalization. However, aspects of internationalization and/or globalization do generate pressures in a variety of often interrelated ways: the relocation of some areas of production to ever-lower labour-cost economies; the increased need to adopt the latest, and often labour-saving, technologies to combat rising competition – actual or anticipated – in both export and domestic markets; and references to the economic imperatives of an internationalizing or globalizing world economy by politicians or employers seeking legitimization for policies and practices pursued for other reasons.[10]

Critical developments within and amongst societies are rarely, if ever, to be explained by any one factor. Growing inequality would not, therefore, generate internal breakdown or external conflict on its own, even if it could be established that it was generally increasing. The profound changes inflicted upon societies by rapid changes in economic systems have, however, often interacted powerfully with other sources, and expressions, of general insecurity to foment dramatic, and often dangerous, developments within the social and political realm.

The twentieth century has provided dramatic evidence of the destabilizing dynamics of economic systems in rapid and profound change, and prompted the seminal studies undertaken by J.A. Schumpeter[11] and Karl Polanyi.[12] For Schumpeter, the inherent dynamism of the market system generated 'waves of creative destruction'.[13] The inherently destabilizing character of this process of turbulent renewal within the market system would, itself, undermine the institutional framework that had facilitated the emergence of that system and, in turn, stimulate pressures to tame it through new political institutions and legal restraints.[14] A widespread tendency towards socialist principles and practices during the earlier part of the twentieth century was one of the more dramatic results of such impulses, in Schumpeter's view.[15]

Karl Polanyi was equally concerned to identify the destabilizing effects of the rapid and profound changes wrought by a vigorous market economy.[16] A central feature of the advance of the market economy, to Polanyi, was the growth of the international market and rapid change in the international division of labour. Established forms of employment were often swept away by such changes and, in their wake, traditional social institutions were placed under threat. Popular resistance was one of the clearer consequences of such transformational and disruptive market processes.

Polanyi thus identified a 'double movement' within a dynamic international market economy: rapid changes in the bases of employment within societies, accompanied by the rise of popular movements aimed at opposing, and even reversing, the general effects of such economic developments. Such apparently diverse phenomena as Bolshevism within early twentieth-century Russia and Nazism in mid-century Germany were both extreme examples of such popular counter-movements.[17] Moreover, many of the forms of popular counter-action to economic transformation assumed, and could be expected to assume, a xenophobic character, as with the virulent racist nationalism of Germany's Nazis.

The impact of increasing internationalization and/or globalization may be given particular force through the effects of periodic cycles of financial boom and collapse. Such cyclical disturbances may be a repetitive symptom of loosely constrained or unconstrained financial systems, which exhibit regular patterns of 'mania', panic, and collapse.[18] At the international level, such speculative bubbles may be encouraged and intensified by a period of increasing financial integration and may, in their aftermath, contribute significantly to periods of increasing constraints upon, and contractions of, international financial transactions.

The spectre raised by some critics of rapid economic internationalization and/or globalization is thus that of domestic dislocation within, and tensions amongst, the affected societies. Internally, the institutional foundations of the market order might be threatened – with attacks upon the principles of private property, market exchange and, where relevant, liberal democratic politics. Externally,

xenophobia or ideological incompatibilities might be fuelled and
generate, individually or in combination, a dangerous slide towards
international, or inter-societal, conflict. Signs of just such developments were identified by some observers in a number of South and
South-Eastern Asian economies in the aftermath of the economic
crisis of 1997–98, as evidenced by the eruption in Indonesia of
violence against the local Chinese business community in February
1998.[19]

Such dystopian views of an internationalizing or globalizing
world, however, rest upon a combination of retrospective diagnoses
of the turbulent history of the first half of the twentieth century
and the more pessimistic interpretations of, and extrapolations from,
contemporary developments during its final decades. Social and
political strife in South and South-East Asia may thus be no more
than a transitory difficulty, rather than a harbinger of regional
upheaval. The central issues that will preoccupy much of the subsequent discussion are, therefore, whether developments during the
first fifty years of the century were historically unique, or whether
repetition can be expected, and whether pessimistic interpretations
of contemporary tendencies are warranted.

Internationalization and/or globalization: the new constraints upon states and societies

Domestic destabilization and international conflict remain at one
extreme of predictions about the ultimate effects of increasing
internationalization and/or globalization. Less extreme views also
warn about the effects of increasing internationalization and/or
globalization with arguments that contemporary states and societies
are now subject to a range of significant, and potentially damaging,
constraints.

The rhetoric and reality of state subordination to the imperatives of a globalized world economy turn, in large part, upon the
extent to which the governments of individual states are now subject to unprecedented limitations on the making and implementation of economic policy. An immediate danger in considering this
issue, or set of issues, is that of assuming an unwarranted degree of
homogeneity amongst contemporary states. The practical implications of the contemporary international political economy will be
influenced, substantially, by a number of characteristics of states,

and their 'national' economies: the size, diversity and level of 'development' of the economy; the economic and industrial policies that have been in force in preceding years; and the general policy-orientation, and ideological outlook, of the current government. Variations in each or any of these factors will increase or decrease the level of 'openness' of the 'national' economy; its structural strengths or weaknesses; its sensitivity to changes in the external economy and/or pressures from foreign influences; and the disposition of the local government to respond positively or negatively to 'signals' from the external system.

Many of the elements of diversity amongst states facing the pressures of an internationalized and globalized world will be examined in greater detail later in the discussion. The present task is to survey the range of possible constraints upon governments that might be created by greater internationalization and/or globalization: constraints in the areas of macro-economic policy and of industrial policy.

In the past, governments were often able to use a range of policy instruments to pursue their broader objectives for the domestic economy: trade policy to protect domestic industry and support exporters; fiscal (or taxation and expenditure) policy to influence the general level of economic activity, generate incentives and/or effect a measure of redistribution; monetary policy (particularly interest rate policy) to influence the general level of economic activity and/or to alter the structure of incentives between consumption and savings/investment; and industrial policy to promote desired structural developments within domestic industry.

The advance of internationalization and/or globalization has involved the progressive limitations of trade policy brought about through the multilateral agreements negotiated under the General Agreement on Tariffs and Trade and in response to past bilateral pressures exerted by the United States of America. General industrial policy has also been weakened by the growing costs of effective governmental support for struggling, or emergent, industries in a world of accelerating and intensifying technological and industrial change and the dominance of a general *laissez-faire* philosophy.

Macro-economic policy-making constraints are also well discussed in the literature on contemporary internationalization and/or globalization, and flow primarily from the integration of the world's financial system. States formerly sought to separate the use, and effects, of interest-rate policy, fiscal (taxation and expenditures) policy, and exchange-rate policy. Today, however, it is contended that the separability of interest-rate policy and exchange-rate policies has been irreversibly compromised.

The problem now facing governments of open economies is that the level of international financial integration is now such that movements of money transnationally have become highly sensitive to changes in 'national' interest rate levels. An increase of domestic interest rates will attract a substantial inflow of funds from abroad, attracted by the higher interest rates now available. This inflow of funds will, in turn, increase demand for the country's currency on international money markets, prompting an increase in its value (its price in terms of other currencies). If, therefore, a country is trying to maintain a fixed exchange rate then it cannot manipulate its domestic interest rates for any purpose other than to support that fixed rate, increasing interest rates only to stem an outflow of funds and reduce downward pressures on the currency, and decreasing rates only to stimulate domestic production and exports and to stem upward pressures on its currency value.[20]

A government that, by contrast, chooses not to maintain a fixed exchange rate for its currency, continues to enjoy a greater freedom of manoeuvre. It can reduce interest rates to stimulate the domestic economy by reducing the costs of investment and credit-based consumption. Equally, it can increase interest rates to dampen down the domestic economy. Financial integration has, however, again increased the risks of such interest-rate manipulation. Increasing interest rates to dampen down the domestic economy can attract considerable inflows of funds. If exchange rates are free to float, the 'national' currency can begin to appreciate rapidly in consequence. Rapid currency appreciation can soon increase the effective price of exports on international markets and, hence, reduce their competitiveness. Equally, the domestic prices of imports can be reduced by the appreciation in the value of the 'national' currency, confronting domestic suppliers with intensified competition from imported goods. The appreciation of the currency may thus reinforce the depressive effect upon the domestic economy of the initial increase in interest rates. The combined effect upon the economy may therefore be both far greater than initially intended by the government that authorized the interest-rate increase and be more unpredictable than the direct effects of an interest-rate increase alone.[21]

The expectation that governments in the past could manipulate interest rates to stimulate domestic economic growth, without subsequent heavy costs in terms of increased inflation, may have been exaggerated.[22] Capital mobility within an increasingly integrated world financial system has, however, clearly increased the constraints upon governments contemplating the manipulation of interest rates. It is also argued, by some observers, that governments' abilities to raise taxes to pay for desired public services has also been compromised.

In the area of taxation, increasing internationalization and/or globalization appears to have generated a growing gap between private taxation and corporate taxation. The majority of individual taxpayers remain relatively immobile with regard to the countries, and therefore the tax-jurisdiction, within which they live and work. Support for tax-cutting political parties thus remains the main legal mechanism for most citizens to pursue tax reductions, and the limited success of such endeavours is reflected in the persistence of relatively high top rates of personal taxation in most of the world's leading economies.[23]

Corporate taxation, however, is quite a different matter from personal taxation in a world of growing internationalization and/or globalization. The growth and spread of transnational corporations, of transnational business associations and alliances, and of complex transnational transactions has posed serious challenges to the tax-raising capacities of state governments. Three features of contemporary conditions have created particular difficulties for governments: the increased freedom of firms over the location, and headquartering, of their activities; the growing problem of deciding where, exactly, a growing number of companies should properly pay their taxes; and, in some circumstances, increasing difficulties in enforcing significantly different consumption taxes in different jurisdictions.[24]

The technological innovations and legal freedoms that have permitted the growth of contemporary transnational corporations have facilitated an increasing locational flexibility for many businesses. Such footloose companies can identify low-tax locations for the siting, or relocation, of their future activities. Moreover, the threat of flight to low-tax locations can prove a potent weapon in bargaining over tax issues with the governments of host countries in which firms are already located, or of higher-tax-level countries that are interested in attracting inward investment by transnational corporations.

Once established on a transnational basis, the activities of companies assume increasing geographical complexity. Networks of activity may spread across a number of separate countries, with all parts of the network contributing to the value of the firm's final product and, hence, profit. Allocation of tax liability under such circumstances becomes a complex and controversial matter. Transnational corporations are able to exploit this complexity to organize their internal accounting in a manner that reveals higher levels of 'profitability' for those activities that take place in countries that have lower rates of 'value added' tax. 'Prices' are thus set for inputs and outputs that their various subsidiaries ship to one another to support such manipulative accounting, high prices being set for the outputs of subsidiaries in low-tax countries and low prices determined for the output of subsidiaries in high-tax countries. 'Intrafirm pricing' – or 'transfer pricing' – of this type has thus been both a common and a somewhat elusive practice among many of the world's leading transnational corporations during the post-war decades.[25]

Governments faced with constraints upon their abilities to tax many of the most profitable of businesses and the wealthier of individuals are clearly faced with a painful choice between cutting services to their populations, increasing the tax burden upon the ordinary, and less mobile, members of their communities, and engaging in deficit financing of the public exchequer.[26]

The option of deficit financing, however, is increasingly limited within the contemporary global order. If the dangerous practice of 'printing money' is to be avoided, deficit financing may be sustained only by governmental borrowing from the public and the private financial system. Such borrowing may encourage increases in interest rates, and will place an increased burden upon taxpayers, who will be called upon to meet the future payments of capital and interest for current borrowings. A further problem with such borrowing, however, is that in an open and global financial system, any effects on the interest rate may have significant effects upon inflows of capital, upon the exchange rate, and thence, relatively rapidly, upon the condition of the domestic economy and domestic industry. Inflows of finance may not result, however, if international financial markets judge the generation of a substantial fiscal deficit to be evidence of the profligacy, or downright incompetence, of a government, and actually withdraw funds.[27] In the face of such complex consequences and volatile responses, governments feel increasingly drawn to the rhetoric of 'fiscal prudence' and 'golden rules' of government expenditure.[28]

Faced with such potential difficulties in a globalized world, governments are drawn towards a combination of increasing the tax burden upon the general population[29] and restraining, and often actively cutting, the level of expenditure upon a range of valued, and valuable, public services.[30] Such a strategy often encounters serious limits of political acceptability, however, as populations rebel against ever-higher taxes and/or reject the continued dilution of public services: a dilemma that encourages the use of indirect, and often less visible, forms of taxation, on the one hand, and the adoption of cosmetic devices to create the illusion of improving public services at a time of reduced real resources, on the other.

The range of constraints that governments now confront has persuaded many that their best efforts should be directed to enhancing the capacities of their economies and populations to respond to, and take best advantage of, the requirements of an internationalized and globalized world economy. Former combinations of demand management and industrial policy have, in places, given way to the pursuit of monetary stability, flexible labour markets, enhanced training of workforces, and a range of allied improvements on the supply side of their home economies. Such a policy adaptation to the perceived imperatives of an internationalized and globalized world economy can be seen either as a natural process of 'progressive enmeshment' within the new global economic order or, from a slightly more critical view, as one of 'coercive socialization'[31] by overweening structures and/or compelling agencies within the contemporary international political economy.[32]

Possible constraints on economic and industrial policies

Many analysts of contemporary economic internationalization and globalization believe that states and their governments are now also subject to a wider set of constraints upon their economic and industrial policies: some 'negative' and some 'positive'.

The 'negative' constraints to which governments are now subject focus upon possible restraints upon business. Policies and practices that constrain the freedom of business to function and to prosper are deemed to be increasingly untenable in a world of mobile capital and intensifying international competition. Thus, the power of trades unions and organized labour to disrupt the productive process will have to be reduced, largely by changes in the legal framework within which they work, as happened under the government of Mrs Thatcher in Britain. Equally seriously, business must be freed from irksome restraints upon its ability to hire and fire workers and change their conditions of work and pay as circumstances 'warrant'. Other restrictions upon the ability to undertake business where and how firms choose may also have to be reduced or eliminated: from the abandonment of controls over the use of land,[33] through to constraints upon the ability of local authorities and governments to impose local taxes upon business to fund local services.

The constraints imposed on states and governments on the 'positive' side by economic internationalization and globalization may be even more widespread and diffuse. Open economies operating within the prevailing 'neo-liberal' ideology will be disinclined to promote domestic industry through explicitly protectionist measures or, indeed, explicit programmes of industrial development and support. A range of other measures may, however, be necessary if the domestic economy is to prosper in an increasingly competitive international environment with ever more mobile businesses. A wide range of measures may, in particular, contribute to the creation of a more welcoming and fruitful environment for business.[34] Measures to improve the attitudes and aptitudes of the local workforce are significant in this respect, as witnessed by the intensifying official concern of both recent Conservative and Labour Governments within the United Kingdom for the quality of education and training and similar concerns at all levels of the federal system of the United States of America.[35]

Attractive environments, stable societies and docile but capable workforces are thus all part of the 'package' that states and their governments feel constrained to supply if new industry is to be attracted and retained in a globalized world. Regional policies may, as will be seen later, constitute a primary means through which the panoply of policies of attraction can be orchestrated and inward investment secured for regions that are most in need of economic and industrial revitalization. Indeed, regional assistance programmes may be one of the few policy instruments that are deemed legitimate

by governments entertaining 'neo-liberal' principles that are subject
to restrictive rules such as those of the European Community, or
are concerned about the possible reactions of international agencies
like the World Trade Organization.

Many of the policies and practices that governments feel constrained to adopt to attract and support business in a world of mobile
capital and intensifying competitive pressures constitute forms of
indirect subsidies. The financial burdens of such policies are shoul-
dered by domestic taxpayers; increasingly, by the less favoured
individual taxpayers, as has been seen earlier in this discussion.
The beneficiaries are, in good part at least, the corporate entities,
whose operations enjoy tax breaks, favourable operating conditions, and 'flexible' workforces. The general good of employment
and economic vitality is thus balanced by the private benefit of
enhanced business profits, much of which may be expatriated, and
increased freedom of action for business enterprises, some of which
may be abused.[36]

The notion of a globalized world political economy thus carries
many implications for the new constraints that states and governments face in the areas of monetary and fiscal policies, and in
economic and industrial policies broadly conceived. Indeed, the
pressures that an integrated global financial system imposed upon
governments complement, and are complemented by, the pressures
created by mobile business and intensifying international competition. States and their governments thus give the impression of being
reduced in competence and capability, with respect to major aspects
of policy, in a manner consonant with notions of 'the end of the
state'[37] or the more measured 'retreat of the state'.[38] Such a diminution of the capacities of the state, however, opens up serious questions about the potency of politics, in general, and of democratic
politics, in particular.

Internationalization, globalization and the opportunities for states

If the advance of internationalization and/or globalization has created
new constraints upon some traditional policy-making capabilities
of states' governments, the interconnections and interdependencies
that constitute many of the emergent economic order offer considerable advantages to some states and their policy-makers. A cardinal myth
of many of the contemporary debates about internationalization

and/or globalization repeats the error of the earlier discussions of international economic interdependence of assuming that the effects of the phenomenon are identical for all states involved. In fact, the contemporary global political economy impacts upon member states in diverse ways and has significantly differing implications for their policy-making capabilities and for the well-being of their populations.

The relationship between individual states and the contemporary political economy thus varies substantially in terms of their dependence upon external developments. Dependence can best be defined as: 'Dependence exists for any actor when a satisfactory outcome on any matter of significance for that actor requires an appropriate situation or development elsewhere.'[39] Such conditions of dependence, however, are a function of the nature and extent of sensitivities and vulnerabilities. Definitions of these terms were developed in Robert Keohane and Joseph Nye's classic study *Power and Interdependence*.[40] The definition of sensitivity therein is relatively straightforward: 'Sensitivity involves the degrees of responsiveness within a policy framework – how quickly do changes in one country bring costly changes in another and how great are the costly effects.'[41] Students of the collective or structural effects of an internationalized and globalized world would merely need to include the phrase 'changes in the external environment' to broaden the definition in a suitable manner.

The vulnerability of any state or society is both a more serious and a somewhat more problematical matter, from the definitional point of view. Keohane and Nye offer two accounts of vulnerability: 'Vulnerability can be defined as an actor's liability to suffer costs imposed by external events even after policies have been altered.'[42] And: 'The vulnerability dimension of interdependence rests on the relative availability and costliness of the alternatives that various actors face',[43] the tension between the two 'definitions' of vulnerability turning around whether it is a function of costs that will persist whatever actors do, or whether it is a function of the relative availability and costliness of policy options that will actually bring about the complete elimination of the direct costs of the vulnerability in question.

Time and costs enter the picture in practice, to produce a two-dimensional range of possibilities. Figure 4.2[44] depicts the polar extremes of the two dimensions. The situation of any state on

Figure 4.2 The sensitivity/vulnerability of states

	Short-term	Long-term
High costs	high sensitivity	high vulnerability
Low/Zero costs	low sensitivity	low vulnerability

any issue of importance to it may thus vary along a sensitivity–vulnerability dimension and along a high–low dimension. Higher levels of vulnerability will thus constrain states far more than lower levels of vulnerability or sensitivity. Higher levels of sensitivity are also likely to impinge upon shorter-term policy-making far more than conditions of low sensitivity. Situations of states, in contrast, with relatively low levels of vulnerability and sensitivity will be less exposed to pressures from the external environment and better placed, therefore, to pursue self-determined goals and policies. Interdependencies may also lie along vertical or horizontal axes, or a combination of the two, with the pattern often being critical to the continued functioning of important industries or the wider economy.

States and societies do not, however, relate only to the generalized structure of the international economy. They are also participants in bilateral relationships with other states and societies. Such relationships give dependencies a bilateral character or, in the case of complex networks of interlinked bilateral relationships, a multilateral character that is more substantive than a structural phenomenon. The occurrence of dependencies within bilateral relationships generates conditions of interdependence. Developing the original definition of dependence provided above, interdependence can be defined thus: 'Interdependence exists for a grouping of two or more actors when each is dependent upon at least one other member of the group for satisfactory outcomes on any issue(s) of concern.'[45]

It is important to note that not all connections between states or societies are really relationships of interdependence. Interconnections may exist between states or societies that are more to do with general structural conditions within the world economy or that do not carry the same implications of direct costs and policy constraints that are signalled by the notion of dependencies.[46] The significance of situations of interdependence is rarely identical for all the participants. The qualitative significance of the dependencies characterizing any bilateral (or set of multilateral) relationships will usually differ for the parties; the levels of dependence amongst the actors are also likely to vary considerably.[47] Such qualitative imbalances and asymmetries provide considerable potential opportunities for influence for those experiencing lower (or even trivial) levels of exposure over those suffering more serious levels of dependence.

There has, however, been a long tradition of regarding the growth of international interdependence as a benign phenomenon. The growth of international trade should, according to this view, prompt the emergence of a new international division of labour and the development of a benign form of interdependence amongst economies, societies and states. Benign international interdependence would, in turn, foster harmony amongst the benefiting peoples and, by increasing their mutual dependencies for an increasing range of goods and services, make it increasingly difficult for those peoples to resort to disruptive and destructive armed conflict with one another. Norman Angell's *The Great Illusion* gave strong expression to such interpretations of, and aspirations for, international developments in 1913,[48] on the virtual eve of the outbreak of the First World War.

The worst wars in humanity's recent history did little to consolidate benign global interdependence during the first half of the twentieth century. Indeed, the critical interdependencies of the years between the two wars were, by transmitting and intensifying the effects of the Great Crash in the USA in 1929,[49] far from benign. Such bitter disappointments, however, failed to destroy liberal optimism and may, indeed, have reinforced the need of many to refine and promote such approaches to future international peace and harmony. The end of the Second World War certainly saw the proliferation of related approaches and proposals: at the theoretical level in the functionalist formulation of David Mitrany;[50] and in the institutional realm, in the Bretton Woods institutions of the International Monetary Fund and the International Bank for Reconstruction and Development,[51] in the later General Agreement on Tariffs and Trade,[52] and in the early moves, via the establishment of a Coal and Steel Community, towards the creation of a new European Economic Community.[53]

The later revival of academic interest in the 1970s in the condition, and implications, of interdependence further reinforced an optimistic liberal view of the international political economy and its prospects. The immediate sources of this intellectual renaissance were varied, including the work of Karl Deutsch on transactional patterns,[54] the growth of security communities,[55] and the birth of new interest in transnational relations and institutions.[56]

The immediate antecedents of the concept of globalization, however, lay in the notion of complex interdependence introduced by Robert Keohane and Joseph Nye in their seminal *Power and Interdependence*.[57] Two ideas within the notion of complex interdependence were central to the later concept of globalization: significant interdependencies among societies;[58] and the emergence of an intensifying complexity in the interrelationships among societies. The notion of complex interdependence, then, rests upon the manner in which the combination of these two conditions places societies, and their governments, under new, and highly significant, constraints. In particular, where a condition of complex interdependence exists among any two or more societies:

- there are, partly by definition, multiple channels of contact amongst governmental and non-governmental elites and other trans-national associations;
- the traditional hierarchy of governmental issues, with military-security issues at the apex, no longer exists;
- military force is no longer used by governments within their own geographical regions or on those issues with regard to which complex interdependence prevails.[59]

The new constraints in the political and military realm under which states, and their governments, are supposed to operate when complex interdependence comes into being are thus clear: under conditions of complex interdependence governments cannot prioritize security issues; cannot use force against other states where complex interdependence prevails; and must remain cautious about any actions that might disrupt harmonious relations with other states with whom valuable relations are maintained. The consequence, however, is the development of zones of persisting peace and security that should last for the foreseeable future.

The situation, however, is not as simple or straightforward as many early adherents to the notion of complex interdependence supposed. Propositions about its supposed causes and connotations are open to similar criticisms and complications to those that confronted the later notion of globalization. The first set of difficulties concerns the empirical uncertainties of the concept. As a concept related to supposedly novel circumstances, the empirical referents of complex interdependence were necessarily limited in number and duration. With very few supportive examples, it was easy to claim that the characteristics of complex interdependence were the product of special circumstances and/or likely to prove fragile in the face of any serious political and security issues that might arise in the future. Moreover, it was inherently uncertain what levels and patterns of interdependence among societies would qualify their relationships as examples of complex interdependence – an uncertainty compounded by the ambiguities affecting the notion of interdependence outlined earlier in this chapter.

The empirical problems of complex interdependence link into its analytical uncertainties. The first, and most fundamental, question is whether the notion of complex interdependence purports to be an empirical model – a simplified version of actual reality – or a heuristic model – an intellectual device intended to answer 'what if' questions, with no necessary correspondence to any aspects of prevailing reality. In *Power and Interdependence* Keohane and Nye make it clear that complex interdependence is being offered as no more than an ideal type to counter that of traditional Realism.[60] Reviewing their seminal volume ten years after its publication, Keohane and Nye re-emphasized the status of complex interdependence as no more than a heuristic model.[61] The temptation to deploy the term 'complex interdependence' as a purported statement about 'reality' was, however, too strong for many analysts of international relations to resist in the later 1970s and the 1980s.

The second analytical ambiguity with the idea of complex interdependence was whether it referred to a fully developed state of affairs or merely to an emergent condition. This is an inherent difficulty confronting models, such as complex interdependence or globalization, where the definitive conditions are variables: that is, there can be varying levels of 'multiple channels of contact' or degrees of financial integration or transnational manufacture. This difficulty is serious only for concepts, such as complex interdependence or globalization, that are supposed, if realized in practice, to have clear, qualitative consequences. If the concept refers only to fully developed conditions, then there is no real problem: the qualitative consequences must follow if the concept is sound. If the concept refers, in contrast, to an emergent (or even variable) condition, then it is not clear at which stage of its development the predicted qualitative consequences should materialize: no simple test of the validity of the concept is thus possible and its veracity must, to an extent, be taken as a matter of faith.

Substantively, the ideas of complex interdependence and the more optimistic versions of globalization herald a new era of peaceful relations among states and societies. Many analysts have argued that international peace and prosperity are primarily the product of democratic regimes and their inherently pacific interrelationships. The popular answerability of such democratic governments, and their greater rationality, is often identified as the source of their pacific dispositions. When interacting with other democratic societies, the lack of mutual provocation complements the constraining influence of the myriad contact acts and interconnections that democratic regimes allow to develop amongst their societies. Complex interdependence is thus encouraged by, and compounds the effects of, democratic politics in generating zones of substantial peace and general security, with reason, reasonableness, multiple contacts and economic constraints all complementing one another in a benign cycle.[62]

The benign syndrome of democratic polities, with open societies and economies, interacting to generate and sustain perpetual peace cannot be taken for granted, however. There have been relatively few genuinely democratic societies in history (by the liberal criteria deployed by 'democratic peace' theorists), and few of these have a long track record. Moreover, definitions of war and peace are highly contestable and contested.[63] If generous definitions of democratic societies are to be allowed, then Britain's involvement in the Boer War at the start of the twentieth century will have to be dealt with; if wider definitions of war are to be tolerated, then US support for action against the democratically elected Allende government in Chile in the 1970s also has to be accommodated. However, the central question for the present discussion concerns the foundations of democratic systems themselves: do genuinely democratic political systems require suitable economic conditions, which, if denied, will either qualify the degree to which genuine democracy can be practised or, in the extreme, precipitate the collapse of democratic regimes themselves and, with their demise, the death of 'democratic zones of peace'.

The ideas of complex interdependence and its successor concept globalization, and the notion of democractic peace thus encounter serious empirical and analytical ambiguities. Such ambiguities relate to, and are compounded by, equally serious questions about the direction of causality for many central developments in human affairs.

Moreover, all complex systems exhibit structural differentiation. In the international political economy this endows some states and actors with far greater power and influence than others. The enjoyment of general structural power,[64] multilateral influence, or strength in bilateral relations is thus a consequence of the varying circumstances enjoyed, or suffered, by different states. A range of structural advantages also allows some societies to maintain advantages from an internationalizing and globalizing world and minimize their exposure to potentially destabilizing external developments. The partial de-localization of many of the larger business enterprises may, however, weaken the past relationship between successful firms and their 'home' countries, leaving the populations of the former 'home' societies increasingly vulnerable to geographically indiscriminate processes and developments. The equations of 'international' advantage and disadvantage are thus becoming increasingly complex and variable in a world of advancing internationalization and/or globalization.

A new global society

One much-discussed consequence of the advance of internationalization and/or globalization is the possible development of a new global society. The forms and foundations of such a new transnational form of association were considered in some detail in Chapter 3. Analytically, one of the first problems generated by the idea of a new global society is whether such a phenomenon should be considered to be a source or a consequence of globalization. However, the interests of this chapter are directed primarily towards the effects of internationalization and/or globalization.

An idea of a new global society as a consequence of internationalization and/or globalization turns upon arguments linking new developments within the global system and the responses that may be necessary at the popular level. Thus, global financial integration, the steady expansion of transnational corporations, the spread of transnational crime and terrorist networks, and the apparent emergence of a growing number of threats to the global environment all create new needs for transnational responses at the societal level. Such responses may assume the form of new links between formerly national political parties and trade union movements, new transnational pressure groups, or internet-linked associations of like-minded individuals. The arguments linking the new global challenges and the new patterns of popular global response are either polemical or functionalist.

Polemical arguments are designed to alert populations to the new challenges and urge activity directed towards the new transnational patterns of response. Such appeals are methodologically unproblematical; their challenges lie purely within the domains of practical popular politics. Functionalist arguments[65] are analytically quite distinct from polemical appeals. Such arguments turn upon the imperative forces that a range of developments within the global political economy are supposed to impose upon human actions and associations.[66] However, arguments that significant developments will occur because they are deemed 'necessary' by some process of argument have rarely been a reliable guide to the conduct of human affairs. Such an *a priori* form of the 'functionalist fallacy' may thus be seriously misleading and carry as many traps for the unwary as the infamous *post hoc* form of the fallacy (the argument that because some significant development has taken place it must have taken place, with the retrospective construction of an apparently compelling account for its occurrence). Unfortunately, many expectations of the emergence of a new global society rest upon just such insecure *a priori* functionalist foundations.

Such responses as may develop in the face of advancing internationalization and/or globalization are thus likely to be varied in their form and effectiveness. Individuals and groups will certainly be motivated to pursue more effective forms of transnational action against those that they perceive to be damaging their interests, and many of the new technologies of transport and communications will undoubtedly assist their efforts. The overall consequences of such efforts are, however, likely to remain open to debate, and possible disruption, for some time ahead.

A globalized world versus a regionalized world

Four visions of the emergent future confront the contemporary observer of the international political economy: continued progress towards a wholly internationalized and globalized system; a dialectical relationship between globalizing and regionalizing trends; a simple retreat to a regional, or even sub-regional, world order; or a general collapse into chaos and anarchy. The first two possibilities will be the subject of this section. They will also be considered further at a later stage of the discussion, in addition to the latter two possibilities.

The simplest vision of a world of advancing internationalization and/or globalization envisages an increasingly homogenized world, in which all local and regional differences will be progressively dissolved. Evidence of steady increase in many of the measures of internationalization and/or globalization is referenced in support of such a view.

A contrasting school of thought, however, identifies severe limits to internationalization and/or globalization which, when once reached, will result in the rapid fragmentation of the international political economy into a set of distinct, competitive and possible conflicting regional groupings. Signs of growing regionalization within the international political economy are deployed in support of this interpretation of contemporary developments.

Developments during the latter decades of the twentieth century provide evidence of growth in both internationalization and regionalization. Such a mixed record encourages the third, and most complex, view of contemporary developments: that internationalization/globalization and regionalization are related to one another in a dynamic dialectic, in which increasing regionalization is, itself, a direct consequence of the pressures generated by growing internationalization and/or globalization.

The statistical evidence provided in the figures and tables of Chapter 1 demonstrates the steady growth of trade, financial transactions, and cross-border acquisitions. This, however, is by no means the entire picture of developments in the late twentieth century. Two other patterns are also important: the persistence of significant differences amongst economies, and some signs of tendencies towards economic and political regionalization. Data on movements of 'national' interest rates, inflation rates, prices of stocks and shares, levels of unemployment and wage rates all continue to show significant levels of variation.[67]

There is also some evidence of a measure of regionalization within the international political economy. In some cases, economic regionalization reflects the force of attraction exerted by a major regional economy, such as the United States of America on the American continent[68] or Japan in East Asia.[69] In cases such as that of the European Union, a clear political commitment to forge a new economic and political regional entity has driven a substantial measure of regionalization, with an increasing portion of the trade of its members being conducted within the Union.[70]

The regional bias of the trade of Western Europe is easy to overstate, however. When the ratio of intra-regional trade to the region's share of world wealth production (GNP) is computed, Europe is a far from exceptional region. Table 4.5 lists the ratios of intra-regional trade to regional GNP for the world's major regions in 1990, and indicates the higher levels of such trade 'gravity' in the other world regions. All, however, suggest that, by this measure, the world in 1990 exhibited a modest level of regionalization.

A new emphasis upon regionalism also appears to have entered the political agenda. The European Union is a clear example of a post-war project to create a new structure of harmony and co-operation amongst the peoples of Western Europe and, if need be,

Table 4.5 Ratios of intra-regional trade to regional Gross National Product as a proportion of global GNP, 1990

Region	Ratio of intra-regional trade to regional GNP
North America	1.91
Latin America	3.42
Western Europe	1.55
Africa	2.42
Middle East	2.00
Asia	2.24

Source: Table 2, pp. 102–3 in Andrew Wyatt-Walter, 'Regionalism, globalization, and world economic order', in Louise Fawcett and Andrew Hurrell, *Regionalism in World Politics: Regional Organization and International Order* (Oxford: Oxford University Press, 1995), pp. 75–121.

to construct a new economic power within which to confront an increasingly competitive international economy.[71]

The negotiation of the North American Free Trade Area, while primarily economic in motivation, also had a strategic and geopolitical facet, with acknowledgement of the common regional problems of drug trafficking, migration and the environment.[72] Wider concerns have also influenced the wide variety of smaller regional associations within the Latin American subcontinent and the much-vaunted scheme for a Free Trade Area of the Americas.[73]

The creation of the Association of South-East Asian Countries (ASEAN) was clearly motivated by political aspirations to stimulate increased levels of intra-regional trade and construct a framework for enhanced regional co-operation.[74] These initiatives, however, were challenged by the eruption of the Asian financial and economic crisis in 1997–98 and by such irresponsible behaviour by member states as the forest-burning within Indonesia and the consequential spread of smog throughout many of the neighbouring countries.[75]

The Middle East and Africa remain even more problematical as arenas of regional co-operation and consolidation. The Middle East has been riven by tensions and conflicts since 1945, not least the long-running confrontation between Israel and its Arab neighbours. Such lines of friction inhibit easy collaboration, but also provide a strong motive for attempts to create new structures of co-operation: in common defence against mutual threats, or as peace-building measures in areas of endemic conflict.[76] In the case of Africa, post-colonial enthusiasm underlay the creation of Organization of African Unity (OAU), and sub-regional interests have prompted such subsequent ventures as the Economic Community of West African States (ECOWAS). The progress of such initiatives has, however, been waylaid by the repeated afflictions and upheavals to which many of Africa's societies have been subject during the last third of the twentieth century.

The future of regionalization remains uncertain. The motives for a regional response to the pressures exerted by the advance of internationalization and/or globalization may be readily identified, and their practical expression is sometimes easy to detect. Whether such impulses will be swamped by the continued progress of internationalization and/or globalization, or merely reinforced and re-invigorated, is not yet clear.

Relocalization and the political economy of global fragmentation

The emergence of cohesive regions is not, however, the only pattern of counteraction to the advance of internationalization and/or globalization. The pressures generated by increasing internationalization and/or globalization may be such as to undermine effective regional initiatives and to stimulate, in marked contrast, more divisive responses and the re-emergence of particularistic and even xenophobic sentiments and structures.

Two patterns of relocalization are possible. The first is a re-emphasis of the 'traditional' states. The identities of such states would not necessarily correspond to the current membership list of the United Nations, but would probably reflect many of the major states and/or their major ethnic, cultural or geographical sub-groupings. The reasons for expecting such a pattern of response to the pressures of internationalization and/or globalization, and any faltering of regionalization, will be reviewed in detail in later sections of this book. The alternative pattern is that of fragmentation at all levels of the established world order: the global, the regional and the state, with sub-state and trans-state groupings emerging to dominate the political scene.

The pattern of future developments might thus resemble more closely James Rosenau's vision of 'turbulence'[77] than one of a cohesively globalized system or a tightly regionalized world. However, the description of such an alternative to a highly globalized, newly regionalized, or resurgent statist world requires considerable care. The conventional, and largely negative, senses of terms like 'turbulence' and 'fragmentation' are not necessarily applicable to such circumstances. Many anti-statists,[78] enthusiasts for the principles of 'small is beautiful',[79] and 'green' activists[80] would extend a positive welcome to the radical relocalization of politics and economics. The issue turns, ultimately, upon two factors: the conditions under which relocalization takes place; and expectations about the capacity of relatively small groups of human beings to order their affairs in a benign and effective manner, while also ensuring harmony with members of other groupings.

The problem posed by the prevailing conditions is that the reversals of trends towards greater internationalization and/or globalization, which are themselves prompted by the pressures created by such trends, are unlikely to be smooth or gentle processes. Far more likely are dramatic developments occasioned by wide-ranging economic and financial crises, such as that witnessed in Asia in 1997 and 1998, and/or vigorous local reactions against political and economic developments reflecting increasing internationalization and/or globalization. Such reactions may all too easily assume unpleasant characteristics, of the type documented by Karl Polanyi[81] and other observers of the eruptions that disfigured the first half of the twentieth century.

The malign character of many past responses to the pressures of rapid economic, social and political change confronts optimistic expectations about the capacity of human beings to reorder themselves in a benign and effective manner with serious questions. Revolutionary enthusiasts have long thrived on great hopes of post-revolutionary human emancipation, only to be disappointed by the post-revolutionary descent into barbarity, self-consumption and a general failure to achieve the 'promised land'. Such experiences in the past might reflect the unpropitious circumstances under which various revolutions were prosecuted; they might equally, however, signal serious limits to the human capacity to effect rapid and profound changes in the behavioural foundations upon which people live their lives.

Whatever the form and character of a fragmented future world, such fragmentation would signal an emphasis upon diversity, rather than the global social and cultural homogenization that is sometimes suggested by prophets of a globalized world and a new global society. Internationalization and/or globalization may thus prompt the reassertion of diversity – a dialectic of difference – rather than the smooth emergence of similarity.

Globalization and the supply of and demand for effective governance

Discussions of the effects of economic internationalization and globalization upon the institutions and capabilities of established governments generally fail to differentiate between their effects on the demand for effective government and on the supply of such government. This distinction, and the complications that it highlights, have been implicit in much of the preceding discussion.

Many of the issues affecting the demand side of the issue will be discussed in detail in subsequent chapters. The current discussion, however, is primarily concerned with the effects of globalization upon the supply of effective government at the level of established states and at the level of the international system.

For good or ill, the primary agent of government in the modern world is the state (nominally organized around, and for, a 'nation'). A range of interacting historical forces and experiences lay behind the emergence of states as the most effective actors in the modern system and as the political agents that won the highest level of acceptance and support from their populations. Governance at the domestic level has been orchestrated by state authorities for most of the more, stable societies for much of the past two centuries or more, and such state authorities have been the final arbiters of disputes when they have arisen within their domestic jurisdiction, as demonstrated dramatically by the example of the Federal State in the American Civil War in the mid-nineteenth century. States have also been the primary actors in the inter-state or inter-governmental agencies that have been formed from time to time to manage the collective affairs of humanity as a whole: the United Nations, and many other international organizations, being essentially a 'club of states'.[82]

The range of constraints imposed by a globalized world that have been discussed earlier in this chapter all conspire to undermine the effectiveness of such state institutions in many important areas of policy and practice. The central problem is that states may be less able to pursue positive economic and industrial policies to ensure the well-being of their populations except to accommodate the imperatives of a globalized world economy, or to promote a range of other policies in other areas of life that might be intrinsically desirable but that conflict, in some manner, with the requirements of the globalized system or its human representatives. States and governments that seek legitimacy and support may have to be more than mere weather-vanes for a globalized world political economy.

The problems of the diminished state compound when the state in question is democratic in form. The wishes of the population are now integral to the legitimacy of the democratic state and the democratic process of deliberation and mutual decision central to its functional integrity. If a globalized world imposes imperatives upon states across a range of the most important policy areas, then democratic politics must necessarily be diminished, because all popular wishes cannot be accommodated, and domestic debate and decision cannot be sovereign. Such a situation challenges the integrity of established democratic states and, paradoxically, confronts societies in transition from dictatorship with the paradox that the democracy towards which they are seeking to move may be no more than a shadow of democracy: democratic in form, but not in fact on most economic issues of substance. The seriousness of this possibility, in turn, is expressed by the view of an authoritative panel of political scientists that the successful transition to democracy requires a political system that is able to engage the genuine support of its population for economic reforms, rather than impose them 'top down', and the creation of an economic system that is supportive of democratic institutions thereafter.[83]

The weakening of established democracies, and the frustrations of expectations amongst the transitional societies, could have the most serious of consequences. Democracy is not inherently perverse: it throws up perverse policies only when populations become alienated by wider developments. Democracies are also robust while they are able to meet the demands and expectations of their populations. Shorn of the capacity to satisfy popular expectations, democracies have demonstrated no more robust a history than any other political orders that have fallen upon bad times. Democracy itself could thus be threatened by the more extreme consequences of a globalized world, if globalization were to have the form and effects envisaged by some of its stronger theorists.

Weakened states would be equally weakened in their activities in the various inter-state fora that currently endeavour to manage world affairs. While neo-liberals might applaud such a development, others would be concerned at the danger of weakened capabilities for effective governance of the world at a time when internationalization and globalization have generated the kinds of increased requirements for effective control and regulation that were revealed by the economic and financial crisis of the late 1990s.

The further danger of a world of diminished states is that other agencies will seek to impose themselves upon the world stage, or even be forced to assume responsibilities for which they are unprepared and ill equipped. These possibilities will be considered in greater detail at a later stage. The important issue at this stage in the discussion, however, is that such alternatives are likely to suffer from one, or both, of two serious shortcomings. The interests that will be promoted by alternative agencies, be they coalitions of commercial interests, alliances of pressure groups or groupings of citizens' associations, will be special and partial interests that will fail to accommodate and promote the general good. The second shortcoming is that such agencies will lack the general resources to ensure effective governance of the global system, i.e. the practical instruments of implementation of rules and regulations and the legitimacy that will provide the popular consent and support for any non-dictatorial form of governance.

Conclusions

The effects of internationalization and/or globalization are thus likely both to be complex and often to be contradictory. The practical diversity of their consequences complicates the task of establishing the character and extent of internationalization and/or globalization from the available evidence. Internationalization and/or globalization are thus doomed to remain controversial theoretically and methodologically, as well as in policy terms, for the foreseeable future.

However, the challenges potentially posed to established states and conventional modes of public governance by economic internationalization and globalization are many, and potentially profound. Traditional priorities in the fields of security and military strength may be overturned by a world in which the physical self-assertion of states is increasingly impossible. Monetary and fiscal policies may also be so reduced in effectiveness, or so compromised by their interconnections, as to reduce governments to near-impotence. Wider economic and industrial policies may also be dominated by the requirements of internationally mobile business and the pressures of intensifying international economic and industrial competition. Popular social choices expressed through democratic political institutions may be particularly constrained, with serious consequences for both established democratic systems and transitional societies. The issue, then, is whether such a vision of the diminished role and capability of the state is valid and, if so, what the consequences are likely to be for a world of growing population, increasing environmental pressure and undiminished cultural and ideological divisions.

Notes

1 Clive Jenkins and Barrie Sherman, *The Collapse of Work* (London: Eyre Methuen, 1979); and Frank Blackaby (ed.), *De-Industrialisation* (London: Heinemann, 1978).

2 Hence the Advanced Industrial Countries' dominance of general microprocessor design and manufacture.

3 China (mainland), Hong Kong, Indonesia, Korea (South), Malaysia, Singapore, Thailand (but not Taiwan). Source: Table 12, World Bank, *World Development Report 1997* (New York: Oxford University Press for the World Bank, 1997), pp. 236–7.

4 Andrew Hurrell and Ngaire Woods, 'Globalisation and inequality', *Millennium*, Vol. 24, No. 3 (Winter 1995), pp. 447–70.

5 'Second thoughts about globalisation', *The Economist*, 21 June 1997, p. 108.

6 'The end of jobs for life?', *The Economist*, 21 February 1998, p. 104.

7 *Ibid.*

8 'The end of the miracle', *The Economist*, 29 November 1997, pp. 25–7; and 'Kim the peacemaker', *The Economist*, 31 January 1998, pp. 67–8.

9 See the contributions to: Barry K. Gills (ed.), *Globalisation and the Politics of Resistance*, special edition of *New Political Economy*, vol. 2, no. 1 (March 1997).

10 On motives for invoking internationalization and globalization, see: R.J. Barry Jones, 'The globalization debate in perspective: purposes and practices in a polymorphous world', in R. Germain, *Globalisation and its Critics: Perspectives from International Political Economy* (London: Macmillan, forthcoming).

11 J.A. Schumpeter, *Capitalism, Socialism and Democracy*, 5th edn (London: George Allen and Unwin, 1976).

12 Karl Polanyi, *The Great Transformation: The Political and Economic Origins of Our Time* (Boston: Beacon Press, 1957).

13 Schumpeter, *Capitalism, Socialism and Democracy*, Ch. 7.

14 *Ibid.*, esp. Chs 12, 13 and 14.

15 *Ibid.*, esp. Chs 15, 16 and 17.

16 Polanyi, *The Great Transformation.*

17 *Ibid.*

18 C.P. Kindleberger, *Manias, Panics and Crashes, A History of Financial Crisis*, 3rd edn (New York: John Wiley, 1996).

19 'Indonesian rioters vent fury on Chinese', *Guardian Weekly*, 8 March 1998, p. 20 (from *Le Monde* of 21 February 1998).

20 See the article, 'Capital goes global', *The Economist*, 25 October 1997, pp. 139–40.

21 'Who's in the driving seat – survey of the World Economy', *The Economist*, 7 October 1997, esp. p. 12.

22 *Ibid.*, p. 15.

23 'Bearing the weight of the market', *The Economist*, 6 December 1997, pp. 124–5, esp. p. 125.

24 'The tap runs dry', *The Economist*, 31 May 1997, pp. 19–21.

25 On intra-firm trade, see: R. Murray, *Multinationals Beyond the Market* (Brighton: Harvester, 1981).

26 James O'Connor, *The Fiscal Crisis of the State* (New York: St Martin's Press, 1973), esp. Ch. 8.

27 On 'disciplinary neo-liberalism' see: Stephen Gill, 'Globalisation, market civilization, and disciplinary neoliberalism', *Millennium*, vol. 24, no. 3 (Winter 1995), pp. 399–423.

28 See: 'A promising party', *The Economist*, 20 May 1995, p. 32.

29 'The tap runs dry', *The Economist*, pp. 19–21.

30 Jan Aart Scholte, 'Global capitalism and the state'. *International Affairs*, vol. 73, no. 3 (July 1997), pp. 427–52, esp. pp. 448–9.

31 Hurrell and Woods, 'Globalization and inequality', p. 457.

32 For a critical view see: Stephen Gill, 'Globalisation, market civilisation, and disciplinary neoliberalism', *Millennium*, vol. 24, no. 3 (Winter 1995), pp. 399–423.

33 'The British disease revisited', *The Economist*, 31 October 1998, pp. 31–4.

34 Many of which are surveyed in: R.J. Barry Jones, *Conflict and Control in the World Economy: Contemporary Economic Realism and Neo-Mercantilism* (Brighton: Harvester/Wheatsheaf, 1986), esp. Ch. 7.

35 On the new US apprenticeship scheme see: 'Generation X-onomics', *The Economist*, 19 March 1994, pp. 55–6.

36 On changing attitudes towards regional assistance policy in the UK, see: Brian Groom, 'Mandelson orders big shake-up for regions', *The Financial Times*, 19 October 1998, p. 1.

37 Kenichi Ohmae, *The End of the Nation State* (New York: Free Press, 1995).

38 Susan Strange, *The Retreat of the State* (Cambridge: Cambridge University Press, 1996).

39 R.J. Barry Jones, *Globalization and Interdependence in the International Political Economy: Rhetoric and Reality* (London: Pinter, 1995), p. 6.

40 R.O. Keohane and J.S. Nye, *Power and Interdependence: World Politics in Transition* (Boston: Little, Brown, 1977).

41 *Ibid.*, p. 12.

42 *Ibid.*, p. 13.

43 *Ibid.*

44 Taken from: Jones, *Globalization and Interdependence*, p. 8.

45 *Ibid.*, p. 6.

46 On the distinction between interconnections (or interconnectedness) and interdependence proper see: Mary Ann Tetreault, 'Measuring interdependence', *International Organization*, vol. 34, no. 3 (Summer 1980), pp. 429–43; David Baldwin, 'Interdependence and power: a conceptual analysis', *International Organization*, vol. 34 (Autumn 1980), pp. 471–506.

47 See: Jones, *Globalization and Interdependence*, esp. Chs 5 and 6; and R.J. Barry Jones, 'The definition and identification of interdependence', in R.J. Barry Jones and Peter Willetts (eds), *Interdependence on Trial: Studies on the Theory and Reality of Contemporary Interdependence* (London: Frances Pinter, 1984), pp. 17–63.

48 Norman Angell, *The Great Illusion* (New York: Putnam, 1909).

49 J.K. Galbraith, *The Great Crash, 1929* (London: Hamish Hamilton, 1995); and on the international transmission of its effects see: C.P. Kindleberger, *Manias, Panics, and Crashes*, 3rd edn (New York: John Wiley and Sons, 1996), pp. 123–5.

50 David Mitrany, *The Road to Security* (London: National Peace Council, 1994); David Mitrany, 'The Functional Approach to World Organisation', *International Affairs*, vol. 24, no. 3 (1948); and David Mitrany, *A Working Peace System* (Chicago, Ill.: Quadrangle Books, 1966).

51 See: J.H. Richards, *International Economic Institutions* (London and New York: Holt, Rinehart and Winston, 1970), Chs 2 and 3.

52 On which, see: *ibid.*, Ch. 7; and M.J. Trebilcock and R. Howse, *The Regulation of International Trade* (London: Routledge, 1995), esp. Chs 1 and 2.

53 John Pinder, *European Community: The Building of a Union* (Oxford: Oxford University Press, 1991), Ch. 1; and Brigid Laffan, *Integration and Co-operation in Europe* (London: Routledge: 1992), Ch. 1.

54 Karl W. Deutsch *et al.*, *Political Community and the North Atlantic Area* (Princeton, NJ: Princeton University Press, 1957).

55 *Ibid.*, p. 58.

56 R.O. Keohane and J.S. Nye, Jr., *Transnational Relations and World Politics* (Cambridge, MA: Harvard University Press, 1972) (originally

a special edition of *International Organization* – vol. 25, no. 3 (Summer 1971).

57 R.O. Keohane and Joseph S. Nye, *Power and Interdependence: World Politics in Transition* (Boston: Little, Brown, 1997).

58 On the problematical definition and identification of which see the discussion in this chapter.

59 Keohane and Nye, *Power and Interdependence*, pp. 24–9.

60 *Ibid.*, p. 23.

61 R.O. Keohane and J.S. Nye, '*Power and Interdependence* revisited', *International Organization*, vol. 41, no. 4 (Autumn 1987), pp. 725–53.

62 For a critical discussion of the 'democratic peace' thesis see: John Macmillan, 'Democracies don't fight: a case of the wrong research agenda', *Review of International Studies*, vol. 22, no. 3 (July 1996), pp. 275–99.

63 See: Raymond Cohen, 'Pacific unions: a reappraisal of the theory that democracies do not go to war with each other', *Review of International Studies*, vol. 20, no. 3 (July 1994); for a response to which see: Bruce Russett and James Lee Ray, 'Raymond Cohen on pacific unions: a response and a reply', *Review of International Studies*, vol. 21, no. 3 (July 1995), pp. 319–23; and for a response from Raymond Cohen see: 'Needed: a disaggregate approach to the democratic-peace theory', *Review of International Studies*, vol. 21, no. 3 (July 1995), pp. 323–5.

64 Susan Strange identifying four basic forms of structural power: politico/military; production; financial; and knowledge-based. Susan Strange, *States and Markets: An Introduction to International Political Economy* (London: Pinter, 1988).

65 A.J.R. Groom and P. Taylor (eds), *Functionalism: Theory and Practice in International Relations* (London: University of London Press, 1975).

66 See: Martin Shaw, *Global Society and International Relations: Sociological Concepts and Political Perspectives* (Cambridge: Polity Press, 1994).

67 Jones, *Globalization and Interdependence*, esp. pp. 105–18.

68 *Ibid.*, esp. pp. 145–8.

69 *Ibid.*, esp. pp. 147–51.

70 *Ibid.*, pp. 143–5.

71 Brigid Laffan, *Integration and Co-operation in Europe* (London: Routledge, 1992); John Pinder, *European Community: The Building of a Union* (Oxford: Oxford University Press, 1991).

72 Andrew Hurrell, 'Regionalism in the Americas', in L. Fawcett and A. Hurrell, *Regionalism in World Politics* (Oxford: Oxford University Press, 1995), pp. 250–82; and Anthony Payne, 'The United States and its Enterprise for the Americas', in A. Gamble and A. Payne (eds), *Regionalism and World Order* (London: Macmillan, 1996), pp. 93–129.

73 Jean Grugel, 'Latin America and the remaking of the Americas', in Gamble and Payne, *Regionalism and World Order*, pp. 131–67.

74 Rosemary Foot, 'Pacific Asia: the development of regional cooperation', in Fawcett and Hurrell, *Regionalism in World Politics*, pp. 228–49; and Ngai-Ling Sum, 'The NICs and competing strategies of East Asian regionalism', in Gamble and Payne, *Regionalism and World Order*, pp. 207–45.

75 The limits of politeness', *The Economist*, 28 February 1998, pp. 73–4; and 'The fire next time', *The Economist*, 28 February 1998, p. 74.

76 See: Charles Tripp, 'Regional organizations in the Arab Middle East', in Fawcett and Hurrell, *Regionalism in World Politics*, pp. 283–308.

77 James N. Rosenau, *Turbulence in World Politics: A Theory of Change and Continuity* (Hemel Hempstead: Harvester Wheatsheaf, 1990).

78 On anti-statist (anarchist) views, see: George Woodcock, *Anarchism* (Harmondsworth: Penguin Books, 1962).

79 For the classic statement of which, see: E.F. Schumacher, *Small is Beautiful: a Study of Economics as if People Mattered* (London: Blond and Briggs, 1973).

80 Richard Douthwaite, *Short Circuit: Strengthening: Local Economies for Security in an Unstable World* (Totnes: Resurgence Books, 1996).

81 Polanyi, *The Great Transformation*.

82 R.J. Barry Jones, 'The United Nations and the international political system', in: D. Bourantonis and J. Wiener (eds), *The United Nations in the New World Order: The World Organization at Fifty* (Houndmills: Macmillan, 1995), pp. 19–40.

83 Adam Przeworski *et al.*, *Sustainable Democracy* (Cambridge: Cambridge University Press, 1995), esp. Chs 5 and 6.

II
State action in question

5

The traditional purposes of state action

The emergence of the modern state did not take place in a vacuum. The state developed in intimate association with evolving patterns of political, economic, social and ideological power and influence: ambitious military leaders, acquisitive landowners and traders and proselytizing religious authorities. The crystallization of the modern state, with its characteristic institutions and ideologies, was thus largely a reflection of those dominant interests and structures.

However, the traditional purposes of the state have been complemented by new and wider concerns that reflect the growth of the institutions of the state itself and the need for wider and deeper ideological justifications for its existence, role and impositions upon society. In part, the broadening of state concerns has been a progressive response to the growth of popular pressures; for democratic representation in, and control of, the state; for an expanding range of services and provisions; and, most particularly, for the preservation of the well-being and security of the general population, rather than merely a high-placed minority.

'National' strength and well-being

The traditional purpose of the state, once its development reached the point of requiring a general justification, was that of ensuring sufficient strength and capability to sustain its existence and that of the society that it serves and by which it is sustained. The element of circularity within this 'traditional' account of the state's purpose – to exist to preserve the conditions necessary for its own survival – lies at the heart of fundamental debates about the state – its nature and ultimate justification.

The Hobbesian defence of the state as the guarantor of domestic tranquility[1] was soon supplemented by the Realists' emphasis on the role of the state as the primary protector of society against external threat.[2] However, critics of the modern state reject both the domestic order and the external defence justifications. Contemporary critical theorists have complemented this long tradition of anti-statist theory[3] with a rejection of the argument that an insecure external situation preceded, and hence justified, the emergence of the security-focused modern state. Critical theorists have subsequently identified the internally coercive and externally threatening modern state as the primary *source* of an 'international' system that, therefore, incorporated threat and insecurity into its very foundations.[4]

The grand debate between the advocates of universal 'realism' and their determined anti-statist critics does little, however, to assist those who seek to understand and deal with the evolving character of a far from invariable 'international' system. For such analysts, the emergence of the state, and the crystallization around it of a complex of security concerns, is a 'reality', albeit a constructed reality, of the modern era. The concentration of security issues in the 'hands' of the state has been the primary consequence of this process. States have asserted control over domestic society and sought to preserve its security within the international environment.

The state's efforts to maintain domestic sovereignty and to preserve external security have had a range of enduring consequences. Most states have sought to reduce and eliminate 'domestic' challenges to their authority and to their capacities for control. The early modern period within Europe thus saw the steady erosion of the influence of religious authorities within secular governance. Centres of competing political authority and military capability were also suppressed, often in a dramatic and violent manner, by those promoting the dominant position of an emergent geopolitical centre within a developing state.[5]

The elimination of opposition is merely the negative side of domestic jurisdiction. Effective domestic governance by the state also required the development of a range of positive capabilities. Rules and regulations required formulation by legislative bodies, adjudication through legal systems and implementation by an expanding range of state agents, from local administrators through to police forces. Such institutions and agencies contributed to, but could not alone ensure, the legitimation of the state and all its doings. Many agencies of popular communication and persuasion, such as the Church or the educational system, were thus recruited to promote popular consent and support for the state.

The maintenance of a society's place in the international system was an equally important influence upon the development of the state. Military forces have long been a primary means for the preservation of security from external threat. Their development and maintenance has thus been central to the modern state since its emergence. However, relations between states have never been a matter purely of armed might or military deterrence. Diplomacy, too, has played a central, and increasingly well-defined, role throughout the modern period. Modern states have, therefore, given birth to ever larger and more elaborate systems of diplomatic representation and activity.

Legislatures, administrators, lawyers and law courts, military forces and diplomatic services are all expensive matters, however. One of the most distinctive characteristics of modern states has thus been the development of larger and ever more elaborate systems for the imposition and collection of the taxes required to pay for the expanding range of their activities and services. Medieval rules could secure finance on the basis of customary payments of money or 'kind' from subordinate members of society and recruit armies from medieval lords, their trained followers and levies of armed citizenry.[6] The professionalization of military activity in the modern era,[7] however, necessitated a new and more systematic approach to the resourcing of a state's armed forces. New systems of tax collection and/or financial credit had to be created. The states that were successful in establishing such new systems for financial extraction were then able to expand their military capabilities and spearhead the steady increase in military establishments. Between the mid-fifteenth and the mid-seventeenth centuries the military manpower of the leading European states increased by a factor of 5 in the case of Spain, 2.5 in the case of France, and just under 3 for England.[8] The expansion of military establishments thus continued without let during the succeeding century and a half,[9] and the financial resources devoted to the maintenance of such levels of armed might also grew remorselessly.[10]

The steady expansion of the activities, resources and authority of the modern state has thus been a central feature for over four centuries. Such extended functions and capabilities have, however, been distinctive of the stronger and more effective states and societies. Many potential states within the European theatre were crushed or absorbed by larger and/or more effective neighbours, as witness the prolonged occupation of Poland and the progressive absorption into a ever-greater Prussia of many German-speaking principalities. Outside Europe, many societies experienced the growing ambitions and capabilities of more dynamic European states as colonial, and then imperial, incursion and occupation.[11]

State-building throughout the modern era thus had a number of features that marked the complexion of the times: politico-military competition and modernization, coupled with the suppression of ineffective competitors within Europe; and the imperial conquest and enforced transformation of much of the world beyond Europe's frontiers. Such a competitive dynamic placed a priority upon the strength and capability of societies; elevated the state as the form of political organization best able to develop and sustain such strength and capability; and fostered the resultant ideology of statism amongst the populations of both the successful new European states and their 'victims' within Europe and throughout the colonial territories.

The 'necessity' of strong and effective states thus entered European, and thence world-wide, consciousness as a self-sustaining doctrine within a world in which intense, and frequently violent, competition amongst the emergent European states gave it a force and presence unmatched by many other developments within human history. Moreover, experience of the chaotic and destructive consequences of religiously motivated conflicts, like the Thirty Years' War, reinforced the developing feeling that the secular and legalistic principles of the state might offer a more promising political order than possible alternatives.

States and social cohesion

Social cohesion and order can rest upon many foundations. Modern states established strong claims to be the entities best able to provide for cohesion and order within complex societies faced with a range of acute pressures and problems. Two influences underlie the emergence of this claim: the wish to secure legitimization and rationalization for their activities by those who were engaged in the process of competitive state-building in the seventeenth and eighteenth centuries; and the understandable concerns of a range of scholars and observers to identify potential restraints upon the excesses witnessed in such struggles as the Thirty Years' War in Europe or the Civil War in England.

Jean Bodin's advocacy of state sovereignty in the late sixteenth century[12] was ideally suited to the interests of princes bent upon the enlargement of their domains, the consolidation of their rule, the enhancement of their capabilities and the maximization of their position *vis-à-vis* their foreign competitors. Thomas Hobbes's *Leviathan* was a reaction to the chaos and destruction of the English Civil War (1642–48).

Reactions against the experience of recent chaos served only to reinforce pro-state sentiments. Without imbuing a strong state with the authority to ensure order within society, Hobbes argued that the unleashing of animal passions would plunge humanity into a destructive 'state of nature', of all against all.[13] The insecurity born into the international environment through the existence of a plurality of sovereign states, owing no allegiances to any higher authorities and subject to the compulsion of no superior power, would be contained by the strength and capabilities that well-founded states would be able to secure from their own resources: a system thus based upon deterrence and restraint, rather than upon deference to a higher power and authority.

Hobbes's prescription could do little, however, to counter the endemic atmosphere of insecurity that is liable to arise in a politically fragmented system and that may, in the most extreme case, allow conflicts to be generated by mere suspicion rather than by substantive incompatibilities of interests, or to pre-empt the historical record of massively destructive conflict within the system of 'sovereign' states. Neither domestic sufficiency nor any of the vaunted mechanisms for managing conflicts within the system of states – alliances, balances of power, unilateral deterrents – have thus proved sufficient to prevent violent explosions of varying, and often awesome, scale and intensity.

The paradoxical implications of state sovereignty do not, however, detract from some of the positive functions for which states have often been welcomed. Ironically, the very failure of states to ensure peace and harmony amongst themselves might contribute to domestic social cohesion by providing populations with external threats that stimulate feelings of group solidarity,[14] drawing their affections and affiliations towards states as major sources of protection against the threats and dangers that have arisen (even if the very existence of the state(s) might itself have been a major source of those 'external' threats).

Such an apparent paradox dissolves entirely in anti-statist theory, in the view of which the state is the embodiment of violence: domestically, against a population that is cowed into submission and involuntary solidarity by the state's monopolization, or near-monopolization, of the means of organized violence and its dominant position within the system of indoctrination; and internationally, against other states that obstruct the ambitions of the state's rulers and/or pose a potential threat to their resource base within their home territory.[15]

States, for good or ill, have thus emerged as a dominant, if not the dominant, source of support for their citizens through the provision of domestic stability and external protection during the modern era. Such security and stability may have been purchased at the expense of the paradoxical intensification of suspicion and insecurity among states and the suppression of alternative foci of affiliation. The more effective states have, however, succeeded to a remarkable extent in maintaining themselves as major poles of attraction for popular loyalties and expectations in the face of even such severe challenges as war, internal strife and economic dislocation.

States and the economy: the pursuit of strength, stability and progress

States have also long been engaged in, and with, economic and industrial systems. This state engagement with the economic and industrial realm has developed through three stages, each of which has expanded upon, while incorporating, the range of concerns and involvements characteristic of its predecessor(s).

Modern states emerged at times of intense political and military rivalry amongst their ruling families and oligarchies. Economic wealth was thus viewed both as a major resource for the support of armed competition and as an objective of such competition when successfully prosecuted. The resources of territorially defined 'domestic' economies were clearly a major source of such economic wealth and, when inhabited by a supportive population, also a major source of military manpower. The feudal system of the proto-states of the Middle Ages, at its most developed, reflected the tight organization of economy and society into a system designed to support and sustain the political and military rivalries and conflicts of ruling groups.

Political and military rivalry is not, however, entirely dependent upon the 'domestic' resources of those engaged in such competition and conflict. Indeed, it is the historical exception, rather than the norm, for a state to sustain its military conflicts with others exclusively from the resources of its own economy and society. The great proportion of major campaigns have absorbed economic resources derived from outside the state(s) involved and/or manpower recruited from 'foreign' countries. Wealth extracted from overseas acquisitions and/or commercial activities has contributed substantially to the military efforts of successive leading states. The major campaigns of most of the leading European states have relied upon troops from outside the 'home' country at one time or another: sometimes pure mercenaries;[16] sometimes foreign 'subjects' of the state's rulers; sometimes citizens of societies maintaining special forms of association with the belligerent state; and, sometimes, inhabitants of territories claimed by, or wishing to be claimed by, the state in question.

However, the economic factor remains central to inter-state competition, and conflict also remains central, whatever the sources of military manpower. Troops have to be supplied, fed and paid. Money, or resources in kind, are therefore essential to the retention of fighting forces and their maintenance in good fighting condition. During the early years of the emergent European states system, before the advent of modern nationalism, rulers could be relatively relaxed about the geographical source of resources for their military systems and efforts: if bullion extracted from foreign conquests could pay for mercenaries recruited outside the home territory, then that was wholly acceptable, just as long as the bullion continued to be received and the mercenary forces continued to secure military success. Domestic resources became critical at such times only if foreign resources could no longer be secured and/or foreign mercenaries no longer paid or supplied. A core of loyal and effective home troops, supplied and sustained by a prosperous domestic economy, then became the primary, and possibly the last, military resource of a hard-pressed state or its rulers.

The emergent states' concern with the economy and industry was largely a matter of their implications for military strength and capabilities. The state regulation of trade and domestic economic activity was designed to secure revenue for the state and to ensure the preservation of important skills and capabilities. Early systems of monitoring social and economic developments were equally directed towards maximizing the extraction of taxes and the assessment of military resources. Indeed, the domestic economy could be, and frequently was, plundered to the point of serious damage as short-sighted rulers made repeated demands for resources to sustain their military ambitions. Again, the acquisition of foreign sources of bullion could be pursued at the cost of domestic economic stability and ultimate prosperity, as in the case of Spain's extraction of precious metals from her colonies in the Americas.

The second major phase in the evolution of the state's involvement with the economy and industry marked a development from the earlier era of militaristic feudalism. By the seventeenth century, mercantilist states had clearly emerged, and posed a frontal challenge to their feudal predecessors.[17] A wider agenda of wealth creation and maintenance had now instilled itself in the minds of the ruling groups of European states. Indeed, ruling groups had, themselves, expanded to incorporate representatives of the wider commercial and economic interests that were playing an increasingly important part in the development of societies and states.

The interests of the state, and of its concerns with the economy, were thus no longer driven exclusively, or even primarily, by political rivalry and military struggle. Commercial success, economic strength and industrial vitality were now a growing concern of policy and policy-makers. Economic and industrial achievements were now valued as ends in themselves, and their growing significance for military strength and political standing was also recognized. The era of mercantilism was thus an era of rapid growth; technological innovation; change within many traditional areas of economic life; the early phases of the industrial revolution; the expansion of international trade and overseas acquisitions by the maritime powers of Europe; the development and elaboration of the state's tax-gathering capabilities; and, of no little significance, a 'revolution' in the scale and technology of military affairs;[18] thereby sowing the early seeds of internationalization and globalization.

Europe in the mercantilist era was a continent marked by competition amongst rival social and political systems. The absolutist monarchies – particularly of Spain and France – were increasingly pitched against the emergent commercial-mercantilist states of North-Western Europe – particularly the Netherlands and the (latterly) the United Kingdom. Success in this frontal, and often bitter struggle, was ultimately to rest with those states that were able to develop new, more flexible, means of resourcing their armed efforts. In the Netherlands, and then the United Kingdom, an increasing acknowledgement of the rule of law, by ruled and ruler alike, encouraged commercial and financial interests to provide resources to the state in times of struggle, confident in the belief that loans would eventually be repaid and bills for supplies ultimately met. The consolidation of the rule of law, and the growth of commercial and financial interests, also encouraged and facilitated a range of economic and industrial developments that might otherwise have lain fallow for lack of investment. A virtuous cycle was thus established within the commercial mercantilist states of North-West Europe that generated a harmony of interests between the state and leading economic groupings; stimulated economic and industrial innovation and growth; and, ultimately, furnished the state with enhanced military strength.[19]

The navies of the commercial mercantilist states, in particular, expanded rapidly in the seventeenth century – the British Navy expanding from some 35 vessels in 1642 to a force of some 151 ships by 1688.[20] Navies of such a size demanded extensive and complex systems of supply, which were furnished in part from commercial sources but also from state-run dockyards – like Chatham, Portsmouth and Plymouth in the United Kingdom – that continued, and extended, such earlier state-organized facilities for the building and supply of ships of war as the Arsenal of the Venetian Republic.[21]

Strategic issues also bore upon the calculations of the mercantilist state. Secure access to strategically important resources was deemed to be of central interest to the state. Domestic economic developments and external trade, initially at least, were thus to be shaped to minimize the state's dependence upon sources of essential *matériel* and resources that were under foreign control. Moreover, where possible, policy would be directed towards fostering the dependence upon one's own economy of potential sources for important supplies to one's enemies.[22] Early mercantilism could thus assume a strategic face that retains echoes in the contemporary era.

Concern and involvement with industry and the economy was thus extended and deepened with the coming of the mercantilist state. Vigorous and prosperous societies were now seen to be increasingly vital to the strength and capability of the state. Equally, the armed strength of the state could be deployed to promote and defend the overseas assets of commercial interests. The coming of modern capitalism, the crystallization of the mercantilist state and the development of overseas empires were thus closely interrelated during the emergence of the modern European state system.

The third phase of the state's involvement with industry and the economy extends the concerns of the mercantilist state into the era of nationalism and, increasingly, democracy. The 'new mercantilism'[23] of the contemporary state reflects a wider appreciation of the range of domestic conditions that might ultimately determine the capacity of a society to undertake effective military action against potential adversaries and the new pressures exerted by the populations of democratic societies for the creation and preservation of acceptable economic conditions.

The discovery (or invention) of the notion of nationhood as the foundational principle of the state sowed the seeds of a progressive shift from the interests and ambitions of ruling groups as the basis of state policy and conduct to the needs and interests of the wider population. The gradual extension of the political franchise further complemented this basis for a widening political agenda. Popular pressures for a wider range of state provision and protection were thus pressed upon increasingly responsive ruling groups.

The widening of the political agenda of modern 'nation'-states was not a matter of the growing enlightenment of governing groups or the assertion of new demands by popular forces, however. War again played a decisive part in redefining the range and content of governmental concerns. The increasing industrialization of modern warfare placed a growing premium upon industrial strength and an extensive economic infrastructure. States that wished to sustain a significant level of influence within the international (but largely European) system of the nineteenth century thus played increasing attention to the maintenance, or development, of industrial strength and economic vitality. State governments thus played a considerable

role in the stimulation, support and direction of the industrialization of Germany, Japan and Tsarist Russia.[24] The governments
of longer-established industrial societies, like the United Kingdom,
could afford a somewhat more *laissez-faire* approach towards their
domestic economies, but were often surprised, and shocked, by
dramatic demonstrations at times of war of the costs of neglect.
After the Boer War, official concern was expressed at the poor
physical and intellectual quality of Britain's military recruits:
deficiencies which, it was believed, reflected the backgrounds of
these recruits in the poorer industrial cities of the country.[25] At the
outbreak of the First World War, the UK government was again
shocked to discover that its neglect of domestic industry had left
the country seriously deficient in a number of vital areas of industrial production: the explosives and propellants required for the
mass artillery engagements of that conflict; optical equipment for
the army and navy; and, indeed, the dyes required for the uniforms
of the massively expanded armed forces.[26]

Industrial and economic strength at times of major conflict was
one major source of the new concern of state governments with the
condition of their industries and economies and the wider associated policy agenda. The human trauma of the First World War
compounded such concerns and reinforced a widening of the policy
agenda with a deep, and loudly proclaimed, moral dimension: the
people who had suffered so grievously from the recent conflagra-
tion deserved the best of care and provision that responsible and
civilized societies could provide. Schemes of general 'insurance' were
introduced widely. Programmes of public housing were instigated.
General education was extended and enhanced.

Further encouragement for the widening of the governmental
agenda then came with the Great Depression of the early 1930s.
The hopes and aspirations of the survivors of the First World War
were sundered by the economic collapse, chronic unemployment and
widespread destitution. Schemes for direct governmental involvement in industry and the economy, of a type and on a scale rarely
adopted in peacetime, were now proposed in many countries and
adopted, with differing motives and means, in a number. President
Roosevelt's *New Deal* in the United States of America exemplified
the benign side of direct governmental action; Adolf Hitler's policies of industrial revitalization and rearmament in Germany, its
malignant face.

The role of government in the economy, industry and society reached new heights with the coming of the Second World War. Under the threat of total destruction and defeat, the United Kingdom was mobilized economically and industrially, under close governmental direction.[27] Nazi Germany later followed suit with a comparable level of mobilization when confronting the twin challenges of an undefeated Britain and her intended war against the Soviet Union. When finally precipitated into war by the Japanese attack upon Pearl Harbor, the United States, with intensive governmental involvement, also created a new military–industrial complex, of unprecedented size and capacity.[28]

The struggles of the Second World War thus generated a massive extension of governmental involvement in industry and the economy. The Great Depression had been banished, and state-led economic efforts on a massive scale proved essential, and effective, in confronting fundamental challenges to 'national' survival. The human costs, and the clearer ideological division between democracies and dictatorships, also reinforced demands for wider governmental protection and provision from the populations of the democratic victors. The immediate post-war years were thus an era of Keynesian management of the macro-economy, designed to maintain economic stability and well-being; widespread direct state involvement in the economy, through the ownership and control of many industries and services; and the introduction of a new and wide range of social provisions and supports.

An unprecedented era of prosperity unfolded for the populations of at least the more advanced industrial societies in the post-Second World War world. The state was now highly involved in the domestic economy and society through macro-economic management, industrial policy and the introduction and management of the new welfare state. Macro-economic policies to stabilize the economy and sustain steady growth were further aided by the considerable stimulus provided by the rapid growth of spending on the armed forces, and their equipment, apparently warranted by the threat posed by Stalin's Soviet Union.[29]

Interpretations of the post-war period of prosperity vary considerably, however. Radical critics of 'Western' capitalism attribute much of this prosperity to the continued exploitation of the less developed, and possible under-developed, majority of the world's societies.[30] Critics from the other end of the interpretative spectrum deemed the post-war period of the welfare state and economic managerialism to be an era of unhealthy developments within the market system, with undue levels of trade union influence; 'feather-bedded' populations; and inflationary governmental interference in the economy.[31] Moreover, a long-term decline of economic strength and industrial competitiveness has been attributed to the efforts of some countries to sustain high levels of armed might and maintain a wide-ranging role in world affairs.[32]

Interpretative controversies aside, the post-war role of the state has remained substantial in most societies. The share of the Gross Domestic Product passing through the hands of the state has remained remarkably high. Total state revenue (tax and non-tax) as a percentage of GDP in 1995 was still: 19.8 per cent in the USA; 45.3 per cent in the UK; 37.3 per cent in Germany; 49.6 per cent in France; 49.6 per cent in Italy; 44 per cent in Sweden; 53.4 per cent in the Netherlands; and 55.1 per cent in Belgium.[33] Actors controlling such a proportion of a society's wealth are actors of considerable significance, whatever their purposes and effects.

States and special interests

Classical Realism identified the actions of the state automatically with the needs and interests of its population. Concepts like 'national interest'[34] expressed the sense that the policies of states' governments were directed by the evolving requirements of the societies that they represented. Such notions of common and enduring interests have, however, proved to be unreliable in practice and controversial in principle. The Realism expounded by Hans Morgenthau equated the interests of states with the preservation of power.[35] Power, however, was far more than a mere assemblage of military force and economic resources, for power, in Morgenthau's vision, was a potentially fungible asset resting, ultimately, upon the psychological relationship established between the state and the other states with which it interacted. The key questions, however, concern the substantive objects being pursued by the state in its international interactions.

A survey of the actions and aspirations of states throughout the modern era reveals considerable variation across time and place. States have changed their primary objectives in response to changing conditions: imperial acquisitions being popular at one time, regional integration at another. States in different circumstances have also revealed quite different patterns of policies and practices: unilateral military strength the object of some states; collective self-defence the option pursued by others. Moreover, states and their governments have not always placed institutional survival above all other objectives. Many states opted for surrender in the face of German invasion in 1940 rather than risk widespread destruction and loss of life through continued resistance.

The clear variability of the 'national interest' across time and place has encouraged more discriminating approaches towards the external behaviour of states. A popular approach in this respect is to de-mythologize the state and to disaggregate it into its constituent parts and interests. The 'national interest', from such a perspective, can be reduced to the particular views and policy commitments of the individuals, groups or parties that happen to be dominant within the governmental system of a state at any time. Not all analysts, however, are happy with such a circumstantial, if not episodic, view of the determinants of state behaviour.

Classical Marxists have thus identified the decisive influence of the needs and interests of the dominant socio-economic class upon the behaviour of the state and the actions of the governments of capitalist societies: 'The executive of the modern State is but a committee for managing the common affairs of the whole bourgeoisie.'[36] From such a perspective, the primary role of government within modern capitalism has been, and remains, the development and maintenance of those conditions that will ensure the well-being of the private enterprise system.[37]

Domestically, the role of the state from such a Marxist perspective has been to create the conditions within which industrial capitalism can survive and flourish. A suitable framework of domestic law had to be developed and applied, to ensure the preservation (and indeed the prioritization) of private property, the reliability of commercial relationships and the general orderliness of society. With the advance of industrial society, the state also had to ensure a suitably educated and enculturalized working population. Such serious dysfunctions as chronic threats to public health were also the province of states and their local representatives.

Externally, the state had to provide the domestic economy with security from direct threats and, if necessary, from the dangers of expropriation of assets or the disruption of commercial exchanges. The determination of state behaviour by the 'needs' of domestic capitalism reached its zenith amongst the Marxists of the late nine-teenth and early twentieth centuries. In Lenin's *Imperialism*, the formal acquisition of overseas colonies by the European Imperial Powers follows directly from the need of domestic capitalist interests to overcome the 'inevitable' decline in the rate of profit by pursuing new opportunities for profitable investments in less developed coun-tries and their consequent need for direct political control of those societies to ensure the safety of those investments.[38]

The problem presented by the state and the record of state behaviour for Marxist analysts, however, rests upon the variability of the behaviour of the leading European states during the twen-tieth century. All was apparently well until the dramatic phase of decolonization began in the decades after the ending of the Second World War. Capitalism's 'requirement' for foreign colonies now appeared to have been disproved by developments. The 'Marxist' theory of neo-colonialism, however, rapidly emerged to fill the theor-etical void, with its central proposition that capitalism's need for profitable investments in less developed countries still existed, but could now be sustained by multinational corporations rather than the (more costly) structures of formal colonial control.[39]

Neo-colonial theory achieved its greatest prominence in the late 1960s and early 1970s. Subsequent developments within rad-ical political economy have, however, presented a more diffuse and diverse picture with regard to the nature, sources and con-sequences of state action. Neo-Gramscians present a more com-plicated vision of state behaviour, in which the ideas that favour, and are favoured by, dominant economic groups exert the greatest influence, rather than the interests of groups operating a simple and open influence directly.[40] Theorists of Dependency and informal empire, in contrast, emphasize the longer-term role of multinational companies rather than of the states from which those companies emanated.[41]

Classical Marxists have not monopolized criticism of the mod-ern state, however. A general anti-statism preceded Marx's radical writings and has continued to exert an influence to the present day. The state, within such perspectives, is seen to be the general locus of action for powerful groups and interests of many types.[42] Milit-ary leaders, ambitious politicians, religious authorities, industrial and commercial interests all seek to influence and exploit a struc-ture to which access is granted unevenly and within which influence is allocated disproportionately. It is, in short, the very nature of a system of governance in which only the few have real access and influence that is at the heart of the problem of the state's repressive behaviour internally and aggressive dispositions externally. Internal opposition has to be controlled by all means, including force if necessary; external behaviour will be dictated by the avarice of influential commercial interests and the ambitions of political and military leaders. The state is thus a central and decisive actor by the very nature of the institutions and capabilities of which it is constituted: a central and decisive actor, however, that is malign in its nature and effects in the views of critical anti-statist theorists.

A further critical approach to the state and government also emerged from the late 1960s onward among a disparate group of formal political economists and radical conservatives who sought to employ many of the traditional tools of economic analysis to the activities of politicians, bureaucracies and governments and, indeed, to all other special interest groups, including industrial and commercial interests. Central concepts within this approach included, 'entrepreneurial politics', rent-seeking behaviour, and budget-maximization.[43] Self-interested behaviour is at the heart of such analysis. All actors, whether individuals or collective agents, political or private actors, are deemed to be benefit maximizers and cost minimizers within whatever arenas they operate. Politicians and bureaucrats will then seek to further their own ends, whether those be the purely personal ends of ambition and avarice, or the more public purposes of institutional well-being and success in shaping policy. Private interests will take advantage of any opportunities that exist to influence public policy in favourable directions.

In the politics of rational actors, then, individual politicians and bureaucrats seek personal advancement, personal benefit, advantages for their departments and success for their policy preferences. Private actors, ranging from business interests through to pressure groups, use all available means to influence politicians and bureaucrats; sway public opinion in democratic systems; and deploy persuasive devices, from threats to bribes to skilled lobbyists, to advance their preferred policies. Actors, of all types, form alliances with other actors, 'log-roll' to secure arrangements that will eventually produce mutual benefits, and use resources over which they have particular control to purchase decisive support from others.

The overall picture of politics and the policy-making process presented by such a perspective is thus reductionist methodologically, in reducing all behaviour to self-interest (albeit broadly defined), and cautionary with regard to the structures of government and politics. Constraint of such behaviour is to be found along one or both of two paths: the general reduction of government, so as to minimize the fruits of, and motives for, its domination by self-interested actors; or, of equal interest, the construction of new, and tighter, constitutional constraints upon the scope and freedom of government, to minimize the damage that distorted public policy can inflict upon the generality of the populace.

Conclusions

The range of actions of the modern state is thus considerable, and the sources of those actions are highly diverse. The close interconnection between the emergence of industrial society and the rise of the modern state within Western Europe belies any simplistic notions of the separability of, or even of chronic tension between, the economy and the political system. As the competition between states has developed and intensified, states have needed more effective domestic economies. The modern industrial economy has, thus far, also demonstrated a growing need for governmental involvement to secure general stability, steady growth and a supportive civil society. Where governments have proved unable or unwilling to play an authoritative role in economic management, the historical record is too often that of industrial decay and/or economic dislocation, with the deeply damaging consequences for the wider society demonstrated by Russia during the late 1990s.

Military competition has repeatedly revitalized the political–economic connection by refocusing governments upon their needs for prosperous and vital economies; by redirecting the focus of domestic economies at times of major war; and by maintaining a general stimulus to industrial innovation, economic reorganization and general modernization.

The forms of action by states have, however, varied considerably from time to time and from place to place. A survey of this variety is necessary before any clear conclusions can be drawn about the possible limitations upon effective state action that might have been generated by the progress of globalization or greater internationalization.

Notes

1 Thomas Hobbes, *The Leviathan*, first published in 1651; and see also:
   H. Warrander, *The Political Philosophy of Hobbes* (Oxford: Oxford
   University Press, 1957).

2 Classically stated in Hans J. Morgenthau, *Politics Among Nations:
   The Struggle for Power and Peace* (New York: Alfred Knopf, 1946).

3 George Woodcock, *Anarchism* (Harmondsworth: Penguin Books,
   1962).

4 Richard K. Ashley, 'The Poverty of Neorealism', *International Organiza-
   tion*, vol. 38, no. 2 (Spring 1984), pp. 225–61; and Richard K. Ashley,
   *The Political Economy of War and Peace: The Sino-Soviet-American
   Triangle and the Modern Security Problematique* (London: Frances
   Pinter; and New York: Nichols, 1980).

5 For instance the French suppression of the Albigensians and the
   Huguenots. See also: Michael Mann, *The Sources of Social Power:
   Volume 1, A History of Power from the Beginning to A.D. 1760*
   (Cambridge: Cambridge University Press, 1986), esp. Chs 13 and 14;
   and R.J. Barry Jones, 'Social Science, globalisation and the problem of
   the state', *Environment and Planning A,* vol. 28, no. 11 (November
   1996), pp. 1948–53.

6 M.M. Postan, *The Medieval Economy and Society* (London: Weidenfeld
   and Nicolson, 1972), esp. Ch. 5.

7 Geoffrey Parker, *The Military Revolution: Military Innovation and the
   Rise of the West, 1500–1800* (Cambridge: Cambridge University Press,
   1988).

8 Paul Kennedy, *The Rise and fall of the Great Powers: Economic Change
   and Military Conflict from 1500 to 2000* (London: Fontana Books,
   1989), Table 1, p. 71.

9 *Ibid.*, Table 4, p. 128.

10 *Ibid.*, Table 2, p. 105.

11 M. Howard, 'The military factor in European expansion', in H. Bull
   and A. Watson (eds), *The Expansion of International Society* (Oxford:
   Clarendon Press, 1984), Ch. 2, esp. pp. 34–40.

12 G. Sabine, *A History of Political Theory*, 3rd edn (London: George
   Harrap, 1963), Ch. 20.

13 Thomas Hobbes, *The Leviathan* (various editions, originally published
   in 1651); and see also: Sabine, *A History of Political Theory*, Ch. 23.

14 See: D.J. Finlay, Ole R. Holsti and R. R. Fagen, *Enemies in Politics*
   (Chicago: Rand McNally, 1967), esp. Ch. 1.

15 Woodcock, *Anarchism*; and A. Carter, *The Political Theory of Anarchism* (London: Routledge & Kegan Paul, 1971).

16 John Keegan, *A History of Warfare* (London: Hutchinson, 1993), Ch. 3, Interlude on 'Armies'.

17 D.C. Coleman (ed.), *Revision in Mercantilism* (London: Methuen, 1969).

18 Geoffrey Parker, *The Military Revolution: Military Innovation and the Rise of the West, 1500–1800* (Cambridge: Cambridge University Press, 1988).

19 Frank Tallet, *War and Society in Early Modern Europe, 1496–1715* (London: Routledge, 1992).

20 J.D. Davies, 'A permanent national maritime fighting force 1642–1689', in J.R. Hill (ed.), *The Oxford Illustrated History of the Royal Navy* (Oxford: Oxford University Press, 1995), p. 57.

21 F.C. Lane, *Venice and History: The Collected Papers of Frederick C. Lane* (Baltimore: Johns Hopkins University Press, 1966).

22 See D.C. Coleman's chapters, 'Introduction', and 'Eli Heckscher and the idea of mercantilism', in D.C. Coleman (ed.), *Revision in Mercantilism* (London: Methuen, 1969), esp. pp. 92–3.

23 On 'new mercantilism' see: H.G. Johnson (ed.), *The New Mercantilism: Some Problems in International Trade, Money and Investment* (Oxford: Basil Blackwell, 1974).

24 Chapters on Germany and Russia and the Soviet Union, in C.M. Cipolla (ed.), *The Fontana Economic History of Europe – The Emergence of Industrial Societies, Vols 1 and 2* (London: Fontana, 1973).

25 Correlli Barnett, *Britain and Her Army, 1509–1970: A Military, Political and Social Survey* (Harmondsworth: Allen Lane the Penguin Press, 1970, esp. pp. 342–3.

26 Correlli Barnett, *The Collapse of British Power* (London: Eyre Methuen, 1972), pp. 85–8.

27 On the mobilization of Great Britain during the Second World War see: Peter Calvocoressi and Guy Wint, *Total War: Causes and Courses of the Second World War* (Harmondsworth: Allen Lane/The Penguin Press, 1972), Ch. 20.

28 On the scale of US mobilization see: *The Oxford Companion to the Second World War*, ed. I.C.B. Dear and M.R.D. Foot (Oxford: Oxford University Press, 1995), pp. 1179–84.

29 See M. Kidron, *Western Capitalism Since the War* (London: Weidenfeld and Nicolson, 1968); and J.K. Galbraith, *The Age of Uncertainty* (London: BBC/Andre Deutsch, 1977), esp. Ch. 8.

30 P. Baran, *The Political Economy of Growth* (New York: Monthly Review Press, 1957); Andre Gunder Frank, *Dependent Accumulation and Underdevelopment* (London: Macmillan, 1978); and M. Caldwell, *The Wealth of Some Nations* (London: Zed Books, 1977).

31 W.H. Hutt, *Politically Impossible?* (London: Institute of Economic Affairs, 1971); Correlli Barnett, *The Audit of War: The Illusion and Reality of Britain as a Great Nation* (London: Macmillan, 1986); and Correlli Barnett, *The Last Victory: British Dreams, British Realities, 1945–1950* (Basingstoke: Macmillan, 1995).

32 Kennedy, *The Rise and Fall of the Great Powers.*

33 World Bank, *World Development Report 1997* (New York: Oxford University Press for the World Bank, 1997), Table 14, pp. 240–1.

34 Joseph Frankel, *National Interest* (London: Pall Mall Press, 1970).

35 Morgenthau, *Politics Among Nations.*

36 Karl Marx and F. Engels, 'Manifesto of the Communist Party', in Karl Marx and Frederick Engels, *Selected Works, Vol. 1* (Moscow: Foreign Languages Publishing House, 1962 – (first published in German in 1848)), p. 36.

37 For the classical Marxist approach see: Ralph Miliband, *The State in Capitalist Society: The Analysis of the Western System of Power* (London: Weidenfeld and Nicolson, 1969).

38 V.I. Lenin, *Imperialism: The Highest Stage of Capitalism*, 1916, various editions – available in vol. 22 of *Collected Works* (Moscow: Progress Publishers).

39 K. Nkrumah, *Neo-Colonialism: The Last Stage of Imperialism* (London: Heinemann, 1965); and Jack Woodis, *Introduction to Neo-Colonialism* (London: Lawrence and Wishart, 1967).

40 S. Gill and D. Law, *The Global Political Economy: Perspectives, Problems and Policies* (London: Harvester/Wheatsheaf, 1998), esp. Chs 5, 6 and 7.

41 Andre Gunder Frank, *On Capitalist Underdevelopment* (Bombay: Oxford University Press, 1975).

42 Woodcock, *Anarchism*; and Carter, *The Political Theory of Anarchism.*

43 N. Frohlich and J.A. Oppenheimer, *Modern Political Economy* (Englewood Cliffs, NJ: 1978), esp. Ch. 4; and James M. Buchanan, *et al.*, *The Economics of Politics* (London: Institute of Economic Affairs, 1978).

6

Traditional forms of state action

The wide range of sources and objectives of state action in the domestic and international economies is matched by the diversity of forms of the state, and its functioning. States have ranged from those that aspired to dominate all aspects of life domestically, and all economic interactions externally, to those that have practised the principles of the minimalist state.

Assertive states in the international economy

Many states throughout recorded history have sought to assert themselves over the economic lives of their subjects or citizens, for a wide variety of purposes. When states have been dominated by personal or sectional interests, then the powers of the state have been directed towards the promotion and protection of those interests.

The popular image of ancient societies presents a picture of the all-powerful ruler. In practice, however, some distinction between the property of the ruler and that of his/her subjects was common, and the ruler's capacity for autocratic action limited, particularly in the larger domains. A range of property rights rested upon a diversity of authorities – some religious, some customary – while patterns of political community and authority were often far more complex than is suggested by simple models of chieftainships and kingdoms.[1]

Where high levels of autocratic rule proved possible in pre-modern 'states', they were either based upon well-entrenched political, social and religious foundations, as in the case of Imperial China, or, if attempting to direct substantial and rapid changes, strictly limited in their territorial scope, as in the case of the Zulu empire,[2] or relatively short-lived. Enduring states with substantial capabilities for directing substantial changes within their societies and economies have required the development of a number of 'modern' conditions: relatively rapid means of transport and communication; mechanisms for direct communication to (rather than with) the mass population; the diminution of attachments to established authorities, religious or secular; and the endowment of a wide range of potent actors, from the top to the bottom of society, with a sufficiency of 'spare' time and resources to allow them to address issues of public interest and direction with effect. States in pursuit of radical changes can exploit such conditions to develop effective infrastructural power[3] and, hence, the ability to rule with and through, rather than over, society.

The development of the Assertive State has, however, been a long and uneven process in respect of the evolving international economy. The medieval state, characteristically, viewed the domestic economy and inter-state trade overwhelmingly in terms of their contribution to the personal wealth and military capability of the ruler and his noble lieges. Feudal vassals administered the countryside and its population to ensure that the ruler could secure supplies of men and *matériel* in time of war. The towns undertook much of the more complex economic activity, albeit through warranted and closely supervised guilds. Taxes were paid to the ruler on traded goods and, when required, on a *per capita* or property basis.[4]

The institutions of the feudal system provided the point of departure for the development of the early-modern state and of mercantilism in Western Europe, as the guild system, serfdom and a myriad constraints upon individual freedom began to wane. The clarity of the mercantilist ideal has been disputed.[5] However, many of the ideas and practices common in the seventeenth and eighteenth centuries approximated to a general notion of mercantilism. The early doctrine of 'bullionism' maintained the concern of the feudal rulers to ensure a sufficiency of treasure to sustain martial endeavours in time of war. An accumulation of silver, gold, and other valuable specie, remained important to the rulers of states and was now to be pursued, in part at least, through the maintenance of a favourable balance of trade with societies that would pay for imports with such precious metals.

Simple bullionism was, however, to be qualified by a growing appreciation of the importance of security of supplies of resources that were of importance to both the economic activity and the military strength of the state. Strategic sensitivity could, in part, be reduced by ensuring against over-dependence upon foreign sources of supply. It could also be reduced by taking control of existing foreign sources of supply or developing new sources in areas that were already under control. The early colonial ventures of the Western European states were thus concurrent, and directly connected with, the coming of the mercantilist era.[6]

The era of mercantilism was, however, also the era of the birth of commercial capitalism, and with it came a gradual loosening of the control of traditional state rules, the rise of an embryonic bourgeoisie and the gradual imposition upon state policy of the interests of the new commercial capitalist class. Such developments culminated in the conflation of state and commercial interests that was to be witnessed in the complex interrelationships between the great trading companies of the Western mercantilist states and their state authorities, exemplified by the case of British involvement in the Indian sub-continent.[7]

The leading states in the new European World system developed an approach that could well be termed martial-mercantilism, in which the pursuit of commercial advantage was intimately interconnected with the promotion and preservation of military strength. The Anglo-Dutch wars of the second half of the seventeenth century marked a frontal confrontation between the two leading military-mercantilist states,[8] was finally resolved only with the effective take-over of Britain by the Dutch William of Orange in 1688, and led to the two centuries during which Britain assumed a virtually hegemonic position within world affairs.[9]

Martial-mercantilism directly encouraged the development of early factories, particularly for the provision of rope and other basic supplies for naval ships. The 'arsenals' and linked manufacturing facilities of the navies of a number of the leading powers of the seventeenth and eighteenth centuries attest to the scale of the activities involved in sustaining large, ocean-going navies and to the extensive role of the state in the organization of such activities. The supply of ever-larger armies and navies also involved growing orders to commercial suppliers, however, and the era of martial-mercantilism also provided a substantial boost to the development of manufacturing within the wider economy. Orders for uniforms and munitions proved to be a fruitful source of stimulus for innovation in the manufacture of textiles and iron products. The emergence of industrial capitalism may not have been entirely the product of martial-mercantilism, but it was far from hindered by its continuous stimulation to innovation in, and the industrialization of, production.[10]

The industrial revolution crystallized the material face of modernity. By embracing and enshrining the fruits of the Enlightenment, technological innovation was finally freed from the constraints of religious authority. A mechanistic vision of the universe, moreover, underpinned the notion of a potentially self-regulating economy. Both technology and the economic system could, within such a new vision of the natural order, thus be self-validating morally and self-managing materially.

The advent of industrial capitalism could not, however, purge economic developments of their moral implications and military connotations, or end the interest of the state in economic and industrial developments. The modern era has thus witnessed a form of Manichaean struggle between a pursuit of self-direction within the realms of economy and technology, and the constant temptation for states, or their current rulers, to seek to exploit the fruits of innovation and economic strength to enhance their strength and capability.

Military industrialization and the command economy

The concern of states with economic and industrial matters was constantly reinforced throughout the eighteenth and nineteenth centuries as the many state rulers witnessesd the accelerating advantages, in terms of military strength and political power, of states like Great Britain that had succeeded in harnessing the potential of the industrial revolution. Early industrialization, within its Western European core, may have been largely unplanned. It was, however, directly encouraged by the military needs of the state. Later industrialization was, however, frequently motivated directly by an appreciation of its fundamental contribution to the military strength and general security of the then less developed societies, with the wholesale creation of new systems of education and technical training, and the construction of new, heavy industries, in Germany, Japan and Tzarist Russia.[11]

The exploitation by the state of the powers of technology and the industrial economy were not the only pattern of state assertiveness within the nineteenth and twentieth centuries, however. Instabilities within the market economy itself also contributed to a periodic re-politicization of economics and a consequential re-emphasis upon the state's role in regulating economic affairs.[12] Controversy thus persists as to whether the real causes of the cataclysmic Second World War lay with the long-standing traditions of German and Japanese militarism, the failings of the international free market economy in the late 1920s or, in the case of Germany at least, the inequities of the settlement of the First World War.[13]

Whatever the relative importance of the causes of the great upheavals of the twentieth century, the enormous efforts of the inter-war Bolshevik regime in Russia to develop heavy industry on an extensive scale owed as much to a concern to enhance military strength and security against a myriad perceived enemies, as it did to general economic growth and prosperity.

Command economies are the natural product of such acute concerns with rapid and substantial industrial militarization. Indeed, when confronted by a fundamental threat to security and survival, as was Great Britain between 1939 and 1945,[14] such patterns of economic direction and control can be adopted by states of a far less dictatorial disposition than the military industrializers of the past.

The state's interest in, and involvement with, the economy has by no means been limited to military industrialization. Throughout the twentieth century, the clear contribution of industrial vitality to general prosperity, when combined with the growing demands expressed by newly enfranchised populations, has convinced many governments of the need for explicit economic and industrial policies: a conviction often reinforced by the effects of domestic and international economic and financial crises. Such policies have however ranged widely in the scale and intensity of their involvement with trade and economic life.

Interventionist states in a competitive and unstable world economy

States of a variety of types, and governments of many political hues, have sought to encourage industrial development and economic vitality. The general imperative of economic strength and general well-being has often reflected specific conditions that have encouraged a range of interventionist patterns that even so fall short of constructing a full command economy.

External threats and the interventionist state

The existence of an external security threat has, as has been suggested earlier, often encouraged a substantial increase in the range and intensity of the state's involvement with the economy and industrial system. The free market ideology of the United States of America proved no check to the massive extension of its government's role in the domestic economy during the Second World War. The massive increase in the size of, and procurements for, the USA's military system revitalized and transformed considerable swathes of the economy.[15] The supply and use of many raw materials was regulated, and unprecedented rationing was introduced for petrol, tyres, meat, sugar, coffee, and butter.[16] Britain, in the face of the wartime threat from Nazi Germany, mobilized her economy and society to an extent unprecedented in any liberal democracy.[17]

External military threats have prompted broadly comparable responses. Industries that are vital to the production and supply of the war effort (or its preparation) have been the object of particular attention. Munitions industries have often been established under state direction, as in the case of the innovative Springfield arsenal in the case of the United States of America, or the Woolwich arsenal in Britain's. Where remaining in the private sector, governments have either established extremely close working relationships with military industries, as in the case of the USA's military–industrial complex,[18] or placed such industries under extremely close regulation, supervision and even direction, as exemplified by the establishment of 'shadow firms' for future munitions production by the British government in the middle and later 1930s.[19] In either case, substantial, and often massive, procurement budgets have exerted a considerable influence upon the form and direction of significant portions of domestic industry.

State-led responses to external military threats can thus have a profound effect upon the domestic economy and industrial system. The economy can receive a massive stimulus, as in the case of the United States of America during the Second World War; but the shape of a major portion of the industrial system can be diverted towards military production. The longer-term consequences of such industrial diversion can be significant. The attractions of supplying a passive client, in the form of a grateful government, can persuade firms to withdraw from the more challenging environment of the competitive market for consumer products – as in the case of many of Britain's leading electrical and electronics firms in the 1960s and 1970s. A significant portion of a country's Research and Development effort can be drawn into the development of new military products.[20] The efforts devoted to the development and production of military equipment may, moreover, encourage an exaggerated emphasis upon military exports as a means of securing a return on past investment and to secure employment for those working in the military industries.[21]

Relative underdevelopment and the interventionist state

External military threats are but the most extreme of the conditions that encourage non-dictatorial governments to greater intervention in the domestic economy. Relative economic backwardness has also been both a recurrent source of interventionist impulses and an influence upon academic analysts during much of the post-Second World War era. Throughout the 1960s, 1970s and early 1980s there was widespread support for a relatively strong role for the state in the development processes. Extensive state bureaucracies for economic and industrial planning were constructed. State ownership, or direct control, of considerable tranches of the industrial and economic system were favoured. Parastatal – state-owned and state-managed – industries flourished, and state-run agricultural organizations were ubiquitous throughout much of Africa. In Latin America, trade barriers provided protection for the development of large, state-owned monopolies and state-encouraged private enterprises. By the early 1980s it was also becoming clear that a further variant of state-directed development was beginning to have dramatic impact within a number of societies in East and South-East Asia, encouraging ideas about a distinctive form of East and South-East Asian capitalism[22] – sometimes dubbed Confucian capitalism – and/or a new pattern of state-led industrialization.[23]

Economic weakness reduces general well-being and undermines the wider prestige of a society. The post-war emphasis upon the economic development of societies, particularly those emerging from long periods of colonial control or general subordination within the international system reflected both considerations. Prescriptions for an intimate involvement of the state in the development of the then less developed countries reflected one, or a combination, of three distinct influences: a local tradition of authoritative, if not authoritarian, rule; a belief that an unguided economy would not produce a rapid and socially acceptable pattern of development; and a general concern to ensure rapid economic growth as a symbol of full independence or as a claim for respect from the wider world.

In the 1960s and 1970s, and particularly the former, such considerations reinforced a favourable view of state intervention in, and direction of, the economy. The Soviet model had yet to be fully discredited; indeed, the heroic performance of the Soviet Union and its economy during the recent Second World War seemed to broadcast only the strengths of such a state-led pattern of economic development.

Experiences within Africa, Latin America and East and South-East Asia during the post-Second World War era were highly varied in form and effect. Two initial observations are, however, in order. First, for good or bad, the role of the state in all these patterns of 'development' was extensive, if uneven in impact. Second, considerable controversy persists over the reasons for the differing effects of state involvement in the three regions (and, indeed, in different countries within each region) and, moreover, over the ultimate consequences of such involvement.

Variations in the resources available to the various regions and countries at the start of their developmental efforts also had a considerable influence upon the nature of state intervention and the direction of initial developmental paths. Some of these critical variations were the products of nature; others the consequence of human actions. Variations in natural resources conditioned many of the initial possibilities. The availability of valuable metals or minerals encouraged an emphasis upon the exports of such commodities as a means of increasing revenues and, hence, funds for development projects. Similar temptations existed where much of the local economy had been devoted to the production of agricultural products for markets in the world's richer countries. The level and form of exploitation of indigenous resources or agricultural potential was, however, a product of past human intervention, and this often established a pattern of production and trade that constrained subsequent developments.

The lack of significant resources was an equal constraint upon developing economies. Small island economies, like Singapore, had to turn to commerce and/or concentrated forms of industrial production for economic advance, rather than to forms of development that emphasized the exploitation of extensive geographical resources. Countries that lack important resources locally – particularly petroleum and metals – had to accommodate the need to pay for such resources as a necessary contribution to their developmental programmes. Countries with abundant, but relatively uneducated, populations often had to make hard choices between low-skill, labour-intensive development programmes or a costly gamble upon expensive programmes of mass education and training. A judiciously phased combination of the two approaches, however, proved to be a source of the eventual success of a few of the East and South-East Asian economies, particularly that of Taiwan.

The Latin American example

The patterns of state intervention in economic and industrial development outside the Soviet sphere of influence varied considerably, however. Such variation reflected the differing conditions prevailing in different regions and countries. The wartime experience of a number of Latin American economies has suggested that the absence of irresistible competition from imports from more advanced industrial economies could encourage the emergence of viable local industries. Import-substitution industrialization, with state support and protection, might thus provide an effective development strategy.

The strength of the local ruling classes in most Latin American societies, moreover, was such as to ensure that the role of the state in most of the region's economies was initially patterned around the defence of established landed interests and the protection of the economic activities of local entrepreneurs. Foreign companies operated extensively throughout Latin America, and frequently formed a symbiotic relationship with local elites. However, such links did not prevent the growth of a form of economic nationalism and a reaction against foreign ownership of important local assets,[24] which blossomed into the formation of such monopolistic state-run companies in strategically central industries as Pemex in Mexico and PetroBras in Brazil. The structure of most of these economies, however, was neither state socialism nor free-market liberalism. The close interconnections among leading politicians, military leaders,[25] the senior management of state-owned companies and the owners of the major private enterprises constitute a form of immovable state-supported crony capitalism, often superficially embellished with populist trappings[26] that particularly inflamed local revolutionaries.[27]

The African economies in the postcolonial era

Anxiety about the substance of the new freedom and the prospects for rapid development was widespread throughout much of postcolonial Africa.[28] Notions of neo-colonialism[29] flourished in such an atmosphere. The essence of neo-colonial doctrine was that formal political independence did not guarantee real independence from the colonial power. The postcolonial economy would, it was argued, continue to be subordinated and underdeveloped under the influence of the continued operations of multinational companies operating from the former colonialist countries and the structural weakness resulting from over-concentration upon the production and export of a narrow range of primary commodities. Leaving matters to the 'market', it was believed, would merely permit continued dominance by the multinationals and protracted over-dependence upon primary commodities, and could be corrected only by determined state-led action. Import-substitution industrialization was again coupled with attempts to localize the advanced processing of the commodities that were traditionally exported.[30]

As a general strategy, the operations of foreign-based multinational companies were discouraged or their assets were nationalized. Receipts of foreign aid were devoted to the creation of large-scale, state-owned industries, urban development and a range of prestige projects intended to enhance the infrastructure, and raise the image, of the societies in question. Agricultural development, and the rural sector, were identified with underdevelopment and generally neglected or, worse, starved of resources by severe government price controls on agricultural goods being supplied to the urban population. Where investment was directed into agricultural projects, it was often over-mechanized, inappropriate to local conditions, and ultimately unsustainable. Throughout much of sub-Saharan Africa, the long-term effects of such policies were collapsing large-scale industrial plants, white-elephant prestige projects, and urban sprawl, with the burgeoning of shanty towns, rural decay and a seemingly unstoppable decline in general economic well-being. The consequence has been an increased reliance upon overseas sources of aid and support and, in particular, dependence upon the assistance and advice – often in the form of structural adjustment programmes – of the World Bank and, to a lesser extent, the International Monetary Fund.[31]

States and development in East and South-East Asia

Economic developments within East and South-East Asia cast a considerable shadow upon the global economy and thinking about economic development during the last two decades of the twentieth century. The experience of economic and industrial development within the region demonstrated both the strengths and weaknesses of state intervention in, and leadership of, the economy and industrial system. For the first two post-Second World War decades or so, Japan stood virtually alone as an industrialized society in Eastern Asia. The fate of most of its regional neighbours was to be fought over, as in the cases of Korea and Vietnam, or to be treated as charity-cases by the world's more advanced industrial societies. By the 1980s, however, it was becoming clear that something of great significance was afoot in the region, as first one and then another 'tiger' economy thrust itself boldly into the world market.

There were two highly significant differences between the Eastern Asian experience and those of Latin America and sub-Saharan Africa earlier: an adoption of an export-orientated industrial development strategy development and a far from hostile attitude towards foreign capital, particularly financial capital.[32] These two features of Eastern Asian development endowed it with some of its distinctive features, underpinned much of its spectacular success in the later 1980s and 1990s, and also underlay its catastrophic collapse in 1997–98.

The details of the development experiences in the various countries of East and South-East Asia differ significantly. Some important similarities are, however, common to the more successful: a governing elite dedicated to rapid economic growth;[33] the creation of a technocratic elite,[34] on the basis of rapidly improving educational systems, particularly in the higher sector; state encouragement for the development of a financial system closely aligned with the needs of a developing economy and industrial system;[35] and a basic commitment to export-led industrialization and growth.[36] Significant differences among these countries included differing attitudes towards direct foreign investment; different rates of opening to incoming financial capital; the level of nepotism within, and between, the governmental and economic systems; and, most significantly, the rate and extent of the development of strong non-governmental institutions within both the economy and the society.

Taiwan and South Korea led the charge to emulate the spectacular post-war performance of the Japanese economy, by which they were explicitly inspired.[37] Special circumstances rendered both societies particularly open to government leadership of the process of economic development. The socio-economic structures of both countries had been profoundly altered by Japanese occupation, with the effective elimination of large (and inherently conservative) landowners.[38] Taiwan's political system had been transformed by the wholesale relocation of the Chinese Nationalist government to Taiwan after the Communist victory on the mainland in 1949. South Korea's also had a longer-term experience of Japanese colonial occupation and then, almost before the dusts of the Second World War had properly settled, the catastrophe of invasion and wholesale destruction during the Korean War. Both sets of circumstances gave the governments of each of these societies particular resources of strength and/or authority that could be deployed when, at last, rapid economic and industrial development became the priority.

Elsewhere in South-East Asia, the immediate post-war years were marked by the effort, with varying levels of violence, to achieve independence from colonial rule. A bitter armed struggle against the Dutch colonialists formed the basis of the strong military system that came to dominate, and largely dictate to, post-independence Indonesia. In the Philippines, a complex mixture of armed Communist revolt (the Huk rebellion) and more constitutional pressure for independence from the United States of America led to the emergence of a somewhat unruly society with some of the bases of democratic government. Malaysia witnessed an anti-British revolt centred upon the local Chinese population of Malaya and the subsequent emergence of a formally democratic, but effectively one-party, postcolonial society.[39] Singapore shared much of the same background as Malaysia, with which it was joined in a federation between 1957 and 1965, and has also prospered under a nominally democratic, but practically authoritarian one-party political system.[40] Hong Kong, in contrast, remained under formal British control during the greater part of its economic development, achieving 'independence', in the form of a reunification with mainland China, only at the end of 1997.

The diversity of experiences and prevailing conditions underlies the significant differences in the patterns of economic and industrial development of the South-East Asian societies, the precise roles played by the state, and the structure and functioning of the resultant economic systems.

The Japanese 'model' Japan, the region's economic leader, developed a remarkable state-led system that, until 1998, was characterized by close liaison between government and business, with a central role for such agencies as the Ministry of International Trade and Industry (MITI) and the Ministry of Finance; the prominence of a significant number of major firms, often groupings of related businesses, supported by a myriad of small and middle-sized components suppliers; a remarkable level of socio-economic stability founded upon general prosperity and the patterns of secure and highly paternalistic employment; and the effective dominance of the political scene by the Liberal Democractic Party. Post-war Japan continued the pre-war practice of 'borrowing' technology from abroad, through the return of technicians with experience of industries overseas and, most significantly, the 'reverse engineering' of advanced technology products from the world's leading industrial states and companies.[41] A major spur to her post-war economic and industrial recovery was provided by the outbreak of the Korean War in 1950 and Japan's use by the USA as a major staging-post and location for the repair and refitting of military equipment throughout the period of the conflict.

Japan's home market remained highly protected during her period of dramatic growth, first through conventional tariffs and latterly through a plethora of non-tariff barriers. Inward investment was generally discouraged. Overseas investment by Japan's leading corporations was eventually encouraged once the competitive consequences of steadily rising wage levels within Japan were fully appreciated.[42]

Political systems The political systems of the East and South-East Asian societies varied considerably during their periods of major economic growth. Taiwan prospered, initially, under the effectively one-party rule of the Nationalist Party, with parliamentary democracy emerging only after the country's ascent to industrial strength and economic prosperity. South Korea, Malaysia, Singapore and the Philippines were all nominally democracies, but were dominated by one party or leader for much of the period of rapid economic development. Indonesia remained, until 1998, an effective dictatorship, resting upon military support or acquiescence. Thailand combined an established monarchy with long periods of effectively military rule. Hong Kong was, as was indicated earlier, a colony of the United Kingdom until 1997 and subsequently a semi-autonomous region of the People's Republic of China. The People's Republic of China, itself, has remained a highly autocratic communist regime throughout the period. Democracy, particularly of the liberal variety, has thus been a far from a necessary condition for the initial processes of economic growth and development throughout the region.

Government–business links   Close links between government and business interests have also characterized many of the other emerging economies of East and South-East Asia. The forms and intensity of these associations have, however, varied considerably: ranging from the relative distance maintained by the government of Taiwan[43] through the complex and close interrelationship between government and the major enterprises – the *Chaebol* – in South Korea,[44] to the rampant government–business cronyism and family nepotism of Thailand and of Suharto's regime in Indonesia.[45]

Inward investment   Direct investment by a foreign company offers many potential attractions to a developing economy: a ready supply of capital; know-how; the latest technology; and ready access to international markets. The majority of East and South-East Asia's 'tiger economies', with the exception of Japan, accepted such inward investment, primarily from Japan or the USA, as a major source of access to capital, technology and market access, with Thailand offering one of the warmest welcomes to foreign firms seeking to take advantage of the very low wage levels of the country once the boom generated by the Vietnam War came to an end.[46]

Strategic considerations may, however, caution against an unqualified welcome for such investment. Unregulated inward investment can, all too easily, discourage or displace local producers; be too much orientated towards its own domestic market; and damage the longer-term balance of payments by increasing the economy's requirements for imports of expensive inputs, while substantial profits are repatriated to the company's home country. Both Taiwan[47] and South Korea[48] were determined to adopt policies that would secure the maximum benefits from inward investment, while minimizing any structural damage that it might inflict upon still weak economies. China's initial hostility towards inward investment into an economy dominated by state-owned enterprises began to soften with the adoption of a more market-orientated approach to development in the 1980s. At the extreme, governments like those of Malaysia chose to support the development of a home-owned automobile industry, rather than to rely upon the more conventional practice of allowing inward investment by established automobile firms from abroad.

Joint ventures between incoming enterprises and local firms have been a popular pattern of managing inward investment. South Korea[49] and mainland China[50] have both adopted this approach extensively, with a surprising amount of participation in such ventures being undertaken in China from firms based in the politically estranged Taiwan.[51] With authoritative, if not authoritarian, regimes, however, foreign investors embarking upon either joint ventures or wholly owned local investments face the danger of rapid changes in local receptivity towards their activities and, hence, in the conditions under which they have to operate.[52]

Technological capabilities General approaches to economic and industrial development have also reflected themselves in the qualitative character of the industrial production that has been developed within different economies. Some governments in East and South-East Asia have been far more concerned to promote a local capability for technological competence and capacity for innovation. Japan led the charge to convert a technology-copying industrial system into a technology-innovating system.[53] Such a technological transformation was to the fore in the South Korean government's promotion of the economically and technologically powerful Chaebol; the Malaysian government's determination to develop a wholly locally-owned automobile industry; and the Taiwanese government's promotion of advanced technical education[54] and high-technology partnerships with foreign firms, particularly in the aerospace sector.[55]

Overall effects   The combined effects of the variations in development programmes and approaches in the various East and South-
East Asian economies are reflected in the differing general conditions
resulting in those economies. Japan is now an advanced industrial
economy, with a relatively mature, if idiosyncratic, democratic polity, with the fate of its population closely tied to the continued
production and export of a wide range of manufactured goods.
Taiwan is rapidly evolving into a smaller version of Japan, with a
newly democratic political system and a vigorous, and technically
advanced, industrial system. The South Korean economy is dominated by its giant Chaebol, the fate of which is intimately interrelated to the viability of its financial system, the stability of its
fragile democracy, and the well-being of the growing proportion of
the population that has moved from the countryside to the towns
during the last two decades. Singapore and Hong Kong remain
intensely urbanized and rapidly evolving economies that are critic-
ally dependent on their intimate involvement in the international
trade system and, in the case of Hong Kong, on its problematical
relationship with the rest of mainland China. Thailand and Indonesia have both, in their different ways, collided dramatically with
the political and economic weaknesses created by a combination
of corruption and cronyism at the highest levels with an emphasis
upon the development of low-wage, low-technology industries.

Disruption, decline and the interventionist state
Relative economic underdevelopment is by no means the only
condition that prompts intervention by states in the economic
and industrial system. Such intervention can be triggered by serious
disruptions to the running of the economic and industrial system
and by the experience of economic decline relative to the past
performance of a society and/or new competitors on the international scene.

Relative economic decline   Great Britain, as the world's first
industrial society, was also the first to anguish about the relative
decline in its economic strength, technological lead and industrial
vitality. Numerous enquiries and reports during the nineteenth century were devoted to measures to reverse such decline, particularly
in the areas of technological training, supply of investment and
managerial efficiency.[56] University reform and the encouragement

of the new technical institutes flowed directly from such periodic concerns.

Comparable concerns to those of nineteenth-century Britain surfaced within the United States of America during the 1970s and 1980s. The spectacular progress and prosperity of the immediate post-Second World War decades seemed to have passed and subsided into a general loss of productivity, international competitiveness and future well-being. Many were the proposed explanations of this 'decline': Paul Kennedy's identification of the economic strains imposed by the USA's 'overstretch' in the post-Second World War international system;[57] Mancur Olson's thesis that mature, and democratic, economies like the USA ossify in the face of the proliferation of special interests with entrenched powers;[58] and the arguments of many that the USA has been disadvantaged by unfair competition orchestrated by foreign firms and their parent governments.[59] State-led policies for industrial regeneration, for changes in the socio-economic institutions of society, or for an outright policy of industrial support and external protection flowed from such an interpretation. However, the unexpected success of the US economy during the 1990s replaced such concerns and their apparent imperatives for state action with the belief that new technology and a more competitive international economy had combined to generate, for the USA at least, a new economic paradigm, capable of delivering sustained growth without inflationary pressures.[60]

Economic disruption and disorder   Sudden dislocations to orderly economic life may also prompt state intervention in the economy, particularly within democratic polities in which governments are exposed to public demands for sustained economic well-being, as has been suggested earlier. The source of such disruptions, other than the outbreak of major wars, has tended to be the onset of major economic depressions, with their widespread, destructive effects upon economic life and industrial vitality. Two general types of state intervention have followed in the aftermath of such catastrophes: programmes to revive damaged economies; and measures to guard against the return of such depressions and, in particular, the repetition of their precipitatory circumstances.

The Great Depression of the 1930s is the outstanding example of a depression that provoked a wide range of state intervention in economic and industrial life, which, ultimately, ensured a restoration of economic activity. Within the United States of America, Franklin D. Roosevelt's new administration introduced a range of controversial measures under the New Deal: the creation of the Tennessee Valley Authority, to build and operate new dams on the Tennessee River; the Civilian Conservation Corps, to provide work relief for younger men; and the Agricultural Adjustment Act, to stabilize the situation of the farming community. The National Recovery Act of 1933 also provided for extensive programmes of public works, to be overseen by a new Public Works Administration, and for new competitive codes for industry, to be developed by a new National Recovery Administration.

The Roosevelt Administration also introduced measures to regulate the financial services industry, a perceived source of the Great Crash of 1929: the Emergency Banking Act to create a new system of federal inspection of banks; and a new Securities and Exchange Commission to enforce a range of new regulations for the securities industry. The Glass–Steagal Act was also enacted to regulate the banking industry and, in particular, to prevent investment banks owning firms that dealt directly in securities, thereby supposedly reducing the danger that a stock exchange collapse would feed through into a banking crisis.

Less benign forms of state intitiative were also under way elsewhere in the world in the 1930s. In Nazi Germany, in particular, a vigorous programme of remilitarization proved a bountiful 'Keynesian' stimulant to the depressed economy and source of new employment opportunities for its dispossessed population. Indeed, while the structural consequences of the Nazi programme of revival were to prove little short of catastrophic, the arms race and world war that resulted proved to be the only source of sustained economic recovery for many societies, including the United States of America, which had experienced a renewed slump in 1937–38.[61]

Relative economic decline can prompt the adoption of policies and arrangements designed to halt and reverse that process, but usually at too slow a rate to secure the desired outcome: sudden economic disruptions and disasters can precipitate the wide-ranging adoption of policies and institutional innovations that may do something to alleviate the prevailing crisis and pre-empt the recurrence of identical difficulties, but that will probably not be sufficient for the troubles that lie ahead and may well act as a brake upon appropriate responses to changing circumstances.

Regimes and regime change   Major extensions of state intervention in the economy often follow changes in the political regime of a country. The management of Russia and Germany was transformed by the advent of the Bolshevik and Nazi regimes respectively. Both went beyond mere intervention to become highly assertive both domestically and internationally. Neither change of regime was entirely spontaneous, however: the Bolshevik revolution followed the collapse of Tsarist Russia under the strains of the First World War; the Nazi revolution followed Germany's defeat in that war and her subsequent economic collapse under the impact of the Great Depression.

Extensions of state intervention of a less dramatic form have also followed upon a change of political regime or, at least, a change in the incumbent government. Circumstances again have a major effect upon the likelihood that an incoming regime or government will expand state intervention in the economy: Roosevelt's new administration arrived in the midst of, and its election was largely occasioned by, the Great Depression. The advent of the post-Second World War Labour Government in the United Kingdom followed upon the wartime experience of extensive state management of the economic and industrial system and was marked by a period of considerable post-war economic strain and necessary redirection. In contrast, the arrival of Mrs Thatcher's government in 1979 in the United Kingdom took place under markedly different circumstances and proved to be the start of a significant reduction of state involvement in the economy.

The pattern of state involvement in the economic and industrial system will clearly reflect the conditions under which new governments come into being and the policy perspectives that they bring to bear. Fashion, for want of a better term, also plays its part, as is signalled by the contrast between the immediate post-war emphasis upon the state ownership of the 'commanding heights of the economy' and the late twentieth-century enthusiasm for privatized, or privatizing, basic industries.

Governments of both a non-democratic and a democratic kind may increase state involvement in the economic and industrial system. Non-democratic governments are more likely to adopt more direct and assertive roles than their democratic counterparts, at least under peacetime conditions. Democractic governments will base intervention upon firm legal foundations; non-democratic governments pay less consistent respect to the law. The intensity of daily involvement of the state in the economic and industrial system will be as much a function of the capabilities of the state as it will of its intentions: thus a democratic state like Great Britain could deploy considerable resources of skilled personnel to man the state-economic apparatus during the Second World War; a contemporary non-democratic regime in a relatively underdeveloped society, by contrast, may find it extremely difficult to staff anything more than the most rudimentary system for economic and industrial management.

Developmental, distributive states and *laissez-faire* states

The variety of the practices and experiences of states during the second half of the twentieth century distils down to four general models of development. The command economy, under the control of the highly directive state, was popular during the early decades of the era, but fell from popularity with the disappointments experienced by much of much of Africa and the later dissolution of the Soviet Union and its empire in Central and Eastern Europe. However, the three other models of state involvement with the economy – the Capitalist Developmental State, the Distributive Social-Democractic State, and the 'Anglo-American' *laissez-faire* state, all retain some level of support in principle and some level of application in practice.

The Capitalist Developmental States[62] of South-East Asia have, as has been seen from their earlier survey, sustained a clear governmental commitment to export-led development, supported by extensive activity to ensure the emergence of institutions and arrangements designed to support and sustain such development. The retention by the state, and its institutions, of sufficient independence from pluralistic economic and social interests, while maintaining effective links with important industrial and economic networks – *embedded autonomy* – has been identified by some observers as an essential condition for the implementation of an effective developmental strategy.[63] Other observers, however, believe that such states are more characterized by a condition of *governed interdependence*, in which strong states are able to survive the rise of, and retain the capacity to set the broad agenda for, an increasingly strong industrial sector, a significant factor in explaining the differences in performance between the South-East Asian economies and many Latin American societies.[64]

An older tradition than that of the South-East Asian Capitalist Developmental State – the Distributive Social Democractic State – also continues to attract adherents in the late twentieth century, however, and its attractions continue to underlie much of the economic policy outlook of the European Union and many of its constituent members.[65]

The appeal of such an approach has been identified with the apparent success in the Scandinavian economies in the 1960s, 1970s and early 1980s of the so-called 'Swedish Model' of economic and social management, which sought to combine equality of income distribution with high levels of employment, economic growth and social stability,[66] through such policies as a solidaristic wage policy, equalizing wages across industries; an active labour-market policy, supporting the retraining and re-employment of workers shed by industries disadvantaged by the solidaristic wages policy; and restrictive policies militating against both inflation and excessive profit-making within the economy.[67]

Moreover, the combination of such policies with the limited size of many of the economies adopting such an approach often encouraged the emergence of surprisingly strong international firms: Ericsson, Volvo and Electrolux in Sweden; and Phillips in Holland.[68] However, the rise in unemployment and other economic problems during the 1990s prompted new doubts about the ultimate viability of the 'Swedish model', particularly in a world of increasing internationalization and/or globalization.[69]

An 'Anglo-Saxon' or 'Anglo-American' model of *laissez-faire* economic and industrial policy reflects the approaches to economic and industrial management adopted by President Reagan in the USA and Mrs Thatcher in the UK in the 1980s. An emphasis upon reliance upon the free market as the primary source of signals about the direction of the economy and as the main source of economic resources prompted policies to weaken the position of organized labour; to reduce public spending; to pursue the privatization of formerly state-owned industries and utilities in the UK; and to reduce social welfare provision in the USA. International economic liberalization, through the General Agreement on Tariffs and Trade, also reflected the prevalent economic philosophy.

The Anglo-Saxon or Anglo-American model has been viewed as a necessary response to a globalizing world economy by commentators and policy-makers alike. Others, however, have seen it as a source of the acceleration of globalization, and of global financial integration, as much as it is a response to them.[70] Whatever the balance in the push–pull equation of globalization and the development of the *laissez-faire* state, the extent to which such states have been realized remains controversial. The US economy retains an extensive military–industrial component, which does not function according to simple market principles. Moreover, the US economy continues to demonstrate extensive state involvement in agriculture – from extensive federal ownership of grazing land to the maintenance of a range of agricultural subsidies – and to support industrial research and development through a variety of conduits, often focused on the military or space. The UK economy retains a substantial public sector, barely smaller than in the year – 1979 – of Mrs Thatcher's' ascent to power, while a range of supports for industrial and regional development remain in place, if under active review. Enthusiasm for fully free international trade also remains subject to significant qualifications.

The Anglo-Saxon/Anglo-American model has been criticized for reducing the capacity of the state to perform important, if not vital, functions for the economy and industrial system and, equally significantly, for encouraging developments that have proved corrosive for the stability and general well-being of society. Domestically, the damaging effects of the *laissez-faire* project have been deemed to include: encouraging short-term views amongst investors and financial institutions with a reluctance to undertake long-term investment;[71] undermining basic research and development; reinforcing self-regarding behaviour amongst senior managers; intensifying inequality across society; and increasing insecurity within the work force.[72] Internationally, the fruits of such an approach have been identified in the rapid integration of the world's financial system; the greater internationalization and globalization of the world economy generally; and the increased volatility of global economic life, with its crystallization in the international economic and financial crisis of 1998/9. At the domestic/international interface, the new world of the Anglo-Saxon state and a globalized world economy might pose profound threats to the efficacy of democracy at the 'national' level and its prospects at the level of global governance.[73]

Dualistic economies

Despite the apparent contrasts between the different models of state action and state–economy relations, many of the more successful of the world's states and economies appear to combine elements of more than one approach to relations between the state and the economy. Sometimes by accident, and often by design, many successful states have demonstrated a mixture of protected, or 'sheltered' sectors of the economy with sectors that are relatively open to the world economy. Conditions within the sheltered and the open economic sectors often differ markedly. Sheltered sectors that have important implications for employment levels will often remain relatively labour-intensive; those that are strategically sensitive will be able to invest and produce in a far more secure environment than that available to sectors that are exposed to, or forced to engage with, unconstrained international competition. Policies towards sheltered sectors will range from outright protectionism, through the imposition of discriminating 'standards', to local purchasing rules and regulations. Policies towards open sectors of the economy will tend to be restricted to the maintenance of a more generally supportive environment, through suitable developments in systems of education and training, the provision of commercially helpful information, the establishment of trade exhibitions and more active trade promotion through embassies and other forms of overseas representation.[74]

Dualism may thus be a variable across states and societies of a range of apparently differing approaches to economic and industrial policy rather than an 'all or nothing' option. In practice, the choices for a state and society will be of which sectors to shelter and which to open to the competitive world economy and of the forms, and extent, of protection for sheltered sections and of general support for open sectors. A dualistic economy, *per se*, may be an economy with substantial sectors in both the sheltered and the open categories. All economies, however, will exhibit dualism in some form and to some extent.

Conclusions

The sources and forms of traditional state action have thus been both extensive and of profound significance for their societies and for the wider world political economy. State purposes that are widely believed to be illegitimate have been intimately linked to economic and industrial policy. Both Hitler and Stalin required a strong and appropriately mobilized economic and industrial system to pursue their domestic and international objectives. Hitler's aggressive policies, in turn, revived the German economy from its depressed state in the early 1930s. Stalin's determination to build a form of industrial communism, and then to create the strength to meet the threat from external foes, drove a massive programme of heavy industrialization and military expansion.

The full range of the legitimate concerns of states also bear upon, and are affected by, economic and industrial performance; security against external threat; the preservation of social stability; and the promotion of general well-being. Measures to ensure these purposes have extensive implications for economic and industrial policy. The functioning of the economic and industrial system is, in turn, critical to a state's ability to pursue such purposes successfully. The mixed record of the economic and industrial policies that have been designed to serve such purposes diminishes neither their necessity nor their ubiquity.

Only if globalization progresses in the manner envisaged by its most optimistic observers will the need for states to retain a concern with the economic and industrial functioning of their societies disappear; only if globalization develops in the way feared by its more pessimistic witnesses will the state lose all capacity for constructive involvement with their economic and industrial systems. It is to the details of the continuing need for state action on the economic and industrial front, and to the problems confronting such involvement, that the discussion now turns.

Notes

1 See: Yale H. Ferguson and Richard W. Mansbach, *Polities: Authority, Identities and Change* (Columbia, SC: University of South Carolina Press, 1996).

2 Donald R. Morris, *The Washing of the Spears* (London: Jonathan Cape, 1966).

3 M. Mann, *The Sources of Social Power: Vol. 1: A History of Power from the Beginning to A.D. 1760* (Cambridge: Cambridge University Press, 1986).

4 M.M. Postan, *The Medieval Economy and Society: An Economic History of Britain in the Middle Ages* (London: Weidenfeld and Nicolson, 1972), esp. Chs 10, 11 and 12.

5 D.C. Coleman, 'Introduction', esp. p. 4 and 'Eli Heckscher and the idea of mercantilism', esp. pp. 92–3, in D.C. Coleman (ed.), *Revision in Mercantilism* (London: Methuen, 1969).

6 Eric Roll, *A History of Economic Thought*, rev. edn (London: Faber, 1973), esp. Ch. 2.

7 On the East India Companies of various Western European states see: M.S. Anderson, *Europe in the Eighteenth Century, 1713–1783* (London: Longman, 1961), pp. 272–8.

8 J.R. Jones, *The Anglo-Dutch Wars of the Seventeenth Century* (London: Longman, 1996).

9 On hegemony, and its bases, see: George Modelski and William R. Thompson, *Leading Sectors and World Powers: The Coevolution of Global Economics and Politics* (Columbia, SC: University of South Carolina Press, 1996).

10 On the link between military competition and industrialization see: Gautam Sen, *The Military Origins of Industrialisation and International Trade Rivalry* (London: Frances Pinter, 1984).

11 See: *ibid.*; and B.M. Supple, 'The State and the Industrial Revolution 1700–1914', in C.M. Cipolla (ed.), *The Fontana Economic History of Europe: The Industrial Revolution* (London: Collins/Fontana, 1973), Ch. 5; Knut Borchardt, 'Germany 1700–1914', in C.M. Cipolla (ed), *The Fontana Economic History of Europe: The Emergence of Industrial Societies – 1* (London: Collins/Fontana, 1973), Ch. 2; and Gregory Grossman, 'Russia and the Soviet Union', in C.M. Cipolla (ed.), *The Fontana Economic History of Europe: The Emergence of Industrial Societies – 2* (London: Collins/Fontana, 1973), Ch. 8.

12 Karl Polanyi in *The Great Transformation: The Political and Economic Origins of Our Time* (Boston: Beacon Press, 1957); and J.A. Schumpeter in *Capitalism, Socialism and Democracy*, new edn with introduction by Tom Bottomore (London: George Allen and Unwin, 1976 (first published in 1943)).

13 See the contributions to: Robert Boyce and Esmond Robertson (eds), *Paths to War: New Essays on the Origins of the Second World War* (Basingstoke: Macmillan, 1989).

14 Corelli Barnett, *The Collapse of British Power* (London: Eyre Methuen, 1972).

15 Richard Overy, *Why the Allies Won* (London: Jonathan Cape, 1995), esp. pp. 190–8.

16 *The Reader's Digest, The World at Arms: The Reader's Digest Illustrated History of World War II* (London and New York: Reader's Digest, 1989), p. 179.

17 Corelli Barnett, *The Collapse of British Power* (London: Eyre Methuen, 1972).

18 S. Lens, *The Military–Industrial Complex* (London: Stanmore Press, 1971).

19 R.J. Barry Jones, 'Challenge and Response in International Politics' (Reading University: unpublished Ph.D. thesis, 1976).

20 A substantial diversion in the case of Great Britain, see Keith Pavitt, 'Technology in British industry: a suitable case for improvement', in C. Carter (ed.), *Industrial Policy and Innovation* (London: Heinemann, 1981), pp. 88–115.

21 For a further discussion of this structural effect see: R.J. Barry Jones, *Conflict and Control in the World Economy: Contemporary Economic Realism and Neo-Mercantilism* (Brighton: Harvester/Wheatsheaf, 1986), pp. 218–22.

22 See, for instance, C. Hampden-Turner and F. Trompenaars, *The Seven Cultures of Capitalism: Value Systems for Creating Wealth in the United States, Britain, Japan, Germany, France, Sweden, and the Netherlands* (New York: Doubleday, 1993), esp. Ch. 8.

23 See, in particular: R. Wade, *Governing the Market: Economic Theory and the Role of Government in East Asian Industrialization* (Princeton, NJ: Princeton University Press, 1990); and L. Weiss and J.M. Hobson, *States and Economic Development: A Comparative Historical Analysis* (Cambridge: Polity Press, 1995), esp. Chs 5 and 6.

24 For a general survey of Latin America, see: R.W. Mansbach, Y.H. Ferguson and D.E. Lampert, *The Web of World Politics: Nonstate Actors in the Global System* (Englewood Cliffs, NJ: Prentice-Hall, 1976), Chs 7 and 8.

25 See: Mauricio Dias David (ed.), *The State and the Military in Latin America: special edition of Ibero-Americana, Vol. VII, no. 2 and Vol. VIII, no. 1* (1978).

26 See: S.J. Burki and S. Edwards, *Dismantling the Populist State: The Unfinished Revolution in Latin America and the Caribbean* (Washington, DC: The World Bank, 1996).

27 S. Andreski, *Parasitism and Subversion: The Case of Latin America* (London: Weidenfeld and Nicolson, 1966).

28 For a general view of the colonial experience and its consequences see: D.K. Fieldhouse, *The Colonial Empires: A Comparative Survey from the Eighteenth Century* (London: Weidenfeld and Nicolson, 1965).

29 See, in particular: Kwame Nkrumah, *Neo-colonialism: The Last Stage of Imperialism* (London: Heineman, 1965) and Jack Woodis, *An Introduction to Neo-Colonialism* (London: Lawrence and Wishart, 1967).

30 See: Peter C.W. Gutkind and I. Wallerstein, *Political Economy of Contemporary Africa* (London: Sage, 1985).

31 Julius E. Nyang'oro and Timothy Shaw, *Beyond Structural Adjustment in Africa: The Political Economy of Sustainable and Democratic Development* (New York and London: Praeger, 1992).

32 Wade, *Governing the Market*, esp. Chs 4, 5, 6, 7, 8, 9, 10 and 11; and Weiss and Hobson, *States and Economic Development*, esp. pp. 148–57 and 169–88.

33 Wade, *Governing the Market*, Ch. 4 and Ch. 8.

34 *Ibid.*, Ch. 7.

35 *Ibid.*, Ch. 6.

36 *Ibid.*, Ch. 5.

37 *Ibid.*, pp. 189–90.

38 *Ibid.*, pp. 72–3.

39 'No room for rivals in Mahathir's Malaysia', *The Economist*, 26 September 1998, pp. 81–2.

40 'Not another boom', *The Economist*, 18 June 1994, p. 88.

41 C. Freeman and L. Soete, *The Economics of Industrial Innovation*, 3rd edn (London: Pinter Publishers, 1997), pp. 148–51.

42 For a popular view of the Japanese economy, see: M.J. Wolf, *The Japanese Conspiracy* (New York: Empire Books, 1983).

43 Wade, *Governing the Market*, esp. pp. 276–80.

44 On the Chaebol and their relations with government see the survey – 'The house that Park built', *The Economist*, 3 June 1995, after p. 66.

45 See 'Suharto's end-game', *The Economist*, 26 July 1997, after p. 60; and 'When the smoke clears in Asia', *The Economist*, 4 October 1997, p. 85.

46 On the weaknesses of Thailand's overall development pattern see: 'The price of Thailand's prosperity', *The Economist*, 15 May 1993, pp. 81–2.

47 Wade, *Governing the Market*, esp. pp. 148–57.

48 'Mexico's alter ego', *The Economist*, 11 February 1995, p. 101.

49 On the nature and difficulties of such joint ventures in South Korea see: 'Look before you leap', *The Economist*, 14 March 1998, p. 94.

50 On the pattern of foreign direct investment in China see: 'A trickle or a flood?', *The Economist*, 6 August 1994, p. 65; 'Hung up', *The Economist*, 22 July 1995, pp. 76–9; 'Going it alone', *The Economist*, 19 April 1997, pp. 84–9; and 'The China Syndrome', *The Economist*, 21 June 1997, pp. 79–80.

51 Taking care of business', *The Economist*, 19 August 1995, pp. 56–7; and 'Unequal partners', *The Economist*, 24 August 1996, pp. 54–5.

52 On new policies to increase local content in China see: 'Slow car to China', *The Economist*, 16 April 1994, pp. 103–4.

53 On the Taiwanese government's support for the indigenous computer industry, see: 'Inside the box', *The Economist*, 9 July 1994, pp. 83–4.

54 See the report that one-quarter of all Ph.D. students in engineering in the USA come from Taiwan: 'Some chicken', *The Economist*, 4 January 1992, pp. 58–9.

55 'Stall on take-off', *The Economist*, 6 June 1992, pp. 78–9.

56 Corelli Barnett, *The Collapse of British Power* (London: Eyre Methuen, 1972); and for contemporary echoes of such concerns and prescriptions see: Will Hutton, *The State We're In* (London: Jonathan Cape, 1995); and Will Hutton, *The State to Come* (London: Vintage Books, 1997).

57 Paul Kennedy, *The Rise and Fall of the Great Powers: Economic Change and Military Conflict from 1500 to 2000* (New York: Random House, 1988), esp. Ch. 6.

58 Mancur Olson, *The Rise and Decline of Nations: Economic Growth, Stagflation and Social Rigidities* (New Haven, CT: Yale University Press, 1982).

59 Lara D'Andrea Tyson, *Who's Bashing Whom?* (Washington, DC: Institute for International Economics, 1992).

60 'Assembling the new economy', *The Economist*, 13 September 1997, pp. 105–11.

61 Eric Hobsbawm, *Age of Extremes: The Short Twentieth Century, 1914–1991* (London: Michael Joseph, 1994), Ch. 3 and particularly p. 101.

62 Ronen Palan and Jason Abbot, with Phil Deans, *State Strategies in the Global Political Economy* (London: Pinter Publishers, 1996), esp. Ch. 4.

63 Peter Evans, *Embedded Autonomy: States and Industrial Transformation* (Princeton, NJ: Princeton University Press, 1995).

64 Linda Weiss, *The Myth of the Powerless State: Governing the Economy in a Global Era* (Cambridge: Polity Press, 1998), esp. pp. 36–9.

65 Hampden-Turner and Trompenaars, *The Seven Cultures of Capitalism*, Ch. 13.

66 On Sweden, see: *ibid.*, Ch. 10.

67 *Ibid.*, pp. 85–8; and see also: Palan, Abbot and Deans, *State Strategies*, Ch. 5.

68 Palan, Abbot and Deans, *State Strategies*, p. 108.

69 Weiss, *The Myth of the Powerless State*, pp. 85–115.

70 R.J. Barry Jones, 'Globalization in perspective', in R.D. Germain, *Globalisation and its Critics: Perspectives from International Political Economy* (Houndmills: Macmillan, 1999); and see also: Stephen Gill, 'Globalization, market civilization, and disciplinary neoliberalism', *Millennium: Journal of International studies*, vol. 24, no. 3 (Winter 1995), pp. 399–423.

71 For the US experience, see: Hampden-Turner and Tromperaars, *The Seven Cultures of Capitalism*, pp. 81–5.

72 Hutton, *The State We're In*, esp. pp. 95–225; and for a wider critique, see: John Gray, *False Dawn: The Delusions of Global Capitalism* (London: Granta Books, 1998), esp. Chs 1, 2 and 4.

73 For a discussion of pertinent issues, see: Jan Aart Scholte, 'Global capitalism and the State', *International Affairs*, vol. 73, no. 3 (July 1997), pp. 427–52.

74 See: R.J. Barry Jones, *Conflict and Control*, pp. 179–200.

III

The future of state action

7

Governance and the future of state action: needs

The challenges posed by contemporary global developments revive age-old questions about the very need for formal government of the affairs of human beings and, if needed, the form and level of such government.

Both egotistical anarchists[1] and extreme libertarians have contested the very need for formal governments to be set above individual human beings. Reason, in harmonious combination with self-interest, would ensure the spontaneous construction of order and common well-being in a world from which the unnecessary, and distorting, influence of governmental institutions had been purged. However, the majority of thinkers, from more communally-orientated anarchists[2] through to more moderate liberals,[3] have accepted the need for some organized self-governance of societies and their constituent groupings, differing only over its particular form. Thus, followers of Proudhon's federalist approach to social governance believed in self-government by smallish communities – or communes – with co-ordination on issues of wider geographical import being addressed by less regular meetings formed by mandated, and recallable, delegates from the more local, and essentially sovereign, communes.[4] However, the history of the leading European states from the sixteenth century onwards has, until recently, been one of the concentration of greater power at the centre of expanding states: a precedent that was followed even after the nominally anti-statist Bolshevik revolution in Russia.

The history of modern Europe does not, however, settle the question of the most appropriate levels of human governance or the most suitable forms. The complex mosaic of sizes and forms of state within modern Europe thus qualifies any simple formula that purports to equate the size and form of state with the demands of contemporary political and military competition. Moreover, increasing internationalization or globalization is, as has been seen, supposed to be overturning the historical link between the state and politico-military competition and conflict, and undermining the state's 'traditional' role in economic management.

The discussion has thus reached the point at which two central questions have to be addressed directly. First, are there continuing needs for the kind of governance that states have traditionally provided for their citizens? Second, if there are continuing requirements for such a form of governance, do traditional states have any role in its provision?

The meaning of governance

The current popularity of the term *governance* has two possible implications. First, a continuing need for the performance of functions akin to those conventionally performed by state governments. Second, that changed conditions are such as to warrant the use of a term like governance, rather than the more institutionally specific notion of government.

Both aspects of the popularity of the term 'governance' are captured in reviews of the many possible meanings of the term[5] and summarized by the 'definition' provided by the recent Commission on Global Governance: 'Governance is the sum of the many ways individuals and institutions, public and private, manage their common affairs',[6] who proceed to describe it as: '... a continuing process through which conflicting or diverse interests may be accommodated and co-operative action may be taken. It includes formal institutions and regimes empowered to enforce compliance, as well as informal arrangements that people and institutions either have agreed to or perceive to be in their interest.'[7]

Forms of governance

While much governance continues to be undertaken by 'conventional' governmental institutions – public governance – an increasing amount of contemporary governance is now undertaken, effectively, by institutions and actors that operate outside the arena of conventional government and politics, by essentially private

Figure 7.1   Forms of governance

	public	private
formal		
informal		

interests: private governance. The bases upon which both public and private governance rest also range from the clear and explicit foundations in treaties, laws or contracts – formal governance – to arrangements that rest upon little more than shared understandings and expectations: informal governance. Four ideal types of governance are suggested by these two dimensions of governance: public–private and formal–informal, as illustrated by Figure 7.1.

At the global level, the United Nations represents an example of public-formal governance; the Group of 8 is closer to public-informal governance; the Féderation Internationale de Football Association (FIFA) exemplifies private-formal governance in control of Association Football world-wide; and implicit cartels among oil companies or car manufacturers provide instances of private-informal governance.

The forms of global governance may be neither stable nor simple, however. With changing conditions, different aspects of governance may pass, in effect, from one form of governance to another. Moreover, the management of many important aspects of the global political economy has long involved a complex mixture of public authorities and private interests, as in the management of commercial shipping.[8] An increasing number of arenas of global management have now been opened to the participation, if only as observers and advisers, of non-state actors, particularly in the environmental arena.[9]

The functions of governance

An appreciation of the range of forms and foundations of governance within the contemporary global system does not, however, answer the central question of their real role. Much discussion of government and politics takes place without any real questioning of its ultimate necessity. Reflection upon this essential issue is, however, vital if a clear perspective is to be established upon the problems confronting effective governance in the evolving global system.

The critical functions of public governance fall under three headings, the second of which is a special case of the first. These functions are: the provision of collective goods; the management of general externalities; and the satisfaction of minority needs. The need for provision in each of these three arenas gives public governance its purpose; its legitimacy; general support; and ultimate resilience.

Collective goods
Collective goods are those arrangements that are desired by the membership of any collectivity; and which, once provided, may be difficult to deny to any members of that collectivity – nonexcludability.[10] Such collective goods may also manifest the characteristics of *jointedness* – that is, they require the contributions of resources by all, or at least most, of the members of the collectivity to bring them into being; and *lumpiness* – that is, that there are critical levels of resourcing and/or supply, below which suboptimal levels of provision will be experienced.

Externalities
Externalities are, in effect, a special case of collective goods that are of particular significance to agencies of public governance and that may also be significant to agencies of private governance. Externalities are effects generated as a side-effect, possibly unanticipated and unintended, of any kind of activity. Such externalities may be negative – as in the generation of pollution by a manufacturing process – or positive – as in the case of the creation of a pool of skilled labour, which may subsequently become available to society at large, by a firm that undertakes high levels of training for its workforce.

Market failures, where the unrestricted functioning of a market economy generates unfortunate effects, including the emergence of distorting monopolies or oligopolies, constitute special cases of the collective goods and externalities that confront agencies of public governance.

The problem of such externalities is that the associated costs or benefits do not translate themselves into costs or benefits for the firm, or other actor, that is creating them. Such an actor can avoid external costs: external benefits, equally, do not bring direct rewards for the generating firm or actor. There may, therefore, be no direct incentive for adopting practices that avoid the external costs or to encourage developments that will produce external benefits. Agencies of public governance have to exist to deal with such externalities – both negative and positive – when they arise or are likely to arise.

There is also a third function of governance, which is primarily of concern to agencies of public governance and which is critical to the current debate about changes in the international political economy, political space and governance. This is:

Minority needs

Minority needs of many kinds are often the needs that are least suitable to satisfaction through market mechanisms, unless the members of the minority possess considerable personal resources, or the needs in question can be met relatively cheaply. Such minority needs include the medical requirements of those who suffer from rare ailments; those who suffer from severe behavioural disorders; those who live in areas with exposure to greater than average threats to stability and personal security; or those who are particularly unfortunate in their current, or continuing, experience of economic or personal life. The defining feature of such minorities is that their needs and wants – current or continuing – will not be met by a market-based mechanism of supply, because the costs would be disproportionate and/or the price would be beyond the means of the members of the minority in question. Such needs and wants may also be beyond the means, in terms of time, personnel and physical resources, of small groups.

New minority needs may also arise unexpectedly and, therefore, not be covered by any forms of commercial insurance or prior provision by small groups – as the devastating floods in Central America in late 1998 demonstrated. The capacity of institutions of public governance to develop a wide range of capabilities and competencies, and to deploy substantial reserves of resources, allows them to deal with such unanticipated minority needs in a manner denied to many other institutions or arrangements.

The range of potential minorities is far wider and more unpredictable than might commonly be supposed. Even the wealthy and well-favoured may suddenly find that a major stock-exchange crash, a collapse of a financial institution, or a financial fraud can leave them in potential penury and acute need of state-like institutions to ensure restitution, where available, or support, where compensation is not feasible. A natural disaster might also leave them deprived of access to their established sources of wealth and well-being, and unexpectedly dependent upon public resources of rescue and succour.

In the face of a wide range of actual and potential minority requirements, agencies of public governance act as an agency of insurance and supply, in which the means of effective supply are secured from the wider community. Securing appropriate means from the wider community, in turn, requires the aggregation of actual or potential minority needs into a wider agenda, or principled programme, that warrants practical concern for such minorities – on the basis either of *moral principles* – that it is right to meet such minority needs; and/or *prudential principles* – that individuals will never know when they may find themselves as members of one or another needy minority. The combination of facilitative and restorative functions on issues of world-wide concern is thus definitive of public governance at the international or global level.

The contested functions of public governance

A review of the general areas of activity that warrant arrangements for public governance does not, however, resolve all the central issues concerning government and politics. Controversy attaches to each of the functions of public governance: to the identity of collective goods, in principle; to the best ways of dealing with externalities, in practice; and to the range of minority needs that it is practicable for public authorities to accommodate.

The problem of collective goods
The general definition of collective goods is relatively uncontroversial: goods that, in contrast to private goods, are characterized by indivisibility and non-excludability and a high degree of 'lumpiness'. Indivisibility signifies the fact that the supply of many collective goods cannot be divided up into smaller quantities when provided for their target population. Non-excludability indicates that it is impossible, or very difficult, to exclude given individuals or groups

from enjoying such a collective good once it has been supplied for the community. Thus, the construction of an effective nuclear deterrent for a society would be a general condition that cannot be parcelled out in varying proportions to different members of that society; nor can it be withheld totally from any individual, while that individual continues to remain within the territory of the society thus protected. A private good such as ice-cream can, in contrast, be supplied in greater or lesser quantities to the members of any society, and can clearly be withheld from those who lack the means to purchase the confection. Finally, many collective goods have minimum levels of provision, below which the collective good will not be provided for a society or other collectivity. Thus, a global Collective Security System that attracted the participation of only a handful of states would not really provide an effective system of security for the global 'community'.

Not only may collective goods be of particular importance for societies or other collectivities; they are also vulnerable to serious under-supply. Members of any collective may genuinely value a specific collective good, but may calculate that, in some circumstances, they can enjoy the benefits of such collective goods while not actually contributing to the costs of their provision – free-riding.[11] A vital role of governments, or other agents of public governance, in this respect is to alter the structure of the calculations that will be made by potential free-riders in such a way as to ensure that sufficient contributions are forthcoming from the members of a collectivity to secure the provision of valued collective goods.[12]

The problem is that such a general view of collective goods does not settle the question of their frequency of occurrence in human affairs. Indeed, one way of defining politics is in terms of the continuous debate, not merely over how best to provide collective goods, but over the range of conditions that are to be identified as legitimate collective goods. The security of a society from external political and military threats has long been widely accepted as a legitimate, and even a self-defining, collective good for states and societies. However, proponents of governmental action over educational provision within a society might seek to define the supply of a high level of education for all its citizens as a real collective good, with many implications for economic, social and political well-being. Others, however, might argue that education is an essentially private matter, of primary consequence only for individual parents and pupils and to be provided for exclusively from personal resources. Even more controversial disagreements have erupted in many societies over whether common patterns of religious belief, social conduct or sexual activity ought to be defined as collective goods to be 'provided' through laws to regulate such areas of personal life and impose common standards of conduct.

Much of politics, traditional government and contemporary governance is thus an issue of first defining legitimate collective goods for pertinent collectivities and then deliberating upon the best means for their provision.

The problems of externalities

Externalities concern a special sub-group of collective goods that encompass all their political problems but add additional difficulties of definition and resolution. Externalities are those collective goods (or bads) that may be generated as side-effects of private actions that are not primarily intended to create those effects. A socially beneficial externality might be provision of a steady supply of trained technicians to the wider economy by a leading firm that undertook, for its own purposes, an advanced level of technical training for its staff, some of whom then moved on to employment with other enteprises. A socially damaging externality might be the environmental pollution generated by an industrial enterprise concerned primarily with the production of some good at minimum direct cost to itself. The problem is that such externalities do not appear directly on the cost–benefit balance sheets of the responsible enterprises or of other actors.

While there is widespread agreement that the existence of such externalities creates a gap between private gains and losses, on the one hand, and social gains and losses, on the other, there are considerable technical difficulties with their identification and even greater difficulties in defining suitable means of dealing with them in practice.

The current complexities of negotiations on the environment and its protection exemplify the problems of policies on externalities. First, there has to be an initial acceptance that there is a worrying effect. Second, it is necessary to be clear and precise about whose actions are creating the undesirable effect. Third, a credible means has to be devised to persuade any environmental violators to modify their behaviour. The debates over global warming demonstrate that acceptance that there is an overall process of global warming has encountered, and continues to encounter, considerable resistance; that many of the major contributors to such global warming proved reluctant to accept their responsibility[13] and/or keen to shift the primary blame elsewhere; and, finally, that measures to persuade reluctant polluters to mend their ways will be highly complicated and unduly costly to put into force,[14] with fears that the more probable responses will be punitive for the Less Developed Countries or result in new restraints upon free international trade.[15]

The encouragement, or reward, of those who generate positive externalities may be equally complicated and controversial. Why, it is often argued, should a firm that undertakes the training of its workforce for its own purposes secure an additional reward from the public purse? Such rewards, it is argued, merely provide firms with a double reward for doing what they would be doing anyway; give additional market advantages to those larger firms that are likely to be in a position to provide programmes of advanced training for their employees; and would, in the final analysis, constitute an unwarranted burden upon inevitably limited public resources. Were, in contrast, effective programmes of training to be provided within the public sector, the benefits would be available to all relevant enterprises within the domestic economy.

Externalities, of both a positive and a negative form, thus create considerable problems for public policy. Their identification is by no means unproblematical, and the construction of effective programmes for their resolution is far from straightforward, involving serious questions of equity and efficiency.

Minority needs and the problem of the unexpected and the potential tyranny of special interests

Meeting minority needs, actual and potential, is an important function of government, but also encounters considerable difficulties. The first task is to reconcile the interests of majorities with those of minorities. A carefully constructed framework of public governance and civic society is necessary if the delicate balance between the majority and minority on any issue is to be maintained, particularly when the issues arouse strong feelings or involve basic interests.

A further problem of dealing with minority needs is that of their future emergence and of the inherent unknowability of the future.

Adequate provision for future needs may fail to be made. However, there is also the danger of over-prediction, and the possibility of the potential waste of resources on minority needs that fail to develop in the manner or on the scale expected. The emergence of Bovine Spongiform Encephalopathy (BSE) from the early 1980s in Great Britain illustrated the dilemmas. Substantial provision from public resources to deal with an epidemic of terminal human illness might be necessary were this disease to spread readily to human consumers of infected beef. When evidence began to emerge of BSE's role in the appearance of a new variant of the human equivalent of BSE – Creutzfeld–Jakob disease – fears of a future mass epidemic revived. Again, however, there was profound uncertainty as to whether this human product of BSE would occur widely within the exposed population. Restraint with regard to the preparation of extensive facilities for the care of the terminally ill was thus seen to be warranted by the inherent uncertainties of the situation.

Substantial provision for some 'minority' needs, or public preparations for their future emergence, can also have perverse effects. New provisions for established minority ailments can encourage mis-diagnosis or phantom afflictions. Preparations for contingencies such as extensive loss of life during the approach of war can precipitate mass panic. Worse, preparations for the protection of populations against threatened attack could persuade a potential adversary that such preparations signalled an intention to precipitate a war and prompt the potential adversary to pre-emptive action. Many forms of public provision can also encounter the problem of 'moral hazard', of discouraging personal precautions against future difficulties by promising public insurance against such difficulties.

Such difficulties are not the most serious problems confronting provision for minority needs. The greatest difficulties concern the cost entailed in meeting some such needs and their potential proliferation. Societies of sufficient size can cope with a significant number of costly minority needs. The problem arises, however, if such costly minority needs begin to proliferate. Such proliferation, in turn, can be encouraged by the development of the technical means of dealing with such needs, for example through medical innovations, and by an awareness amongst minorities that the costly needs of other minorities are being met from public resources. The two dangers inherent in such a proliferation of demanding minority needs are that public resources will come under serious strain and/or that society will begin to disaggregate into a multitude of contrasting, and ultimately competing, special interests.

Systems of governance thus confront a constant tension between the inclusive effects of acknowledging and meeting the needs of minorities and the divisive consequences of over-emphasizing differences and their costly accommodation. Meeting the needs of many significant minorities may remain, however, important to the legitimization of governance and the maintenance of the loyalty of those represented.

A central function of effective public governance, therefore, is that of balancing divergent and possibly incompatible interests. The institutions of public governance can provide the arena within which such interests are expressed, debated and adjudicated. Authoritative judgements over disputed interests, whether between minorities and minorities or between minorities and majorities, can then be implemented and enforced by the institutions of the system of public governance. A form of social cohesion can thus be maintained even in the face of profound divergences and disagreements; forcefully, if that is ultimately necessary.

The provision of collective goods, the management of externalities and the meeting of minority needs thus encapsulate the essential functions of governance. The conceptual complexities that confront these functions and the difficulties that are encountered in their practical performance, however, define many of the abiding challenges of governance. Yet it is just such conceptual issues and practical challenges, that are central to an evaluation of the continuing requirements for governance within the contemporary global system and to the prospects for its effective execution within changing circumstances.

The continuing agenda for public governance

The core functions of supplying collective goods, managing externalities and accommodating minority needs are thus central to public governance. Small-scale societies may be able to fulfil these functions to a limited extent, through relatively informal and highly participatory forms of collective self-governance. More elaborate institutions and procedures rapidly become necessary, however, once these functions have to be provided for larger communities with wider geographical distributions. Indeed, the larger the number of these functions that are to be fulfilled effectively, the more elaborate the institutions of public governance may have to become and the larger the community embraced. Thus, building a village hall may be feasible at the village level; dealing with global warming may require a form of public governance at the global level.

States have, thus far, proved to be the pivotal form, and level, of organization of public governance, orchestrating, at their most effective, a high level of provision within their areas of jurisdiction, while marking a far more fragmented and generally less effective mode of governance in the space(s) outside their frontiers. States, when functioning 'properly', have thus assumed a range of responsibilities for the well-being of their populations at all levels and in all arenas, from individual well-being, to stability of the economy and the security of the entire community. States, through myriad intergovernmental associations and agencies, have also formed the basic components of what public governance has proved possible at the international and global levels: being the formal members of most international organizations and the actors whose mutually regarding interactions are the essence of the international system, the socialization of whose governments and bureaucrats gives what substance it has to the notion of an 'international society'.[16]

Individual well-being

The state, or its functional equivalent, has often been assigned a crucial role in the maintenance of the well-being of individuals in all but the smallest, self-managing societies. The security of the person is the first, and most vital, function of the state. The maintenance of police forces, in function if not always in name, has thus been common to most forms of public governance. The distinctive feature of the modern state is to bring agencies of public order and protection into the public domain: to be financed from the public purse and controlled by public authorities, and to operate in the public good.

The emergence of state-based policing also concerned the preservation of the personal property. Provision in this area has, however, remained more mixed than in the area of personal security for all but the richest or most prominent of individuals. Private insurance of property continues within market economies and provides a second source of reassurance against personal loss for those who can afford the necessary premiums. Indeed, with the high levels of property crime, and the relatively low levels of detection of theft and recovery of property, personal insurance actually constitutes the primary source of practical security for the citizens of many industrial societies.

The earlier practice of private insurance companies providing fire-fighting for their policy-holders proved to be seriously inadequate both for individual and communal protection. Fire-fighting services were therefore progressively brought under the auspices of local authorities, and then of national fire-fighting services.

The well-being of the individual is also promoted finally, but by no means leastly, by the provision of a general framework of law. Access to legal resolution of disputes, and the authoritative enforcement of judgements, is the ultimate guarantee of security of personal property for the majority. Recourse to the law is also the primary means to the preservation of personal physical security, both as a source of redress against those who have inflicted harm and as a form of deterrent against those who might seek to inflict harm in the future. Indeed, a failure to sustain a fair and accessible structure of law is often offered as significant evidence of an imperfect, or even failing, state and is a major source of criticism and/or rejection.

Social stability and welfare

The stability of the social whole, and the welfare of its population in general, becomes an issue of public governance as the size and complexity of a society expands. The security of neither the person nor property can be ensured in the absence of a measure of social stability. The good functioning of the economy is also conditional upon some level of general social stability: economic activity is jeopardized, investment is discouraged, and the emigration of valued workers and the deterrence of constructive inward investment may also flow from social instability.

Many valued objectives are also dependent upon the attitudes, educational qualifications and level of physical fitness of populations. A vigorous economy requires an active and capable population. The effectiveness of a society's military forces rests upon the capabilities and physical condition of its younger members. Policies on public fitness and health have also become common within industrialized societies: ranging from authoritative polices on issues of public hygiene and sanitation, to the regulation, and often provision, of systems of mass health-care.[17]

Acknowledgement of the general need for states, or their functional equivalents, to promote social stability and well-being does not, however, clarify the nature, or range, of the specific conditions for concern or the most appropriate policies. Politics is, as has been previously argued, quintessentially a matter of debate about the nature of the conditions that should be defined as collective goods, or pertinent externalities, as well as the means of their provision or management. That debate and disagreement inevitably attach to such issues does not diminish their centrality to effective public governance.

Regional prosperity and well-being

The economic and social problems of specific regions provide a further spur to action by the wider society. A disadvantaged region creates a minority 'need' on a distinctive scale and of an interesting kind. Regional difficulties create a minority that is defined by its geographical location. Moreover, the reasons for the disadvantage of a particular region may be remote from the experiences and expectations of many of the other regions of any particular society or state, encouraging the neglect of the needs of disadvantaged regions by the more favoured areas.

Moreover, any regional policy adopted by the central state might merely serve the interests and/or ideology of the central government, or reflect its wish to assert its authority, rather than meet the real needs of the localities concerned. Such critical notions contribute, in part at least, to the growing appeal of regional devolution, if not outright secession, within many of the distinctive regions and 'national' sub-groupings of many European states.

Regional policies have thus enjoyed a mixed record. However, many of the problems confronting disadvantaged regions still require the mobilization of resources from beyond their territories, including natural disasters and economic backwardness, or decline. However, the quality of the design and implementation of regional policies remains critical to their effectiveness. When ill-conceived or misapplied, such policies can merely contribute to disillusionment, misallocation of scarce resources and even outright corruption.[18]

'National' economic strength and capability

The role of the state in the promotion of economic strength and capability is one of the outstanding features of modern world history, as was seen in the earlier discussion. Controversy continues to attach to this role of the state, however, with neo-liberals[19] against a range of analysts who believe in the continuation of a vital role for states, or their functional equivalents, in the management of economic and industrial developments. However, all but the most extreme of neo-liberals acknowledge the need for some role for the state, or its functional equivalent, to correct the distortions, dysfunctions and/or excesses that arise in any complex market system, from fraud and dishonesty to cyclical instabilities in some product areas to the damage of unanticipated economic shocks, to the wider dangers of systemic crisis.

A more extensive economic and industrial role for the state, or its functional equivalent, rests upon a view of economic and industrial developments that gives greater emphasis to the imperfections of knowledge, the availability of critical resources, access to markets, and the occurrence of external shocks. The state is thus likely to maintain: macro-economic policies; explicit industrial policies; the provision of essential resources, particularly financial; and policies directed against the emergence of damaging monopolies or oligopolies, to preserve a 'level playing field' within critical market sectors. Protection against external shocks, and particularly unanticipated shocks, also underlies many schemes for shorter-term support for affected industries and lies at the heart of longer-term support for agricultural producers.

State policies may also be informed by a view of the desirable shape of the 'national' economy and its relationship with the wider world economy, including: the size and pattern of domestic agricultural production, particularly when under the threat of war, especially its military production potential; the general sources of 'national' economic growth; and the overall balance of trade with the wider world economy.

State leaders generally aspire to diverse economies with strength in innovation, production and supply in high-value-added areas of manufacturing and service industries. Combinations of experience, observations of the successes of other societies, and doubts about the qualities of completely undirected free markets have encouraged the governments of many states to sustain some policies designed to shape general economic and industrial developments and, in particular, to encourage pivotal industries and the creation of locationally specific, dynamic industrial clusters,[20] with positive interconnections, of considerable benefit to the local economy and, ultimately, to the wide national economy. Such clusters have been identified as playing a vital part in such diverse sectors as the textile industry of North and North-Eastern Italy;[21] the animation industry of Cardiff in South Wales; the micro-electronics and computing concentration in California's 'silicon valley'; the surprising concentration of expertise in the design and construction of Formula 1 racing cars in Central–South England; and many regional concentrations of motor vehicle manufacture.[22]

The balance of trade, and balance of payments, with the wider world economy has also been a source of concern for state authorities. Persistent deficits in these respects will, unless compensated by capital inflows, create downward pressure on the international value of the country's currency, challenging fixed exchange-rate policies. Persistent balance of payments problems have often prompted policies to reduce the external trade imbalance, thereby relieving the persistence of pressure on the balance of payments and the exchange rate.

The widespread abandonment of fixed exchange rates and the adoption of floating exchange-rate regimes has encouraged a more relaxed official attitude towards shorter-term movements in the balance of trade and the resulting balance of payments. However, a protracted balance of trade deficit will still have uncomfortable consequences. Continued deficits in the balance of payments can be compensated by inflows of capital, which, if in the form of short-term financial flows, may leave the economy vulnerable to rapid outflows of funds and resultant currency crises if conditions change adversely. If, however, incoming capital assumes the form of longer-term investments, then the effect will be to transfer increasing proportions of the domestic economy and industry to foreign ownership and control. Whatever the strategic effects of an increase in foreign ownership, such a development is likely to generate increased outward flows of repatriated profits, which, without a compensatory increase of exports of goods and services, will reinforce any future pressures upon the balance of payments and the exchange rate.

Exchange-rate crises are one ever-present, and possibly increasing, danger of a world in which private financial flows have become massive and almost instantaneous, while state governments remain responsible for the maintenance of national currencies. Governments may, as has been seen, be forced to subordinate monetary policy, and to a lesser extent fiscal policy, to exchange-rate stability. Capital and exchange controls remain available, however,[23] as is demonstrated by the actions of some of the governments of South-East Asia in the face of the economic and financial crisis of 1997–98.[24]

Externalities of various kinds also concern those who favour a significant economic role for states, including the positive benefits of: regional industrial clusters; strategically significant industries; the advantages of local suppliers; the development of economic trust and confidence through personal contacts; and the diffusion of technical knowledge and competencies throughout the local region. State polices to support new, or established, industries in strategically critical areas reflect a recognition of many such positive externalities.

Negative externalities are also a major source of the regulative activities of state authorities, however, ranging across: the dangers from uncontrolled monopolists or oligopolists; the damaging effects of irresponsible financial institutions; and the depredations of industrial decline. A wide raft of laws, rules and regulations reflect the wide range of such negative externalities within a complex modern market economy.

Minority needs can also prompt interventionist economic and industrial policies, regional, occupational, or industrial. Such intervention may merely preserve 'lame duck' industries; but the impulse to intervene remains strong within states of many types, and has often been at its sharpest in policies to preserve agricultural activity and rural life.[25]

International and global stability and well-being

Serious externalities also arise at the international or global level, embracing such issues as: financial stability; general economic well-being and the preservation of the global environment; and the management of its natural resources.

The maintenance of international financial stability and probity
International financial regulation evokes disputes between free-marketeers and those who favour state-based management.[26]

Repeated economic and financial crises prompted the gradual establishment of mechanisms and institutions for the management of the world's financial system: from the Bank for International Settlements (BIS), established in Geneva in 1930, to the Washington-based International Monetary Fund (IMF), established at the Bretton Woods Conference on the post-Second World War international economic order in 1944.

The advancing scale and pace of global financial integration,[27] however, reinforced the perceived need to develop and enhance the capacity for regulation of the world's financial system:[28] a perceived need that was reinforced, somewhat sharply, by the economic and financial crisis of 1997–98.[29] Such concerns followed upon earlier anxieties about the need to establish mechanisms for regulating the growth of new and highly risky trading in derivatives on international markets.[30]

Efforts to regulate global financial flows can take place at both the state and the global level. States can, and do, impose unilateral exchange controls on capital movements and regulations on the conduct of financial enterprises that operate within their jurisdiction. Such unilateral measures can moderate some of the dangers of a volatile global financial system, if taken in good time and implemented effectively. To secure the benefits of both global financial mobility and global financial stability, however, requires appropriate policies and practices at the international level.[31] James Tobin's proposal for a universal turnover tax on foreign exchange transactions was offered as one means of dampening speculative enthusiasms.[32] Proposals for ensuring the robustness of those institutions that engage in substantial international financial transactions were inherent in the Bank for International Settlements' proposals for new global standards of capital adequacy for banks,[33] and in suggestions for the differentiation of 'narrow' banks, dealing with the general public, from 'broad' banks, operating with fewer restrictions.[34]

The stability of longer-term international capital flows is also in need of regulatory support in a complex and rapidly changing world. Foreign direct investment has been complicated, and often blighted, by inconsistent accountancy standards amongst countries. Would-be purchasers may thus be misled by unfamiliar, and sometimes markedly inferior, accountancy rules and procedures when considering foreign acquisitions. The risk of serious disappointment, at best, or of outright fraud, at worst, inhibits potentially beneficial foreign direct investment and lies behind hitherto unsuccessful attempts to establish new, universal standards of financial accounting.[35]

The problems created by disparate standards of accounting in a world of fragmented sovereignties links into one of the most serious problems to confront the contemporary global system, in general, and its financial system, in particular: that of fraud and the movement of criminal funds. The remorseless growth of the trade in illegal drugs, the collapse of law and order in much of the former Soviet Union and the expanding opportunities presented by an integrated global financial system have combined to make illicit financial transactions one of the world's major growth 'industries'.[36] The more powerful states can take unilateral actions against some aspects of this sinister economic subculture, with some effect. However, a comprehensive approach to the problem requires extensive international co-operation and co-ordination in the formulation of laws and the instruments of implementation, to suppress substandard 'offshore' financial shelters,[37] share knowledge and intelligence, and take joint action to apprehend and punish malefactors, irrespective of where they offend or reside. States, acting alone or in concert, however, remain the only actors capable of instituting any form of public governance of this increasingly central aspect of the new global economy.

The promotion of global economic well-being

The preservation of any kind of international market system, beyond the most primitive, remains dependent upon the ability of states to sustain order and prosperity domestically and to contribute to the maintenance of orderly trading relations externally. It is still states that sign international trade treaties, are responsible for honouring them, and are the primary subjects of actions taken in international tribunals when free-trade commitments are violated.

States, acting alone or together, also remain major sources of support for those societies that continue to encounter obstacles to their development or experience overwhelming disasters, like the hurricane-induced flooding in Honduras of November 1998. Despite the steady reduction in the relative size of their aid budgets,[38] Official Development Assistance by the world's more prosperous states – both unilateral and multilateral – thus continued to contribute 4.3 per cent of the GNP of the world's 'low-income' countries in

1994 – 12.6 per cent in the case of the 'low-income' countries excluding China and India.[39]

The agenda for international economic negotiation also continues to be established primarily by the major economies: the United States of America and, increasingly, the European Union. The outcomes of such negotiations are, moreover, determined primarily by the interests and dispositions of these actors. Thus the Uruguay Round of the General Agreement on Tariffs and Trade could not be concluded until a deal on agricultural trade had been concluded between the European Union and the United States of America.[40]

The negotiation of a new Multilateral Agreement on Investment (MAI) also reveals the dominant influence of the major economies, but raises further questions about the interests that are being served, or promoted, by state action. The intention of the MAI was to encourage an increase in international investment by introducing new, mandatory rules to ensure that the investments and operations of transnational corporations in various countries would not be subject to discriminatory or unreasonable behaviour: discriminatory rules and regulations; differential tax regimes; or arbitrary expropriation.

However, there was widespread suspicion that the enthusiastic initial promotion of the MAI by the government of the United States of America owed more to the interests, and urgings, of leading US-based transnational corporations than to the general wellbeing of the world's population, in general, or of the less developed countries, in particular.[41] Moreover, once the configuration of forces within the US political system altered, views about the desirability of the MAI began to change and the approach of the US administration began to become more reserved and move into line with the more critical attitude of the European Union, and of France in particular.[42]

The preservation of the global commons
The continuing need for effective state action is revealed by the issues of environmental protection and the preservation of vital natural resources. The sources of pressure upon the natural environment lie in the behaviour of both states and private commercial interests. States have manufactured and exploded nuclear bombs, and many state-owned industries have committed major acts of environmental pollution. Private enterprise, however, is often tempted

to undertake polluting behaviour, neglect of resource conservation and the generation of a range of negative externalities by the pressures of competition and the need to return satisfactory profits to its owners. While the 'demand' side of environmental governance may thus come from both public and private sources, the supply side lies overwhelmingly in the public domain.

The actions of the world's largest economies can, as elsewhere, have a considerable unilateral impact upon many global environmental problems. Any real solutions to many of the most pressing problems of environmental degradation and resource exhaustion, however, require widespread support. Ensuring world-wide participation in measures of environmental protection, in turn, requires appropriate structures of agreement and implementation. New forms of global governance might offer a path to such an end; but new forms of 'top-down' global governance would require the prior surrender of substantial components of state sovereignty, or even the complete dissolution of states themselves, while 'bottom-up' forms of participatory governance would require a level of popular cohesion that is far from apparent currently.

The focus for most feasible arrangements for global environmental governance thus rests in international – or more properly intergovernmental – institutions. Effective regulations to protect the environment will thus be based upon international (inter-state) treaties or agreements and implemented, in large part, via appropriate international organizations that can monitor the performance of states and their constituent enterprises and, possibly, enforce compliance.

There are dangers, however, that individual states will continue to be free to 'free ride' on the efforts of others and to defect from regimes of environmental management unless subject to compulsion from stronger states and/or powerful coalitions of concerned states. The policies that states will promote through inter-state institutions will, again, be open to manipulation by the interests that are able to exercise greatest influence within the most influential states. Thus, petrochemical and vehicle manufacturing industries have devoted massive resources to convert US governments to a sceptical attitude on many measures to reduce the polluting emissions that contribute to global warming.[43] However, it is now possible that the growing size and frequency of environmental disasters may be persuading major insurance companies to influence leading governments, like that of the USA, towards a more pro-regulatory approach to pollution and environmental protection.[44] States like the United States of America will, however, remain central to any effective regime for environmental protection and resource management, through the treaties that they sign and the organizations that they support with resources, compliance and practical enforcement.

Conclusion

The contemporary world is characterized by increased internationalization and some evidence of globalization. It also encompasses a complex mosaic of polities, authorities and institutions of both public and private governance.[45] States are by no means the only human institution that is theoretically capable of providing humanity with effective governance. However, states have emerged as the dominant political form during the modern era, and have established a substantial institutional basis and a considerable hold over the imagination of much of humanity. The replacement of states by other forms or modes of public governance requires both that states, themselves, are dislodged and that the alternatives prove capable of equal, if not better, governance at both the 'domestic' and the global levels of human concern and activity. In the absence of such a development, the weakening of the established state cannot be viewed with any equanimity.

Notes

1 See: George Woodcock, *Anarchism* (Harmondsworth: Penguin Books, 1962), Ch. 4.
2 *Ibid.*, various sections.
3 For a wide-ranging review of which see: E.K. Bramstead and K.J. Melhuish, *Western Liberalism: A History in Documents from Locke to Croce* (London: Longman, 1978).
4 On Proudhon, see: Woodcock, *Anarchism*, Ch. 5.
5 R.A.W. Rhodes, 'The new governance: governing without government', *Political Studies*, vol. 44 (1996), pp. 652–67.
6 The Commission on Global Governance, *Our Global Neighbourhood* (Oxford: Oxford University Press, 1995), p. 2.
7 *Ibid.*

8 Mark W. Zacher, with Brent A. Sutton, *Governing Global Networks: International Regimes for Transportation and Communications* (Cambridge: Cambridge University Press, 1996), Ch. 3.

9 See the account of the international Tropical Timber Organization, in David Humphreys, 'Hegemonic ideology and the International Tropical Timber Organization', in J. Vogler and M.F. Imber, *The Environment and International Relations* (London: Routledge, 1996), pp. 215–33.

10 N. Frohlich and J.A. Oppenheimer, *Modern Political Economy* (Englewood Cliffs, NJ: Prentice-Hall, 1978), Chs 2, 3 and 4.

11 *Ibid.*, esp. pp. 61–5.

12 N. Frohlich, J.A. Oppenheimer and O.R. Young, *Political Leadership and Collective Goods* (Princeton, NJ: Princeton University Press, 1971).

13 'Worries about Rio', *The Economist*, 7 January 1995, pp. 22–3.

14 'Carbonated growth', *The Economist*, 8 August 1992, p. 61; 'Greened', *The Economist*, 2 December 1993, p. 117; and 'Cool costing', *The Economist*, 6 March 1993, pp. 106–9.

15 'The greening of protectionism', *The Economist*, 27 February 1993, pp. 19–24.

16 David Armstrong, 'Globalization and the social state', *Review of International Studies*, vol. 24, no. 4 (October 1998), pp. 461–78.

17 R.J. Barry Jones, *Conflict and Control in the World Economy: Contemporary Economic Realism and Neo-Mercantilism* (Brighton: Harverster/Wheatsheaf, 1986), esp. pp. 193–5 and pp. 197–200.

18 For reports on reappraisals of UK regional aid policy see: Brian Groom, 'Ageing regional aid policy is feeling the strain', *Financial Times*, 19 October 1998, p. 8; Brian Groom, 'Mandelson orders big shake-up for regions', *Financial Times*, 19 October 1998, p. 1; and Brian Groom, 'New ways to help industry', *Financial Times*, 23 October 1998, p. 22.

19 In the sense of extreme believers in the power and efficacy of the free market, rather than those theorists of the international relations who stress the central significance of international institutions. See C.W. Kegley jr. (ed.), *Controversies in International Relations Theory: Realism and the Neoliberal Challenge* (New York: St Martin's Press, 1995); D.A. Baldwin (ed.), *Neorealism and Neoliberalism: The Contemporary Debate* (New York: Columbia University Press, 1993).

20 Michael Porter, *The Competitive Advantage of Nations* (Houndmills: Macmillan, 1990), esp. pp. 148–59, 159–65.

21 *Ibid.*, pp. 155.

22 Alan Henry, 'Why British engineering is the pits' pick,' *The Guardian*, 6 February 1996, p. 21.

23 'Of take-offs and tempests', *The Economist*, 14 March 1998, p. 116; and see also: 'Keeping the hot money out', *The Economist*, 14 January 1998, pp. 85–6.

24 'Fashionable', *The Economist*, 5 September 1998, p. 89; and 'Time to turn off the tap?', *The Economist*, 12 September 1998, pp. 99–101.

25 'Tobacco country fights back', *The Economist*, 21 March 1998, pp. 59–60 on the scale of US subsidies for the tobacco industry; 'How subsidies destroy the land', *The Economist*, 13 December 1997, pp. 49–50, on the significance of the use of federal land at subsidized rents in the USA; and 'Aggro money', *The Economist*, 25 September 1993, p. 10; 'Snout slimmed, not for long', *The Economist*, 8 July 1995, p. 40; and 'Milking it', *The Economist*, 20 Jan. 1996, p. 76, on the nature of funding under Europe's Common Agricultural Policy.

26 See 'Hooked on financial red tape', *The Economist*, 22 July 1995, pp. 83–5; and 'The perils of global capital', *The Economist*, 11 April 1998, pp. 76–8.

27 'Capital goes global', The Economist, 25 October 1997, pp. 139–40.

28 Particularly derivatives trading; see: 'Deriving in the fast lane', *The Economist*, 26 June 1993, p. 106.

29 'Emerging-market measles', *The Economist*, 22 August 1998, pp. 62–3; 'Stressed out on Wall Street', *The Economist*, 5 September 1998, pp. 83–4; 'A refresher on the 1930s', *The Economist*, 19 September 1998, p. 122; and, 'The bankers take cover', *The Economist*, 1998, 19 September 1998, pp. 109–13.

30 On the contribution of the collapse of Long-Term Capital Management to the deepening the economic and financial crisis of 1997/8, see: Philip Coggan and Clay Harris, 'Shock Waves from LTCM hit bank shares again', *Financial Times*, 20 October 1998, p. 1.

31 Despite difficulties; see: 'Transparent hype', *The Economist*, 7 November 1998, p. 142.

32 Susan Strange, *Mad Money* (Manchester: Manchester University Press, 1998), pp. 173–4.

33 'The domino effect', *The Economist*, 27 April 1996, p. 76; and 'When borrowers go bad', *The Economist*, 28 February 1998, pp. 97–100.

34 Strange, *Mad Money*, p. 174; and 'The domino effect', *The Economist*, 27 April 1996, p. 76.

35 'Global accounting's roadblocks', *The Economist*, 27 April 1996, pp. 105–6.

36 On the scale and nature of international money 'laundering', see: 'Money-launderers on the line', *The Economist*, 25 June 1994, pp. 101–4.

37 Ronen Palan, 'Trying to have your cake and eat it: how the state system created Offshore', *International Studies Quarterly*, vol. 42, no. 4 (December 1998), pp. 625–43.

38 'Falling fast', *The Economist*, 22 June 1996, pp. 63–4.

39 World Bank, *World Development Report, 1997* (New York: World Bank, 1997), Table 3, pp. 218–19.

40 B. Hoekman and M. Kostecki, *The Political Economy of the World Trading System: From GATT to WTO* (Oxford: Oxford University Press, 1995), pp. 202–4; and 'Make my day', *The Economist*, 7 November 1992, pp. 104–5.

41 David Rowan, 'Meet the new world government', *The Guardian Weekly*, 22 February 1998, p. 14.

42 'The talking FDI blues', *The Economist*, 14 March 1998, pp. 20–2; and 'The sinking of the MAI', *The Economist*, 14 March 1998, pp. 105–6.

43 'Clinton tries to calm storm over climate', *Financial Times*, 6 October 1997, p. 5.

44 Peter Newell and Mathew Patterson, 'A climate for business: global warming, the state and capital', *Review of International Political Economy*, vol. 5, no. 4 (Winter 1998), pp. 679–703.

45 Yale H. Ferguson and Richard W. Mansbach, *Polities: Authority, Identities and Change* (Columbia, SC: University of South Carolina Press, 1996), esp. Chs 1 and 15.

8

Modes of governance in a globalizing world

The need for effective governance in a world of increasing internationalization and/or globalization does not answer the questions of whether such governance will prove possible or which forms will prove most feasible. The demands for public governance created by global developments may be clear and present; its effective supply, however, remains a far more uncertain matter. Moreover, changing international circumstances accentuate the possibilities of governance by a range of actors at various levels of human activity.

Regionalism and public governance

Governance, by the wide-ranging 'definition' offered in Chapter 7, can clearly be undertaken at many levels, beyond that of the isolated individual. The 'traditional' state is the best established agent, and level, of public governance. Notions of regionalism, however, suggest a range of possible alternative forms of public governance to the state. Regionalism is, however, an ambiguous concept that embraces at least three distinct levels, or scales, of activity: micro-regionalism; meso-regionalism; and macro-regionalism.

Micro-regionalism

Micro-regionalism suggests relatively small geographical areas that are usually located within established states:[1] 'Silicon Valley' in the United States of America; the North-East within the United Kingdom; or Brittany within France. Such micro-regions promise to combine geographical proximity with a greater level of social and cultural cohesion than is possible for many established states. The rationale of regional development organizations often reflects such considerations. Responsiveness to, and knowledge of, conditions and requirements within the region is often emphasized as the distinctive advantage of such institutions.

The suitability of micro-regionalism as an effective response to contemporary global developments does, however, raise a number of serious questions. The first concerns that of the real cohesiveness of micro-regions that are promoted as natural and coherent. The issue of devolution within the United Kingdom demonstrated the diversity that can exist even with micro-regions affecting a clear 'national' identity, such as Scotland and Wales. In a referendum on a possible devolved Scottish assembly in 1979, only 32.9 per cent of the eligible electorate voted for devolution and in the second, decisive referendum on devolution in 1997 the favourable vote was still only 44.8 per cent of the eligible electorate.[2] Moreover, in a slightly later referendum on devolution to a new Welsh Assembly, a slight majority in favour, of only 50.3 per cent of a turn-out of only 51.3 per cent of the eligible electorate, embraced wide variations in sub-regional support for devolution, from 66.5 per cent in Neath/Port Talbot down to a mere 32.1 per cent in Monmouthshire.[3] Such diversity reflects varying patterns of economic activity and outlook; local political differences; and the persistence of cultural diversity even within regions that are supposed to be relatively unified and cohesive.

Micro-regions may thus be less cohesive internally than is often supposed. They are also, by definition, relatively small, and such smallness may be a source of weaknesses as well as advantages. The real problems of size concern the narrow economic and resource base that is often entailed by limitations of geographical span. A narrow base, in turn, increases the need for external sources of many important commodities, goods and services and, with it, increased external dependence. The micro-region has a lesser world impact than a larger entity and, unless it is in exclusive possession of a decisive resource, it remains weaker in its relations with global markets, transnational corporations and other elements of the global economy. Size continues to matter in the shaping of the global order, and many micro-regions are likely to continue to turn to states or other, and larger, forms of regional organization when seeking influence in wider arenas.

Micro-regionalism may, finally, be an unstable condition within the contemporary international system. The relative autonomy of micro-regions has often, in practice, been conditional upon the toleration of over-arching states: the structure of 'local government' within the United Kingdom has certainly been reshaped at will by central, state-level governments in the past. Full independence, and the formation of a new state, has been the other possibility where micro-regions have enjoyed, or asserted, a relatively high degree of local autonomy for some time, as the fate of the former Yugoslavia demonstrated so dramatically. Where micro-regions evolve into full states, the resultant states will be small – even microstates – with all the problems and weaknesses of such actors upon the world stage: very limited security capabilities, small domestic markets and a general limitation of capability in economic and political matters.[4]

Meso-regionalism

Meso-regionalism has attracted growing interest and attention in recent years.[5] It relates to the emergence of regions of intense economic activity within geographical areas that are often quite large, but that bridge the formal frontiers of established states.

Both economic and political developments may contribute to the emergence of meso-regions. Formal integration within the European Economic Community has encouraged the emergence of meso-regions within Western Europe, such as the Rhône-Alps region, from Lyons through to Northern Italy.[6] However, economic dynamics may prove sufficient without formal political integration and merely with official toleration, as in the case of the pre-unification association between the then colony of Hong Kong, and Shenzhen and the Pearl River Delta in mainland China.[7] Complementary economic and industrial development within such meso-regions may underpin economic growth and prosperity. The size of such meso-regions may also increase their weight in, and influence upon, the wider world economy. However, the lack of the legitimacy, and the formal institutions and instruments, of 'traditional' states places significant limits upon the ability of such meso-regions to regulate the activities of private enterprises operating within their territories or to participate in the formal institutions of global governance. Again, meso-regions are faced with the need to acquire state-like characteristics and capabilities if they are to supply effective public governance in an ever more complex and demanding world, or to suffer continued weakness in their relations with transnational enterprises and global markets. However, the acquisition of state-like attributes runs directly against the competing claims of states and any wider institutions of public governance, like the European Union.

Macro-regionalism

Formal associations amongst formally sovereign states have become a prominent pattern of response to the increase of economic internationalization and/or advance of globalization. Increasing the size and scale of the agents of public governance offers one obvious path to counter the growing scale and power of private enterprise within the contemporary international system. The origins of the European Community, the most advanced and most prominent of such regional associations, lie outside the dynamic of an internationalizing and/or globalizing world economy; but its continued vitality is intimately connected to this phenomenon.

At their most effective, macro-regions encompass a wide range of economic resources, incorporate the headquarters of many major transnational enterprises, and control access to some of the world's largest markets. The combination of these features provides the macro-region with considerable potential in influencing the development of the world economy and in regulating the activities of private economic interests. However, such effectiveness turns, itself, upon a number of conditions that may be difficult to realize in practice.

Macro-regions may remain little more than areas of intense economic interaction unless they develop formal institutions for the determination and implementation of measures of public governance. The European Union, with its complex, wide-ranging and highly developed institutions, contrasts markedly with the relatively casual character of the Association of South East Asian Countries (ASEAN) in this respect. The North Atlantic Trade Agreement, with its regulatory capacities limited to the adjudication of trade issues arising specifically in connection with the terms of the Agreement,[8] stands between the two extremes of the EU and ASEAN.

Effective public governance is not, however, merely a matter of the appropriate institutions and instruments. In the longer term, it is also, essentially, a matter of securing and sustaining legitimacy. Durable and stable states have succeeded precisely because of their ability to combine effective institutions with the widespread support of those for, and over, whom they rule. The problems confronting macro-regions in emerging as major agents of public governance in a world of increasing internationalization and/or globalization are illustrated by the case of the European Union.

The European Union has established a clear presence within the global political economy: negotiating collectively during the Uruguay Round of the General Agreement on Tariffs and Trade (GATT) that led to the creation of the World Trade Organization (WTO)[9] and, indeed, during earlier GATT rounds; negotiating the successive Lomé agreements with the African, Caribbean and Pacific Countries;[10] and overseeing agreements of association with potential applicants for membership of the European Union, particularly from Central and Eastern Europe.[11] However, the complex structures and processes of policy-making within the European Union raise considerable doubts about its cohesiveness, with some analysts arguing that it remains little more than an inter-governmental regime.[12]

The citizenry of the European Union also remains seriously divided over the development of the European Union, in general, and the advent of Economic and Monetary Union, in particular:[13] divisions that may reflect or underlie the persistence of a supposed deficit in the development of genuine democratic control of the institutions and policies of the European Union.[14] Such divisions, in turn, reflect a combination of doubts about the efficacy of a number of the institutions and central policies of the European Union, itself, and the persistence of considerable differences of culture and national outlook amongst the peoples of the European 'community'.

Macro-regions, finally, will prove to be effective bases for the public governance of the evolving global system only if their leaders can develop sufficient commonality of purpose to act cohesively on the world stage. The persistence of free rider temptations, reinforced by the divisive pressures of diverse domestic constituencies, can prove all too powerful in undermining clear and decisive action by aggregate regional actors upon the world stage, as almost proved to be the case with French obstuctionism[15] during the final stages of the negotiations under the Uruguay Round of the GATT.

Macro-regional bodies may thus offer one of the more promising approaches to the management of a world of increasing internationalization and/or globalization. However, the European Union reveals the formidable problems confronted by even the most advanced of macro-regional organizations. Problems of coherence and cohesion that have only just been overcome by the more stable of states, and then not always permanently, persist in even more intense and insistent forms at the level of macro-regional associations.

The state and public governance

The state remains the best institutionalized form of public governance within the contemporary world. Smaller-scale forms of governance have often been forced to defer to the state level when major problems have been encountered or major disputes of jurisdiction have arisen. Wider forms of political and economic association have rarely proved sufficiently durable to prevent the reassertion of the state. The endurance of the state thus far cannot, however, preserve any but the largest and most powerful from the adverse effects of increasing internationalization and/or globalization or enhance its capacities to deal with the growing range of problems confronting the global system.

The state thus remains at the pivot of a moving kaleidoscope of competing pressures and influences. Micro-regional forces threaten its cohesion from below, while meso-regional developments dilute its integrity from within and beyond. Regional and global pressures encourage moves towards macro-regional integration, but these, in turn, confront, and sometimes engender, powerful centrifugal forces. A myriad of non-governmental actors and interests clamour for the attention of, policy responses from, and increasingly participation in the activities of, state governments. The activities of a range of private commercial interests, finally, encroach increasingly upon the effective jurisdiction of state governments in a variety of areas of real public concern.

States are also the source of one of the most serious obstacles to effective public global governance. The fragmentation of the world into a myriad of jealously sovereign states has traditionally undermined attempts to establish world-wide authorities. The absence of any form of world government, with the capacity for authoritative resolution of differences and disputes, and the forceful implementation of judgements, has, moreover, generated a chronic sense of physical insecurity in international relations combined with an ever-present temptation to 'free ride' on collective goods provided by others.[16] Theoretical and practical solutions to the problems of a politically fragmented world have thus absorbed the energies of a wide range of theorists and practitioners down the ages.

Intergovernmental modes of global public governance

The solution to the problems of global political fragmentation, and thereby to the problems of wielding global influence for most state governments, has thus traditionally been sought through participation in a range of inter-state associations and institutions: some macro-regional, some based upon common interests, and some global in scope and membership. Macro-regional associations of states have already been considered earlier in this discussion. World-wide intergovernmental associations and organizations are, however, numerous and active in many areas of public global governance.

The range and continued growth of intergovernmental arrangements underlies the optimism of a range of observers of international relations over the prospects for effective management of the global system, even in a world fragmented into formally sovereign states. Two major strands of thought reflect such optimism. The first is integral to the long-established notion of an *international society*.[17] The central question for theorists of international society is whether the disorder and potential conflict of a world without a central power and authority can be contained. The answer is in the affirmative, emphasizing the combined effects of international law, and law-based international institutions, with the progressive socialization of states, and their rulers, into the evolving norms of reasonable and restrained international (or inter-state) behaviour.[18]

Such a perspective upon international relations raises a number of basic questions and sits rather uneasily with the vision of a world of increasing internationalization and/or globalization that is progressively eroding the role of the traditional state. The first, and rather obvious point, is that the idea of international society (or more properly inter-state society) enshrines and prioritizes the state: it remains quintessentially a form of State-Centric Realism, however qualified and moderated. The second problem is that notions of international society often imply, or even entail, inter-subjective foundations. The participants in any international society, even in the loosest sense of the word, have to be aware of that participation and the norms and principles of appropriate participation.[19]

The question arises, however, as to whether such aggregate actors as states can be said to have awareness, or whether the relevant ideas and understandings actually reside (or fail to do so) in the minds of the political leaders and diplomatic representatives of participating states.[20] Moreover, it is far from clear that all societies, or even states, have participated fully and equally in 'international society' in the past or can hope to do so in the present and the future.[21]

The central question raised by the idea of international society, however, remains that of the need, and extent of, shared values, understandings and expectations amongst the participants: whether a structure based on minimal ties of attachment – *gesellschaften* – is sufficient, or whether 'thicker' patterns of mutual involvement, with deep cultural foundations – *gemeinschaften* – are necessary for the ordering of world affairs – and, if so, whether such a condition is possible.

The second strand of optimism about a system of effective global governance founded upon sovereign states rests upon the notion of international *regimes*. The relationship between theories of international society and of international regimes is complex and much debated.[22] The mode of analysis of students of international regimes is couched in the neo-utilitarian[23] language of the rational self-interested decisions of the actors that participate in international institutions and other arrangements. However, the widely-accepted definition of international regimes as: '. . . sets of implicit or explicit principles, norms, rules, and decision-making procedures around which actors' expectations converge in a given area of international relations[24] acknowledges, and even emphasizes, the central role of the ideas entertained, and shared, by participants. Such patterns of intersubjectivity may provide the lubricant for day-to-day participation within any international regime, but its ultimate cement remains the self-interest of members. However, participation in a well-established regime affects the structure of costs and benefits that actors have to consider when calculating day-to-day actions or the more serious possibilities of defection.[25]

In the views of some regime theorists, therefore, the existence and successful operation of international regimes offer a promising solution to the problems of sustaining collective action internationally. Temptations to free-ride are checked by the alterations in cost–benefit calculations induced by the successful functioning of regimes themselves. Webs of such international regimes, in turn, might provide the basis for wider public global governance, particularly when they develop and function in the more critical areas of the contemporary global political economy. Sceptics, however, continue to doubt the substance and durability of such regimes in many areas of contemporary international and global governance, and are particularly dubious about their capacity to address the most pressing global problems and processes, or to provide an effective counterweight to global business interests and institutions.

States do, in practice, participate in a wide variety of international institutions and arrangements, many of which warrant the term 'regime'. Such world-wide inter-state institutions of pertinence to global governance are of four general types: long-standing quasi-administrative organizations for technical regulation, such as the World Radio Conferences, the World Conferences on International Communications, and the related International Telegraphic Union;[26] the more recent range of 'universal' institutions of the United Nations and its associated organizations; the specialist financial agencies established by the Bretton Woods Conference of 1944 – the International Monetary Fund and the International Bank for Reconstruction and Development (the World Bank);[27] and relatively informal, but often regular, meetings of groups of states with common interests, like the Group of 8 (G8).[28]

Quasi-intergovernmental institutions also exist, such as the Geneva-based Bank for International Settlements and the Basle Committee on Bank Supervision,[29] with their 'ownership' by the Central Bankers of the major industrial countries and their responsibilities for overseeing orderly financial international inter-bank payments and settlements and for more general international financial co-ordination. The semi-autonomous status of Central Bankers in many advanced industrial societies endows their meetings with a peculiar status: neither fully intergovernmental, in the strict sense, nor non-governmental.

The functioning of many long-established intergovernmental and quasi-intergovernmental institutions, particularly in the more technical areas, gives some hope to those who believe that the formation and operation of 'epistemic communities' constitutes the basis of future public global governance. The hope, here, is that the formation of international groupings of technical experts will provide solutions to immediate international problems, will provide a model for the co-operative solution of other, possibly less technical, issues and might, ultimately, lead to the creation of complex web of institutions for global governance.[30] The record of international institutions and associations is far too mixed to support unqualified optimism in such respects, however. As the issues of concern have borne more closely upon interests that are defined as basic to the well-being of contributing states, or central to their views about the desirable course of world developments, so partiality of interests or outlook have impacted upon the deliberative process and often distorted, or destroyed, the prospects for collective progress: as witness the acrimonious debates over the New International Economic Order in the late 1970s,[31] or continued arguments over the proper policies and practices for institutions like the International Monetary Fund.[32]

Non-governmental actors and global governance

The picture regarding state-based public global governance is thus complex and highly varied. Extensive intergovernmental association certainly takes place through a plethora of institutions. The effectiveness of such institutions is highly varied, however, and states generally continue to guard their independence jealously. The fragmentation of the global political system continues to place real limits upon the effectiveness of public global governance. Moreover, increasing internationalization and/or globalization is, in the eyes of many, placing states, and hence state-based governance, under growing pressure and constraint. Some believe that these new conditions will compel states to work more closely to construct new, and more effective, forms of public global governance – in effect, to pool sovereignty. However, substantial obstacles to such new departures continue to lie within the states themselves and within the hearts and minds of the peoples that they serve.

If state-based governance is insufficient for the new global economy and new forms of public global governance are difficult, if not impossible, to create, a serious vacuum threatens to emerge at the heart of the global system. In the short and medium term, it is possible that such a vacuum will be met, partially, by essentially private interests and associations. Such forms of private global governance, however, would be complex in form, controversial in character, and ultimately limited in effect.

Private governance in the international system has been varied in form and breadth of effect. Private financial actors have long played an important, and often controversial, role in the international political economy. Financial assistance from moneylenders was often essential to the funding of the military operations of medieval rulers. The Rothschild brothers acted as financial agents for Britain's extensive financial operations during the Napoleonic wars.[33] By the end of the nineteenth century, *haute finance* had come to play a central part in orchestrating the world's financial system and, with it, the basis of its burgeoning trade system[34] – a role that laid it open to demonization within contemporary radical discourse.

Major financial interests have continued to play a prominent role in the global financial and, hence, economic system. Banks, insurance companies, pension funds and such recent exotica as 'hedge funds' dispose of vast sums of internationally mobile financial capital. Decisions to move funds into or out of any country can exert a stronger disciplinary influence upon its government than anything else short of armed force or, in the case of Less Developed Countries, decisions on the deployment of aid. Some observers thus attribute a central significance and pivotal influence to the private global financial system.[35]

The range of private economic interests whose activities are pertinent to global governance, broadly defined, is not confined to banks, insurance companies, pension funds and 'hedge funds', however. Credit-rating agencies, like Moody's, also exert a considerable public influence in their public judgements upon the creditworthiness of various countries. The downgrading of a country's credit rating can trigger a substantial loss of international confidence in its prospects, massive outflows of financial resources and, hence, damage to the economic position of the country in question. The policy changes that may well have to follow in the wake of such a *démarche* demonstrate the significance of such credit rating agencies to contemporary global governance.

The managements of national stock exchanges and other commodity exchanges also have a role of considerable pertinence to global economic governance. Such exchanges now play a crucial role in the economic well-being of societies, in general and in the vitality of many of their business enterprises, in particular. Poorly managed stock exchanges threaten the ability of firms to raise capital effectively through the issue of new equity. Poorly managed exchanges of all kinds can be prey to fraud and mismanagement in a manner that undermines general confidence and, hence, the smooth functioning of related financial and economic operations.

Regulation of various forms can also be undertaken through a range of associations, including tactical alliances, that bring together the major commercial producers or consumers, or some combination of the two. The major standards in personal computing and domestic electronics have been established, *de facto*, by combinations of dominant producers: the 'Wintel' standard created by Microsoft and Intel in the case of personal computers; the VHS standard for domestic video-recorders; Phillips' compact cassette in the case of domestic audio recorders, and, in the case of the Digital Versatile Disc standard for both domestic video play and computers, new and complex coalitions.

Cartels of dominant industrial actors have also been a common feature of the international political economy. The Liner Conferences, of operators of the major international cargo fleets, dominated the routing of international shipping and the pricing of cargoes before the container revolution.[36] Less formal cartels have also dominated a number of pivotal industries at various times. The oil industry has long been dominated by a relatively small number of major producers, whose market position has allowed them to exert disproportionate influence upon prices at the petrol station when such collaborative behaviour has been thought to be in the interests of most, if not all, the members of the virtual cartel.[37] The supply and pricing of motor cars in many markets, like those of the various member countries of the European Union, are also widely believed to be carefully controlled and aligned by the major suppliers in order to maintain a high price and ensure comfortable profit levels.[38] All industries that are dominated by monopolistic, or oligopolistic, suppliers are vulnerable to manipulation in such a manner, with substantial implications for public well-being.

Private governance in areas of global public concern has often played a role in the global political economy. Where effective public global governance is undermined by the fragmentation of authority in a system of sovereign states, or weakened by the cumulative effects of increased internationalization or globalization, the opportunities for private agencies to step into the vacuum are enhanced. Such developments do not worry many of those who extend an enthusiastic welcome to the 'new globalization', believing the ever more integrated world market system to be the harbinger of general prosperity and well-being. Private governance in the public sphere does, however, suffer from a number of serious, and ultimately fatal, shortcomings.

The first and most obvious shortcoming of private governance of the public sphere is that such private governance is inevitably founded upon partiality of interest and perspective. Private enteprises and other actors exist to promote the purposes of shareholders, members and others who lend their resources and support to such entities. In practice and in principle the interests and aspirations of such immediate 'stakeholders' must prevail in the discussions and decisions of private-interest actors. The public interest may figure in such deliberative processes, but will rarely be the primary consideration, as is demonstrated by the $43 million spent during the first half of 1998 by the US tobacco industry to defeat legislation aimed at restricting the promotion and sale of tobacco products,[39] or by the more generous levels of the annuities paid to smokers by insurance companies.

Private actors operating in the sphere of public governance will also lack the full range of the means of implementing decisions and adjudications that will be available to well-established agencies of public governance, such as states. Few private actors are able to deploy substantial levels of armed force, with the partial exception of mercenaries on hire to transnational corporations or the armed thugs of internationally active criminal organizations. Few private actors also possess the police forces to enforce policies, and the gaols to incarcerate malefactors, that states have conventionally maintained. Moreover, the acquisition of necessary resources – such as taxes or other costly contributions – is far more problematical for private agencies, contributions to the costs of desired collective goods being essentially voluntary for all those operating within an association or cartel unless it is dominated by the equivalent of a hegemon that is able to enforce such contributions.

Such constraints reflect, and in part underlie, the lack of wider legitimacy that attaches to private actors seeking to engage in areas of public governance. The governments and populations of a number of the countries most affected by the economic and financial crisis of 1997–98 were seriously unimpressed by the credentials of those international financial actors who withdrew massive finances precipitously when the crisis began to crystallize. Drivers in many countries within the European Union are equally doubtful about the legitimacy of those private firms who set the high prices of new motor cars. International traders were equally dubious about the rights of Liner Conferences to set the high prices for maritime shipments in the days before the container revolution.

The problem of the legitimacy of public governance by private agencies leads to the central problem of democracy in a world of increasing interationalization and/or globalization. The debate about the nature of democracy and the conditions under which it can function remains intense.[40] The ability of citizens to exert influence upon those who make decisions that have an effect upon their lives is, however, common to most of the more acceptable interpretations of democracy. Private actors and interests may be subject to quasi-democratic constraints from within the body of those who make up the relevant association or agency. Beyond that, however, they are essentially undemocratic, being free from constraints from the wider community, in the absence of the countervailing capabilities of governments, the operation of boycotts and other forms of peaceful popular pressure, or of outbreaks of riot. The quintessentially undemocratic character of private governance in the public sphere merely compounds its general lack of legitimacy.

The shortcomings of private governance in the public domain are further compounded by a general lack of foresight by the relevant agencies. The tightening of rules for traders on most national stock exchanges has followed, rather than preceded, the exposure of major misdeeds by their members. Indeed, the growth of doubts about self-regulation within the national financial services systems, and the wider world financial system, fully reflect the partial and myopic performance of such private agents of governance in areas of clear public interests and concern.[41]

Governments may not always have earned the highest points for perspicacity, as is evidenced by the lamentable record of the government of the United Kingdom over the Bovine Spongiform Encephalopathy crisis; but they have often showed themselves more perspicacious, as with the UK government's support for the development of radar and the creation of shadow munitions industries in the years preceding the Second World War. Private agencies of governance, however, have no better a record than the poorer of governments, as crises and scandals within the financial sector repeatedly demonstrate. Indeed, such private agencies have frequently turned to government to make good any failings in private governance and, in particular, restore public confidence in the probity and efficiency of the enterprises represented by them.[42]

Private governance in the public domain might thus become a significant response to any failure of effective public governance at the global level. Such private governance of the public realm will, however, offer a seriously second-best, if not third- or fourth-best, alternative to well-founded, properly resourced and legitimate institutions of public global governance, be they truly global or merely intergovernmental.

Mixed modes of governance

One mode of governance in the global system that holds some promise for the future, and that is far from uncommon currently, is that of mixed modes of governance, in which private interests join with the representatives of states and state-like entities to regulate and manage aspects of the international political economy. Governments, as such, participate in framework-setting discussions and decisions and may retain oversight authority. However, detailed responsibility from some area of public governance is delegated to technical groupings, and/or essentially private agencies, under such arrangements. The regulation of the aviation industries in the UK and the USA is undertaken by the semi-autonomous Civil Aviation Authority and Federal Aviation Authority, respectively. The UK government's proposals for the regulation of the British accountancy industry in later 1998 envisaged a new structure of self-regulation, within which the regular participation of government would be confined to the presence of nominees of quasi-governmental bodies like the Bank of England on the management board of the regulatory 'foundation'.[43] Both forms of 'mixed' governance give prominence to specialists whose careers have been devoted to the study of, or participation in, the relevant spheres of activity. Knowledge-based 'epistemic communities' may thus be formed around, and become singularly influential within, appropriate issue-areas within national systems, or the global political economy more widely.

Mixed regimes of governance may thus be created and function reasonably effectively, especially within those areas of the global political economy that are particularly amenable to technical management.

However, such mixed regimes continue to rest, and rely, upon authority from formal institutions of public governance for their ultimate implementational capacities, legitimacy and, where pertinent, democratic credentials. Governments and intergovernmental agencies can withdraw support from mixed regimes of governance and replace them with more conventional managerial institutions where desired.[44] Such mixed regimes may, finally, be vulnerable to capture by a range of those special interests that become involved in their activities.

Multi-level governance

The evolving experience of the European Union also suggests that effective governance in a world system that is fragmented into sovereign states might be secured through a complex system of multi-level governance.[45] The central idea here is that of functional differentiation of sovereignty. Institutions of public governance are established, and endowed with clear sovereignty, at appropriate levels of human activity. Issues requiring a global level would thus be addressed by a global agency with full sovereignty in respect of those issues. Where issues could be dealt with satisfactorily by agencies operating across smaller geographical spaces, then governmental agencies with appropriate sovereignty would operate at those levels, down from regional, through state, to small-community levels.

Multi-level governance could also accommodate a variable public–private mix, as needs and possibilities dictated. However, the resultant complex mosaic of governance might encounter considerable problems of coherence, consistency and ultimate durability. The lack of clear foci of authority and responsibility within the global system, comparable to that traditionally established by the state within domestic polities, could generate conflict amongst competing sovereignties, inconsistencies between divergent policy orientations and, most seriously, an ability for powerful private interests to manoeuvre advantageously through regulatory interstices.

Hegemony

The unanswered issue in all the preceding discussions of possible forms of governance within a world of increasing internationalization and/or globalization is that of hegemony: of the exercise of preponderant influence within the international or global system by one state or a small number of like-minded states – hegemons.[46]

Two pressing questions arise. First, can any cohesive and coherent system of public governance at the global level operate in the absence of a supportive hegemony? Problems of effective collective action persuaded many theorists of the vital role of hegemons in establishing international regimes.[47] Regimes could then, in the view of Robert Keohane, ensure the survival of valuable forms of international co-operation and collaboration even in the face of the subsequent decline of the hegemon.[48] The problems created by a world of complex forms of governance, and of the growing activity and influence of private, transnational economic actors, however, are such as to raise serious questions about the enduring efficacy of regimes in the face of such potential challenges to coherent and authoritative governance in the absence of a decisive hegemon. Indeed, if hegemonic powers are disinclined to assert effective authority within the global system, then private interests are likely to prevail and effective management and regulation to be undermined.

The second question concerns the possibility, if not probability, that the inherent tendency of the global political economy to generate difficulties will be merely compounded by an over-complex pattern of governance, and that this will, in turn, eventually encourage potential hegemons to assert their power and authority within the system: a 'double movement'[49] of growing complexity and disruption generating increasing pressures for the reimposition of relatively centralized order and control.

The attempt to reassert hegemonic influence over the global system might, however, encounter a further paradox of political economy: that control may be ceded with relative ease, but only reimposed with considerable difficulty and at substantial political and economic cost. This central asymmetry remains a fundamental problem for the future of the international and global political economy and a central intellectual issue for its students. Such questions will, however, be the subject of much of the discussion in the next chapter.

Notes

1 But sometimes also cross-frontier 'communities', such as the Basques of Northern Spain and South-Western France.

2 The majority for devolution amongst those actually voting in each case being: 51.6 per cent (of a turnout of 62.9 per cent) in 1979 and 74.3 per cent (of a 60.4 per cent turnout). See the report: 'Surprisingly brave', *The Economist*, 20 September 1997, pp. 34–7.

3 'Winning the peace', *The Economist*, 27 September 1997, p. 36.

4 Patricia Wohlgemuth, *The Ministate Dilemma*, Occasional Paper No. 6 (New York: Carnegie Endowment for International Peace, 1996); and Benedict Burton, *Problems of Smaller Territories* (London: Athlone Press, 1967).

5 Kenichi Ohmae, *The End of the Nation State: The Rise of Regional Economies* (New York: Free Press, 1995).

6 *Ibid.*, p. 80.

7 *Ibid.*, pp. 82–3.

8 'Goes on itching', *The Economist*, 21 May 1994, p. 66; 'Northern rumblings', *The Economist*, 14 January 1995, pp. 50–1; and 'The trucks that hold back the NAFTA', *The Economist*, 13 December 1997, pp. 51–2.

9 Keith Penketh, 'External trade policy', in F. McDonald and S. Dearden, *European Economic Integration* (London: Longman, 1992), pp. 146–58.

10 Stephen Dearden, The European Community and the Third World, in McDonald and Dearden, *European Economic Integration*, pp. 159–74.

11 Barbara Lippert, 'EC-CMEA relations: normalization and beyond', in G. Edwards and E. Regelsberger, *Europe's Global Links: The European Community and Inter-Regional Cooperation* (London: Pinter Publishers, 1990), pp. 119–40.

12 Andrew Moravcsik, 'Negotiating the Single European Act', *International Organization*, vol. 45, no. 1, pp. 19–56; and Andrew Moravcsik, 'Preferences and power in the European Community: a liberal intergovernmentalist approach', *Journal of Common Market Studies*, vol. 31, no. 4 (December 1993), pp. 473–524.

13 On divisions over the Maastricht Treaty on EMU see: on French divisions – 'If', *The Economist*, 22 August 1992; on British reservations – 'The Great Euro soap opera', *The Economist*, 25 October, 1997, pp. 35–6; on Danish difficulties – 'Those Vikings are at it again', *The Economist*, 7 November 1992; and, in general, 'A rough year', *The Economist*, 19 December 1992, pp. 17–19.

14 See: 'Democrats at work', *The Economist*, 20 May 1995, p. 48.

15 'Bushwhacked', *The Economist*, 24 October 1992, pp. 92–8; and 'French dread', *The Economist*, 18 September 1993, pp. 95–8.

16 See the discussion in Chapter 7.

17 Hedley Bull, *The Anarchical Society: A Study of Order in World Politics* (London: Macmillan, 1977).

18 H. Bull and A. Watson (eds), *The Expansion of International Society* (Oxford: Clarendon Press/Oxford University Press, 1984).

19 See: B.A. Roberson (ed.), *International Society and the Development of International Relations Theory* (London: Pinter, 1998).

20 R.J. Barry Jones, 'The English School and the political construction of international society', in Roberson, *International Society*, pp. 231–45.

21 J.D.B. Miller, 'The Third World', in J.D.B. Miller and J. Vincent, *Order and Violence* (Oxford: Clarendon Press, 1990), Ch. 4.

22 Barry Buzan, 'From international system to international society: structural realism and regime theory meet the English School', *International Organization*, vol. 47, no. 3 (1993), pp. 327–52; Andrew Hurrell, 'International society and the study of regimes: a reflective approach', in V. Rittberger (ed.), *Regime Theory and International Relations* (Oxford: Oxford University Press, 1993), Ch. 3; and Ole Weaver, 'Four meanings of international society: a trans-Atlantic dialogue', in Roberson, *International Society*, Ch. 5.

23 John Gerrard Ruggie, *Constructing the World Polity: Essays on International Institutionalization* (London: Routledge, 1998), Introduction.

24 S. Krasner, 'Structural causes and regime consequences: regimes as intervening variables', p. 2, in S.D. Krasner (ed.), *International Regimes* (Ithaca, NY: Cornell University Press, 1983), pp. 1–21.

25 R.O. Keohane, *After Hegemony: Cooperation and Discord in the World Political Economy* (Princeton, NJ: Princeton University Press, 1984).

26 Mark Zacher, with Brent A. Sutton, *Governing Global Networks: International Regimes for Transportation and Communications* (Cambridge: Cambridge University Press, 1996), Ch. 5.

27 See: J.H. Richards, *International Economic Institutions* (New York: Holt, Rinehart and Winston Ltd., 1970), Chs 2, 3 and 4.

28 Formerly the Group of 5 (G5). See: J.E. Spero and J.A. Hart, *The Politics of International Economic Relations*, 5th edn (London: Routledge, 1997), pp. 42–3 and 200–1.

29 Ethen B. Kapstein, *Governing the Global Economy: International Finance and the State* (Cambridge, MA: Harvard University Press, 1994), pp. 44–57.

30 Peter M. Haas, 'Epistemic communities and the dynamics of international environmental co-operation', in Rittberger, *Regime Theory*, Ch. 8.

31 Fred Hirsch, 'Is there a new international economic order?', *International Organization*, vol. 30, no. 3 (Summer 1976), pp. 521–31; and E. Laszlo, *et al.*, *The Obstacles to the New International Economic Order* (New York: Pergamon for UNITAR and CEESTEM, 1980); and on general international divisions see: Stephen D. Krasner, *Structural Conflict: The Third World Against Global Liberalism* (Berkeley, CA: University of California Press, 1985).

32 See the response of the First Deputy of the IMF, Stanley Fischer, 'Reforming world finance – lessons from a crisis', *The Economist*, 3 October 1998, pp. 27–9.

33 Niall Ferguson, *The World's Banker, The History of the House of Rothschild* (London: Weidenfeld and Nicolson, 1998).

34 Andrew Walter, *World Power and World Money: The Role of Hegemony and International Monetary Order* (Hemel Hempstead: Harvester/Wheatsheaf, 1991).

35 Philip G. Cerny, 'The political economy of international finance', in Philip G. Cerny, *Finance and World Politics: Markets, Regimes and States in the Post-hegemonic Era* (Aldershot: Edward Elgar, 1993), pp. 3–19.

36 See: S. Strange, 'Who runs world shipping', *International Affairs*, vol. 52, no. 3 (July 1976), pp. 346–67.

37 Peter Odell, *Oil and World Power: Background to the Oil Crisis*, 3rd edn (Harmondsworth: Penguin Books, 1974); and Daniel Yergin, *The Prize: The Epic Quest for Oil, Money and Power* (New York: Simon and Schuster, 1991).

38 'Carved up', *The Economist*, 31 October 1992, p. 94.

39 'Tobacco firms spent $43 m to kill legislation', *Guardian Weekly*, 8 November 1998, p. 17.

40 David Held, *Models of Democracy*, 2nd edn (Cambridge: Polity Press, 1996).

41 'Self-regulation's last stand?', *The Economist*, 5 December 1992, pp. 109–10.

42 On the role of governmental authorities see C.P. Kindleberger, *Manias, Panics, and Crashes: A History of Financial Crises*, 3rd edn (New York: John Wiley and Sons, 1996), esp. Chs 10 and 11; and for a wider discussion of re-regulatory possibilities, see: Eric Helleiner, 'Post-globalization: is the financial liberalization trend likely to be reversed?' in R. Boyer and D. Drache (eds), *States Against Markets: The Limits of Globalization* (London: Routledge, 1996), pp. 193–210.

43 'Regulatory regime for accountants unveiled', *Financial Times*, 1 December 1998, p. 11.

44 On the UK government's proposals see 'Regulatory regime for account-
    ants unveiled'.
45 Gary Marks, Liesbet Hooghe and Kermit Blank, 'European integration
    from the 1980s – state-centric versus multi-level governance', *Journal
    of Common Market Studies*, vol. 34, no. 3 (1996), pp. 341–78.
46 For a neo-utilitarian view of hegemony see: Keohane, *After Hegemony*;
    and for a critical, neo-Gramscian view, see: S. Gill and D. Law, *The
    Global Political Economy: Perspectives, Problems and Policies* (Hemel
    Hempstead: Harvester/Wheatsheaf, 1988), esp. Ch. 6.
47 Keohane, *After Hegemony*.
48 *Ibid.*
49 After Karl Polanyi, *The Great Transformation: The Political and Eco-
    nomic Origins of Our Time* (Boston: Beacon Press, 1957).

9

'State action' in an unmanageable world

Many observers of the contemporary growth of internationalization and/or globalization believe, as has been seen, in a decline in the relevance and potency of the traditional state. The purpose of the discussion in this chapter is to consider some of the less agreeable consequences that might flow from such a development.

Analysts differ considerably in their views of the likelihood of the various alternatives to a state-based global political order and in their judgements about the relative merits of such alternatives. Anti-statists generally extend a warm welcome to any alternatives to the primacy of the state. Some enthusiasts for unconstrained free markets also believe that the dissolution of a state-based order will merely unleash the full, benign potency of the market system, ushering in a new golden age for humanity as a whole.

Many other observers of the evolving human condition are, however, more uncertain in their predictions of alternatives to the statist order and in their judgements about their desirability. They are, in particular, concerned about two dangers that might follow from the erosion of the role and capacities of states without the emergence of their functional equivalents at regional or global levels. The first, general danger, is that the world will still lack institutions capable of dealing with global problems on a world-wide basis. The second, slightly more specific danger, is that of a worsened asymmetry between the power and capacities of transnational business enterprises and associations, on the one hand, and the weakening capacities of small-scale agencies of public governance, on the other – an asymmetry that would reinforce tendencies for private agencies to displace public authorities in the realm of global governance, and thus further compound any possible global democratic deficit.

Disintegration and the global system

The general disintegration of the global system is one clear danger in a world in which increasing internationalization and globalization undermine the role and capability of the established states, and in which new regional or global agents of public governance fail to emerge. Such disintegration could follow a number of patterns, with varying implications.

The patterns of meso- and micro-regionalism, discussed in Chapter 8, suggest two, possibly complementary, paths towards a form of political disintegration in a post-statist world. Zones of close economic interaction and/or cross-border cultural affiliation would provide the basis for an alternative pattern of affiliation in the case of growing meso-regionalization. Historical, cultural and/or more limited patterns of economic involvement would furnish the foundations for greater micro-regionalization. Some meso-regions might embrace economies and populations akin in size and strength to contemporary states. They would, however, be subject to precisely the same enervating processes and conditions wrought by increasing internationalization and/or globalization upon traditional states, and would, therefore, be subject to comparable policy constraints.

Micro-regionalism would merely compound the problems encountered by states in a world of increasing internationalization and/or globalization. The cohesiveness of the new political entities might be greater in a number of cases than that of the states from which they had emerged. Such micro-regions would, however, be smaller in size and encompass fewer resources than their predecessor states. Such entities would still have to perform many of the functions of public governance for their populations that established states have undertaken. They would thus possess many of the attributes of states, but be no more than small states or even micro-states. Moreover, such new small states and micro-states would continue to be exposed to precisely the same pressures and constraints that had supposedly undermined the position and power of established states. Rather than enhancing the position of agencies of public governance in the face of increasing internationalization and/or globalization, the proliferation of small states and micro-states would merely weaken further the practical power of governments (democratic or otherwise).

World cities and the new global order/disorder

One distinctive view of the future is provided by those who emphasize the emergence of a set of new world cities within the global political economy.[1] This view rejects the notion that the modern technologies of transport and communication will completely deterritorialize all economic, social and ultimately political life. Rather, a range of vital services and support mechanisms will be provided for even the most geographically dispersed industries and production systems with footloose headquarters, by clusterings of experts that have developed, or will form, in a number of major cities to which such expertise has been attracted historically, or that will emerge in response to new incentives.

The focus of world cities, and their core specialists, is increasingly global. Experts connect with similar experts in other world cities or with the representatives of the enterprises that they serve around the world. Such elite urban groups share an increasingly common set of values, understandings and expectations. The involvement of such a world city, and its population, with surrounding territory is increasingly hierarchical, with the peripheral communities merely providing more basic commodities, services and dormitories for the city and its leading inhabitants and/or the location of basic production activities. The world city, in return, assumes an authoritative role – economically, socially and politically – over its periphery and its population.

The hierarchical character of the world that stimulated the emergence of such world cities, however, highlights the disintegrative potential that accompanies a development that might otherwise suggest a new pattern of global integration. Sharpened patterns of differentiation and inequality are possible within a world of world cities. Division and inequality are possible within the world cities themselves; between those who are members of the globally orientated elites and those who are not, and who are therefore increasingly marginalized from the new global prosperity. Greater inequality is also possible between the populations of the world cities and those of peripheries, with wealth and economic power being progressively accumulated in the cities at the expense of their increasingly subordinated environs. Such an intensification of local and regional inequalities might thus compound long-term patterns of inequality between core and peripheral (or core, semi-peripheral and peripheral) economies internationally.[2]

The final product of such an ever more unequal world might be the nightmare vision propounded so vividly in many of the pessimistic futuristic films produced by Hollywood during the last few decades of the twentieth century. A common theme of such dystopian images is that of the urban area sharply divided into heavily protected enclaves of the powerful and prosperous, surrounded by large 'no-go' areas of comprehensive degradation and disorder. The positive orientations of the engaged elite groups of such world cities are directed exclusively towards themselves and their fellows in other world cities. 'Fellow citizens' beyond the walls of comfort and security are regarded with unqualified hostility and fear, and subject to increasingly draconian measures of social control and containment.[3] Such visions remain at the extreme end of the range of possibilities attendant upon the dynamics of a world of increasing internationalization and/or globalization, but are, nevertheless, suggested by the emergence of protected estates in the suburbs of many of the major cities in the United States of America and, to a lesser extent, the United Kingdom.[4]

The new medievalism

The notion of world cities relates in a general way to the idea that the effects of increasing internationalization and/or globalization will generate a 'new medievalism'. Any loosening of the bonds of the 'traditional state' in, or by, a world increasingly orientated towards international commerce and world-wide production will, it has been argued, generate a world closer to that of late medieval Europe, with its elaborate networks of trading cities, than to the system of national economies that emerged with the coming of the mercantilist era and the later start of the industrial revolution. Moreover, the availability of new forms of interpersonal communication on a global scale, when combined with the emergence of new global 'cultures', might also establish new patterns of de-territorialized authority more akin to those of the medieval Europe of universal Catholicism and widespread chivalric values than to the statist normative order of more recent centuries.

The medieval analogy for the new global order may, however, be misleading in a number of important respects. The cement of a common belief and value system may be absent. The integrative function of new means of transport and communication, and of a global market, may be overstated in this respect. The spread and penetration of new global values, be they consumerist or environmentalist, may be constrained by the differential levels of access to long-distance travel and to the new media of interpersonal communication or of participation in the global market economy. Moreover, there is no one-to-one relationship between exposure to these new global influences and responses at the individual or communal levels. New technologies may be adopted world-wide, but adapted to enduring cultural differences. Such technologies may be widely adopted but directed to varying ends in different societies, as with the deployment in India of cinematographic techniques developed in the 'West' for the production of films that are quintessentially Indian in their cultural referents and appeal.

Exposure to global influences may also stimulate negative reactions. Cultural imports may prompt a re-emphasis of traditional cultural values and expressions. Experience of a global economy might encourage popular pressures for measures of resistance to, and restraint of, the resultant pressures.[5] A cultural 'double movement', or a 'dialectic of difference', in a world of increasing internationalization and/or globalization might thus lead to a world of diversity and fragmentation rather than common popular response.

Moreover, the new means of long-distance transport and interpersonal communication might also facilitate the spread and consolidation of diverse viewpoints and competing agendas. One of the notable features of the development of the internet has been the proliferation of special-interest discussion groups, bulletin boards and web pages. The consolidation of partiality of purpose and perspective that is reflected in such a development could herald the fragmentation of 'society' – both domestic and global – rather than its consolidation into a new 'global society' as anticipated by some contemporary observers.[6] The result could be a world of internet (and worse) wars: of 'alternative life styles' against religious fundamentalists of various persuasions; feminists against advocates of 'traditional' family structures; environmentalists against producer interest groups; free-marketeers against socialists; and European integrationists against 'Euro-sceptics'.

Not only may the 'new-medieval' world be more diverse and divisive than its historical predecessor; it will also be exposed to more severe stresses and strains. The density of the world's population, the physical interconnectedness of communities and societies, the speed with which economic, environmental and epidemiological effects can be generated and transmitted across societies, have all increased massively since the Middle Ages. These differences, in turn, intensify the problems confronting humanity and its structures of public governance. The relatively dispersed pattern of supply of public governance in the medieval era is thus unlikely to prove appropriate in a world of substantially increased potential need for cohesive public governance. Further social and political fragmentation may thus prove fatal, given the problems and pressures facing today's world: problems that include not merely the intensification of international competitive pressures, and the labour-displacing effects of many new, computer-based productive technologies, but also the steady proliferation of weapons of mass destruction. The 'Dark Ages' that intervened between the end of the Roman Empire and the emergence of feudal society might thus prove to be a better analogy for a world in which increasing internationalization and/ or globalization induces the collapse of the state.

The horizontal fragmentation of societies is also an increasingly serious prospect in a world of increasing internationalization and/ or globalization, and adds its own impact and threat to the possibility of increasing vertical fragmentation. Traditional forms of democracy may be weakened by the former form of fragmentation, and the prospects of harmonious global governance threatened by the latter.

The dangers attendant upon the advance of internationalization and/or globalization will not, however, materialize in all places with the same speed and strength. As with so much else within the contemporary global political economy, poorer societies with weaker social structures and institutions of public governance are likely to succumb sooner and with greater drama. The virtual disintegration of a number of African societies in recent decades is by no means solely the product of the impact of developments in the global political economy. Such disintegration does, however, illustrate some of the more extreme possibilities. However, the parlous condition of Russia in the last years of the twentieth century, with prospects of economic and political disintegration, warlordism and the predominance of the criminal economy,[7] does demonstrate the serious consequences of the exposure of a fragile and institutionally weak society to the pressures of an ever more competitive and increasingly unforgiving global political economy.

Complacency amongst the world's richer and more industrialized societies in the face of the pressures of a globalizing world would not be warranted, however. While their institutions and capacities may be far more robust than those of poorer and less developed societies, they are also more complex and less able to fall back upon more basic forms of general existence if conditions begin to deteriorate seriously. The acute danger of mass starvation that faced the United Kingdom during the submarine war against its merchant shipping during the Second World War exemplifies the real need of complex and highly populated societies to maintain a range of systems of supply and support in order to ensure the survival of both their populations and their social, economic and political institutions. When facing the dangers generated by the developing global system, the further societies have climbed, the further they may have to fall.

Responses to disintegration

The authoritarian path

Well-established agencies of public governance have often proved able to restore societies from partial breakdown. Wide-ranging social, economic and political breakdown, however, has either led to the terminal disintegration of societies or, more generally, authoritarian responses of one type or another. 'Right-wing' authoritarian regimes commonly justify their arrival as a 'necessary' response to breakdown and disorder, and proclaim their purpose as that of restoring order and 'traditional' values. Radical revolutionary regimes have also found it easier to come to power at times of widespread dislocation, and, despite their benign rhetoric, have commonly resorted to repressive and authoritarian means to restore order and establish new policies and institutions.

The central point here is that authoritarians and revolutionaries are an ever-present component of the political tapestry of complex societies. The stability of established institutions and the relative well-being of their populations, however, prevents such political activists from exerting a decisive influence in such societies for much of the time. Support for the Nazi Party in Germany remained low, and even declining, during the more prosperous middle to late

1920s. It is only with the onset of serious pressures, and consequential socio-economic dislocation, that the influence of such potentially authoritarian political movements begins to rise, as it did in the case of support for the Nazis after the onset of the Great Depression in 1929.[8]

The pattern behind the emergence of authoritarian regimes is thus relatively clear. Damaging pressures arise within, or from the international environment of, a society. Social and economic damage is inflicted upon the society, and general dislocation begins to develop. Established institutions come under pressure, with particular challenges to established institutions of public governance. Disorder and dislocation reach high, and ultimately unsustainable, levels, at which stage authoritarian movements seize power within society and deploy forceful means to reimpose order, create new institutions and restore economic vitality (or precipitate economic mayhem).[9]

External tension and conflict

Conflict can develop between a disintegrating, or disintegrated, society and other states in one of two primary ways. First, domestic disorder may encourage intervention by other states that are concerned either to contain, or even to reverse, the contagion of economic, social and political breakdown. Second, external intervention may be prompted as neighbours succumb to the temptation to acquire additional territory or resources from a society that is no longer capable of defending its frontiers and protecting its population. Developments in various parts of Africa during the late twentieth century illustrated elements of both forms of external incursions into disordered societies.

External conflict may also be generated because the regimes that come to power in the aftermath of domestic economic dislocation and political disorder have often adopted a bellicose posture externally. Such external aggressiveness serves the purposes of revivalist regimes in a number of ways. First, the population can be reunified by the invention of a common external threat or the promise of new external achievements and acquisitions: a malignant form of the 'politics of identity'.[10] Second, domestic economic dislocation may be reversed, in the short term at least, through state-directed rearmament and remilitarization programmes. The early achievements of the new Nazi regime in Germany from 1933 onwards owed much to such psychological and material effects of rearmament and, ultimately, preparations for external aggression.[11] Ideological elements may reinforce such impulses, as indicated by both the case of Nazi Germany and the zeal to export revolution of the new Bolshevik regime in Russia from 1917 onwards. Finally, the authoritarian leaders of a newly reassertive state may find that they have engendered so much external hostility, and/or mortgaged themselves so heavily economically, that armed conflict is precipitated by the anxieties of neighbours or the pursuit of economic tribute from any societies that can be subordinated.

The ultimate domestic consequences of the external conflict engendered by authoritarian regimes that come to power after domestic disorder are varied, but generally poor. Napoleon's France ended, after two decades of astonishing military victories, in total defeat. Nazi Germany and militaristic Japan both drove their countries to ruin in the Second World War. The Soviet Union's 70-year-long confrontation with the non-communist world generated a seriously distorted pattern of economic development, danger of nuclear annihilation and, ultimately the collapse of the Soviet regime and much of the socio-economic system that it had created. One of the few exceptions to such a general experience is to be found in the way in which the United Kingdom's renewed external assertiveness under Oliver Cromwell's Protectorate, after the English Civil War, laid the foundations for steady advance towards future prosperity and international dominance.[12]

Fragmentation and paradox in a globalizing world

The danger inherent within a world in which traditional states wither in the face of increasing internationalization and/or globalization is thus that domestic disorder will ultimately spawn the kinds of authoritarian regimes that will both reassert the role of the state in a particularly unpleasant manner and contribute to a future of greater international instability and even armed conflict. Conflicts within such a world might configure along the lines of Samuel Huntingdon's 'clash of civilizations'.[13] However, 'civilizations' are rather more elusive in practice than they are envisaged by Huntingdon, while the identification of 'incompatible cultures' is likely to be a circular matter: that is, the actual outbreak of conflict will form the basis for the identification of those cultures that are supposed to be incompatible. Indeed, bitter armed conflicts have erupted in the past between societies and cultures that are closely associated by universal and historical standards, as the American War of Independence and the later American Civil War demonstrate. International conflict can thus develop wherever suitable lines of friction develop between societies, and may be particularly encouraged where domestic disorder within one or more of the potential participants has led to the emergence of authoritarian regimes. The defence that some analysts believe that democracy, and particularly liberal democracy, provides against the outbreak of armed conflict amongst such societies will persist, moreover, for only so long as those democracies are able to survive in the face of the potentially disruptive effects of the unconstrained advance of internationalization and/or globalization.

The central paradox of a world of increasing internationalization and/or globalization, then, is that if such a pattern of development does weaken the state, and undermine domestic economic, social and political stability, then the conditions under which internationalization and/or globalization can advance, or even survive, may also be undermined. Domestic disorder threatens, in the first instance, the stability of the social and legal framework that is vital for orderly economic activity of any scale or complexity.[14]

If increasing internationalization and/or globalization does generate domestic disorder, and thence authoritarian and potentially bellicose regimes, international peace and stability might also be threatened. While many leading businesses have survived, and even prospered, during periods of major conflict, existing patterns of international economic interaction are profoundly affected, if not abruptly riven, by such experiences. Some forms of economic exchange may remain possible between adversaries, as with the financial payments that the Bank for International Settlements, and various Swiss banks, arranged between Nazi Germany and the Allied Powers during the Second World War. The maintenance of such links is, however, rather the exception that proves the general rule of ruptured economic relations between adversaries at time of major conflict.

Conclusions

Increasing internationalization and/or globalization thus carries dangers for the global system that cannot merely be wished away.

Uncontrolled market processes are not necessarily benign in all their effects and may, if advancing with a sufficient speed and intensity, have profound disruptive consequences. The intensification of competition and the volatility of the international financial system both overlie the growing pressure being exerted by technological advances upon the scale and nature of employment in many societies. No simple sets of data capture fully the combined effects of these developments and pressures. Trade balances and growth rates are often poor indicators of the economic and social experiences of populations.

Indicators of possible disorder within the societies that are exposed to a world of increasing internationalization and/or globalization abound in the social realm. Here again, however, it is often difficult to differentiate general cultural, social and technological trends from the effects of the global economy. Indeed, common exposure to external economic pressures may have actually contributed to greater social cohesion in many communities in the past. General social developments thus reflect a complex equation in which it is difficult, if not impossible, to tease out any single, decisive influence.

Such caveats do not, however, warrant complacency in the face of the growing pressures created by a world of increasing internationalization and/or globalization. The decline in the position and capacity of the state is not a matter of indifference in a world in which the position and power of transnational business enterprises continues to grow; in which transnational criminality flourishes; in which technology may endow rogue countries and criminal cartels with lethal capabilities; in which a potentially disintegrating post-Soviet Russia is the uneasy home to literally thousands of decaying nuclear weapons; and in which damage to many vital aspects of the human environment continues to advance. The established state may not offer a complete answer to all such issues, if only because of the fragmentation of global governance and authority that is entailed by the existence of sovereign states. However, the state, whether acting along or in concert with others, remains the only agency with anything like the necessary level of capability to begin to deal with most of the more pressing problems now confronting humanity.

Notes

1 P.L. Knox and P.J. Taylor, *World Cities in a World-System* (Cambridge: Cambridge University Press, 1995); and for one of the original

statements of the view see: Saskia Sassen, *The Global City* (Princeton, NJ: Princeton University Press, 1991).

2 David Simon, 'The world city hypothesis', in Knox and Taylor, *World Cities*, pp. 132–55.

3 On the containment character of US criminal and penal policy see: Loic Wacquant, 'Imprisoning the American poor', *Guardian Weekly*, 8 September 1998.

4 'The birth of Enclave Man', *Financial Times*, 20/21 September 1997, p. 11.

5 See the contributions to the special edition of *New Political Economy, Globalisation and the Politics of Resistance*, ed. Barry Gills, vol. 2, no. 1 (March 1997).

6 See: Vincent Cable, *The World's New Fissures: Identities in Crisis* (London: Demos, 1994).

7 'A country where the awful has already happened', *Financial Times*, 24/25 October 1998, p. xxiv; and 'A cold, hungry, pointless Russian army', *The Economist*, 21 November 1998, p. 46; and see, also, the general description provided in John Gray, *False Dawn: The Delusions of Global Capitalism* (London: Granta Books, 1998), Ch. 6.

8 Robert Boyce, 'World depression, world war: some economic origins of the Second World War', in R. Boyce and E.M. Robertson, *Paths to War: New Essays on the Origins of the Second World War* (Basingstoke: Macmillan, 1989), pp. 55–95; and William L. Shirer, *The Rise and Fall of the Third Reich* (London: Secker and Warburg, 1960), esp. Ch. 5.

9 For prospects within post-Soviet Russia see: 'Could it lead to Fascism?', *The Economist*, 11 July 1998, pp. 21–5.

10 Cable, *The World's New Fissures*.

11 Richard Overy, 'Hitler's war plans and the German economy', in Boyce and Robertson, *Paths to War*, pp. 96–127.

12 Corelli Barnett, *Britain and Her Army 1509–1970* (Harmondsworth: Allen Lane/The Penguin Press, 1970), Chs 5, 6 and 7.

13 Samuel P. Huntington, *The Clash of Civilizations and the Remaking of World Order* (New York: Simon and Schuster, 1996).

14 Gray, *False Dawn*.

10

Order, disorder and globalization: the East and South-East Asian crisis of 1997–98

Developments within East and South-East Asia during 1997 and 1998 serve to illustrate the complex and controversial connections between economic development, increasing internationalization and/or globalization, and the complex continuing role of the state.

The background to the crisis of the late 1990s

A number of the economies of East and South-East Asia enjoyed spectacular levels of economic growth during the 1980s and 1990s, as indicated by Table 10.1. The sources of this growth,

Table 10.1   Growth of Gross National Product per capita in East and South-East Asia, 1972–92 ($US)

Country	1972	1976	1980	1984	1988	1992
S. Korea	330	740	1,620	2,250	3,650	6,790
Singapore	1,410	3,040	4,820	8,050	9,170	15,730
Hong Kong	1,230	2,730	5,220	6,350	9,430	15,360
Indonesia	90	270	470	590	490	670
Malaysia	450	920	1,690	2,050	1,940	2,790
Thailand	220	410	670	840	1,050	1,840
Philippines	200	390	650	610	620	770

Source: *World Tables 1994* (New York: Johns Hopkins University Press for World Bank, 1994).
Note: The World Bank does not furnish data for Taiwan.

however, have continued to attract controversy: to some a triumph of neo-liberal economics; to others a tribute to 'Confucian' values; to yet others evidence of the effectiveness of governments committed to state support[1] for export-orientated and market-sensitive industrialization.[2]

Moreover, the sustained period of growth within the United States during the 1990s encouraged optimistic observers to argue that the combination of the emergence of the newly industrialized economies of East and South-East Asia with the wider effects of a world of increasing internationalization and/or globalization had generated a 'new economic paradigm' for the US in which healthy levels of growth could be sustained more or less indefinitely without the emergence of inflationary pressures,[3] since the growth was sustained until well into the Asian economic and financial crisis in October 1997.[4]

However, a high degree of dependence upon exports to the world's geographically concentrated, rich markets was one obvious weakness in the economic position of many East and South-East Asian economies: any faltering of demand in the importing countries would have a major impact upon the export patterns and revenue earnings of too many of the 'emerging' economies. Moreover, there were some serious doubts about the political and economic structures of the region's newly industrializing economies, with suspicions of extensive cronyism among politicians and the leaders of major businesses and growing worries about the patterns of industrial development in some economies.

In the view of sceptical economists like Paul Krugman, the rapid growth of many East and South-East Asian economies had resulted from nothing more exotic than high levels of investment in economies with extensive underemployed resources. Moreover, the deployment of such high levels of inputs could not be sustained indefinitely, and particularly not when opportunities of high levels of return began to wane and structural obstacles within the domestic economy were encountered.[5]

By the early 1990s, the complexion of the future 'crisis' was beginning to emerge. Levels of short-term external debt had been high and rising for South Korea, Malaysia, Indonesia and Thailand throughout the 1980s and 1990s. In 1984, in the middle of the so-called 'debt crisis' of the Less Developed Countries (mainly Latin American), the short-term debt of South Korea and Thailand was

Figure 10.1   East and South-East Asia – short-term debt ($US million)

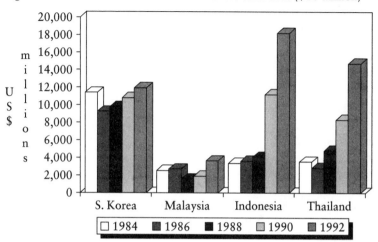

Table 10.2   Short-term external debt as a percentage of overall external debt

	1984	1986	1988	1990	1992
S. Korea	27.1	19.8	27.4	30.9	27.7
Malaysia	13.5	12.4	8.6	11.9	18.3
Indonesia	11.3	9.0	7.9	16.7	21.6
Thailand	23.6	15.3	22.2	29.5	37.4
Argentina	21.9	8.4	9.7	13.0	20.6
Brazil	10.6	8.5	9.4	20.8	17.4
Mexico	6.8	5.8	7.9	15.2	22.5

Source: World Bank, *World Tables, 1994* (Baltimore: Johns Hopkins University Press, 1994), country tables.
Note: no debt data given for Singapore and Hong Kong.

already high, as indicated by Figure 10.1, and higher as a proportion of their overall debt than the three major Latin American debtor countries, as Table 10.2 demonstrates. Much of this increased short-term borrowing, it eventually transpired, had been undertaken by commercial interests to finance ambitious expansion plans at home and abroad[6] and was made possible, in part, by currencies that many analysts feared were overvalued.[7] Indeed, South

Korea's giant *Chaebol* had increased their average levels of indebtedness to a remarkable 550 per cent of their equity value, with extensive cross-lending to their own affiliates.[8]

Anxieties had also been stimulated by the dominant, if not overweening, position acquired by the *Chaebol* in the South Korean economy[9] and their responsibility for some 60 per cent of the country's exports.[10] Moreover, the process of economic development during the 1970s and 1980s had in no way diminished the dependence of the 'emerging' East and South-East Asian economies upon export markets in the Advanced Industrial Economies, which absorbed 63.5 per cent of East and South-East Asia's exports in 1970 and the same proportion of 63.5 per cent in 1989.[11] The major change was the increase of the share of manufactured goods in East and South-East Asia's exports to the Advanced Industrial Countries: increasing from 44.8 per cent of such exports in 1970 to 79.8 per cent by 1989.[12]

Anxieties were dampened, however, by the view that prudential forms of 'sterilization' had ensured that much of the inflow of funds into the East and South-East Asian economies could not, and would not, lead to the kinds of financial crises that had beset so many major Latin American debtors.[13]

The unfolding crisis

The financial and economic crisis that was to engulf East and South-East Asia, and then spread throughout much of the rest of the world economy, started to unfold in 1997. Early signs of impending problems emerged as early as April, with evidence of flagging economic growth within the region.[14] Concern was then reinforced by reports in May of the increase in South Korea's external indebtedness by 33 per cent in 1996, to a total of $104.5 billion, with comparisons with the case of Mexico before its financial crash in 1994.[15]

The seriousness of the developing situation began to become clear in the early summer of 1997 as Thailand plunged into an acute currency crisis, with concerns of a contagious currency crisis within the region.[16] As the Thai currency crisis continued to worsen, general anxiety was reinforced by a range of political disputes and dangers that also crystallized within South-East Asia: a dispute between China and the Philippines over the Spratly Islands;[17] continuing worries over China's intentions towards Taiwan; and the worsening economic conditions in North Korea, with their attendant dangers of political disorder and/or diversionary military aggression against South Korea.[18]

By the summer of 1997, the East and South-East Asian financial and economic crisis was unfolding rapidly. In late June the Thai finance minister resigned in the face of mounting problems and criticisms[19] and with no substantive progress on the economic and financial front.[20] Then, at the start of July 1997, Thailand was forced to devalue the baht[21] and appeal for support to the International Monetary Fund.[22] Thailand's forced devaluation prompted a general loss of confidence in the majority of the regional economies, the flight of short-term capital, and a series of currency crises in first one and then another East and South-East Asian economy.[23] The continuous currency crises throughout the summer of 1997[24] began to affect the ability of manufacturing industries to purchase imported inputs and maintain levels of production. By the end of August, US managers of Asian investment funds were repatriating their funds on a substantial scale.[25] Fragile enterprises, like the relatively young South Korean car manufacturer Kia, soon faltered in the face of such adverse developments.[26]

The climatic effects of the irregular El Niño current also plunged much of South-East Asia into deep drought during 1997. With the outbreak of widespread fires on a number of the main islands of Indonesia[27] suspicions grew that major landowners in the country, including some leading members of the government, had been complicit in starting many of the fires for short-term commercial reasons.[28] Whatever the causes of the fires, much of central South-East Asia was enveloped by a dense smog that ruined tourism and inflicted considerable additional damage upon economic and industrial activity.[29]

By October 1997 the East and South-East Asian economic and financial crisis was in full flood and spreading rapidly throughout the region. The woes of the Kia car manufacturing company, with plans to nationalize it by the government,[30] were by now merely a symptom of the wider malaise afflicting South Korea's overstretched Chaebol generally.[31] By the end of the month, Hong Kong's stock exchange was falling rapidly and pressures on the Hong Kong Dollar were building.[32] By the end of the year stock exchanges were collapsing throughout the region.[33]

With spreading disorder, the International Monetary Fund, the main instrument for intergovernmental management and troubleshooting within the global financial system, became increasingly active throughout the region. Indonesia[34] and the new government of South Korea[35] had followed Thailand's lead in negotiating for support packages from the IMF by the end of 1997, after earlier, but ultimately ineffectual, World Bank support for the former country's currency.[36]

Finally, a severe financial and economic crisis also began to crystallize in Japan.[37] The government decided to let the Hokkaido Takushoku bank fail without an official bail-out,[38] as the onset of the regional economic crisis exposed long-term weaknesses of many of its leading financial institutions.[39] By the end of 1997, Japanese financial institutions were facing the prospect of a downward spiral, as the falling value of their assets constrained lending into an economy in desperate need of increased credit and liquidity to stave off a deep and intractable recession.[40]

The crisis

By the start of 1998 it was apparent generally that East and South-East Asia were in the midst of an extremely serious economic and financial crisis, from which only such cautious regional economies as Taiwan had partially escaped,[41] and that now threatened to spread its effects throughout the rest of the global economy.

The course of the 'Asian Crisis' during 1998 exhibited a number of notable patterns and persistent problems, many of which may become characteristic of international economic and financial dislocations in an era of increasing internationalization and/or globalization. Prominent among these characteristics were: the fluctuating levels of optimism and pessimism; the uncertain responses of the governments of the states most immediately affected by the deepening crisis and the growing anxieties of governments in other regions of the global economy; the problematical, and increasingly controversial, involvement of the International Monetary Fund in the 'management' of the crisis; and the general panic among those private financial institutions that had become embroiled in the financial cauldron of East and South-East Asia through earlier loans and credits.

Optimism and pessimism in the deepening crisis
The South-East Asian economic and financial crisis faced observers and participants alike with conditions and developments that were

in important respects novel and worrying. The resultant combination of high levels of uncertainty and anxiety prompted considerable fluctuations in sentiment and expectation.

As early as July 1997, observers were arguing that even the forced devaluation of the Thai baht need not necessarily signal the end of Thailand's 'economic miracle'.[42] On 3 and 4 September 1997 evidence of optimism about the general economic prospects was evident on Wall Street,[43] in European stock markets,[44] on the Japanese stock exchange[45] and even on the Hong Kong stock exchange.[46] However, by 5 September pessimism was already reasserting itself in New York[47] and deepening rapidly in Malaysia.[48]

Daily developments altered expectations about the future course of events. A one-day drop of share prices of 10 per cent on the Hong Kong stock exchange prompted analysts to predict disaster on the Hong Kong stock exchange in late October[49] and induced marked reductions in share prices on stock-exchanges around the world.[50] A sharp reduction in the international value of the South Korean currency in mid-November[51] spread further alarm through world markets.[52] However, optimism revived briefly later in November, with encouraging signs from the Tokyo stock exchange[53] and a resurgence of confidence in Wall Street,[54] even though developments in Malaysia were far from encouraging.[55] Overall, the year had seen a major fall in the international values of the currencies of Indonesia, Malaysia, the Philippines, South Korea and Thailand, as indicated by Table 10.3.

Table 10.3 Currency values of East and South-East Asian economies December 1996 to December 1997 (currency units per $US)

Country	mid-Dec. 1996	mid-Dec. 1997	mid-Dec. 1998
Hong Kong	7.74	7.75	7.75
Indonesia	2,353.00	5,445.00	7,750.00
Malaysia	2.52	3.81	3.80
Philippines	26.30	40.00	39.40
Singapore	1.40	1.68	1.65
S. Korea	844.00	1,483.00	1,209.00
Taiwan	27.50	32.50	32.30
Thailand	25.60	46.30	36.40

Despite growing evidence of profound and potentially protracted problems in many of the East and South-East Asian economies at the end of 1997,[56] 1998 started with general optimism[57] and expectations of regional reconstruction within the region.[58] However, the prospects of debt default by Indonesia and of currency devaluation by China,[59] and the impact of the collapse of Hong Kong's largest investment bank, Peregrine Investment Holdings,[60] soon revived fears.

Serious concerns about regional prospects and their impact upon the wider world economy were still warranted, however. Devaluation, it had been hoped, would reduce the international prices of the region's exports. Unfortunately, devaluation increased the prices of imported resources, components and energy supplies, while the general economic and financial crisis sharply reduced local producers' access to working capital and confronted them with the problems of maintaining their businesses in the face of general economic disorder.[61] The problems of motor vehicle manufacturers reflected the twin problems of collapsing local and regional markets and the general difficulties of increasing exports.[62] Only exporters of locally-produced food were able to benefit fully from the effects of the currency devaluations.[63]

The region's reprieve was thus short-lived, and by mid-February concern was rising about the possible need for Hong Kong to abandon the parity of its dollar with the US dollar[64] and general currency instability within the region.[65] By the early summer of 1998 the autocratic ruler of Indonesia – President Suharto – was coming under growing pressures as political instability rose throughout his country,[66] and by the end of May he had been forced from office.[67] Trade statistics also revealed that exports from East and South-East Asia, as a whole, had been reduced by a half over the past year.[68]

Expectations during the last quarter of 1998 that the worst might now be past were accompanied by continued concerns about the scale of domestic restructuring that still had to be completed before a stable and prosperous future could be assured.[69] The South Korean economy continued to contract[70] and economic fundamentals remained weak in many of the East and South-East Asian economies.[71] The region seemed to be facing further financial crises,[72] with any recovery likely to be short-lived, in the face of a debt-ridden banking system, rising unemployment and collapsing industrial investment.[73] Uncertainties and doubts thus continued through the November and December of 1998.[74] However, the deep currency crises experienced by the majority of the East and South-East Asian economies during the latter half of 1997 were repeated only by Indonesia during 1998, as Table 10.3 demonstrates.

The spreading contagion
The second major feature of the South-East Asian economic and financial crisis of 1997 and 1998 was its contagious[75] effects. The spread of the crisis to other regions of the world economy had three sources: first, the psychological effects of the South-East Asian crisis upon bankers and investors throughout the rest of the world economy; second, the collapse of many regional markets for the exports of the region's own economies; and third, the more diffuse effects upon world markets of the collapse of demand in many East and South-East Asian economies: effects upon the producers of primary commodities and upon the exporters of advanced goods and services formerly imported in volume by the previously buoyant economies of the region. The loss of confidence of lenders and investors, based mainly in Advanced Industrial Economies, in emerging markets generally owed more to the demonstration effect created by the sudden and catastrophic collapse in so many East and South-East Asian economies, as lenders and investors re-evaluated the wisdom of their past financial decisions and the ultimate reliability of those to whom they had advanced resources,[76] and was particularly evident in the renewed pressure upon the Brazilian[77] and Russian[78] economies and their currencies from the summer of 1998 onwards. Once under way, however, the collapse of economic activity had clearly contagious effects, as demand for real goods and services declined sharply, with clear effects upon commodity prices.[79]

Businesses with considerable direct interests in the South-East Asian economies were amongst the first to suffer serious effects, ranging from the Swiss-Swedish engineering firm ABB's loss of a hydroelectric dam contract in Malaysia[80] to the loss by Boeing of an order for four new Boeing 747-400 aircraft from Philippines Airlines,[81] with other East and South-East Asian airlines considering similar moves.[82] By the end of 1998 the UK's Export Credits and Guarantee Department was anticipating a substantial increase in the value of claims to be received from unpaid exporters to emerging economies, from some £153 million in 1997 to an estimated £300 million for 1998.[83] The wider impact upon the 'real economy' of East and South-East Asia took longer to crystallize than the more immediate financial crisis of middle to late 1997, as Figures 10.2 and 10.3 on industrial production and the growth of Gross Domestic Product indicate.

Figure 10.2 East and South-East Asia – industrial production (% change from previous year)

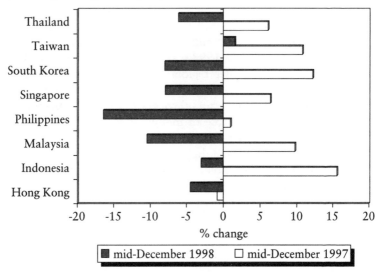

Figure 10.3 East and South-East Asia – change in Gross Domestic Product (% change from previous year)

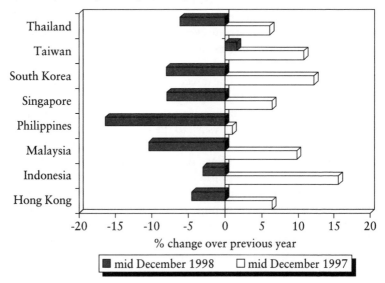

By February 1998, the exposure of banks and other financial institutions around the world to the adverse effects of the Asian economic and financial crisis was beginning to become a matter of growing concern.[84] Leading 'hedge funds' like Long Term Capital Management appeared to be highly vulnerable to the effects of adverse developments in the East and South-East Asian economies, in particular, and to world-wide economic dislocations, in general.[85] The volumes of mobile finance within the new global economy, the speed of financial movements, which had been facilitated by the new computer-based technologies, and the financial leverage that relatively unregulated financial operators could generate had combined together to create the risks of rapid and very serious financial collapse in the wake of a development like the Asian economic and financial crisis.

State responses within East and South-East Asia

The responses of the governments of the East and South-East Asian economies to the crisis of 1997–98 were marked by the alarm and confusion that follows upon the sudden emergence of unexpected, and potentially disastrous, developments. The varied, and often confused, pattern of reaction was a product of local uncertainties and the influence of powerful external agencies like the International Monetary Fund.

Mainland China moved rapidly to reverse its hesitant moves towards domestic economic liberalization and, in particular, to greater external financial openness.[86] Singapore and Taiwan[87] were able to limit themselves to relatively mild adjustments, such as the modest devaluation of the Taiwanese currency on 14 October 1997. Elsewhere, however, responses were often dramatic, and the presence of agencies like the IMF was pervasive.

Thailand[88]   After the floating of the baht on 2 July, the government of Thailand had introduced a reduction of governmental spending by $3 billion in 1998, an increase in value-added tax from 7 per cent to 10 per cent and a suspension of a growing number of financial companies that were no longer deemed to be viable,[89] to secure agreement on the IMF support of $17 billion of 10 August 1997. Widespread domestic economic and financial reform, with closer regulation of banking, the establishment of a new privatization secretariat, the issue of governmental bonds to fund rescue measures for the financial system, and the adoption of a generally restrictive monetary policy were to follow.[90] With recession proving to be more deep-seated than had been appreciated initially, however, the Thai government was forced to announce a relaxation of its restrictive fiscal and monetary policies in its letter of intent to the IMF of late May 1997.[91] Growth could not, however, be revived immediately,[92] as Figures 10.2 and 10.3 demonstrate.

Indonesia[93]   Indonesia's flotation of the rupiah on 14 August 1997 was followed by difficult negotiations with the IMF. However, rather than offering real concessions on the issues of corruption, the controversial project to create a national motor car manufacturer and the dubious development of a new commuter aircraft with \$2 billion of governmental support,[94] President Suharto and his government preferred to stall the International Monetary Fund, while talking publicly about a possible \$10 billion loan from Singapore.[95]

The scale of the problems afflicting Indonesia, however, compelled a more responsive approach to the IMF and its requirements. By early November, President Suharto's government had announced a domestic reform package, including the closure of 16 failing banks, the phased withdrawal of financial support for the national car manufacturing programme, the deregulation of a network of trading monopolies related closely to members of the Suharto family and the reduction of a range of import tariff protection for major local industries.[96] Indonesia's economic and financial woes were not so easily to be resolved, however, and on 15 January 1998 a commitment to a revised IMF package, which would secure the release of a second \$38 billion tranche of IMF support, was announced.[97]

Profound structural weaknesses within Indonesia's economy and a reluctance to undertake serious reform were, however, to ensure that her 'crisis' was to prove one of the more intractable and long-lasting of those among the East and South-East Asian economies. The international exchange value of the rupiah effectively collapsed on 22 January 1998, necessitating a temporary freeze on Indonesia's payments of external debts.[98] Rioting and violence against the local Chinese population[99] signalled a marked deterioration of the situation. President Suharto's government then turned to the idea of imposing a 'currency board' for the Indonesian currency and money supply[100] – a form of updated 'Gold Standard', whereby the local money supply would be tied, irrevocably, to holdings of US dollars or a wider basket of reserves. [101]

The Suharto regime combined brinkmanship in its dealings with the IMF with the limited pursuit of domestic economic reform[102] until its eventual collapse on 21 May 1998 after widespread student rioting. Limited measures of bank reform[103] could not disguise official recalcitrance towards the terms of the earlier IMF agreements.[104] However, a further agreement was reached between the government and the IMF on 8 April. After the fall of Suharto, the IMF concluded a new agreement with President Habibie's new government, which pressed ahead with financial reforms and the controlled sale of the assets of failed banks.[105]

South Korea[106]   The fate of the South Korean economy proved to be of the greatest significance for the region and for the wider world economy. It had been by far the most significant of the 'tiger' economies: symbolically, given its sensational rate of its economic growth during the 1980s, and objectively, given its growing place in the international trade system.

The Asian crisis exposed many of the basic shortcomings of the developmental model that had been pursued by South Korea. However, the government sought to maintain the value of the currency, the won, until mid-November 1997; but by 4 December it was forced to call upon the resources of the IMF and negotiate a $57 billion rescue package. The scale of financial exposure of Korea's leading Chaebol was now becoming apparent,[107] however, and with it the parlous condition of South Korea's financial system. By 12 December, therefore, pressure was growing for South Korea to renegotiate its arrangement with the IMF.[108]

The primary obstacle to government-led reform of the South Korean economy and financial system remained the power and position of the leading Chaebol, which resisted the rationalization of their activities and their complex patterns of cross-financing with their subsidiaries.[109] Continued currency pressure, however, forced the government into rescheduling (on 28 January 1998) $24 billion of the country's external debt,[110] promises to open the country's financial markets to foreign investors, the suspension of investment banks specializing in short-term corporate lending, and the rationalization of the Chaebols' debts.[111]

South Korea's Gross Domestic Product fell by 3.8 per cent in the first quarter of 1998; however, private consumption fell by 10 per cent and unemployment increased to 6.7 per cent of the work-force in April 1998.[112] Trade unions opposed labour-shedding policies. Bankers resorted to 'emergency' loans to corporate borrowers facing potential bankruptcy. Within the government bureaucracy, there were also many who remained wedded to the principles and practices upon which South Korea's earlier spectacular growth had been based and resistant, therefore, to the rather more 'neo-liberal' prescriptions that were being proffered in the face of the current crisis.[113]

The South Korean government felt compelled to impose its new direction in economic and financial policy, however. In July 1998, record fines of £34 million were imposed upon the five largest Chaebol for continuing to provide improper subsidies to their weaker subsidiaries.[114] Greater interest in the role, and well-being, of small and medium-sized companies was also signalled in November 1998 by a new corporate restructuring fund of some $1.2 billion.[115]

Malaysia[116]   The onset of the Asian crisis exposed significant weak-nesses in the infrastructure, the quality of the labour force and the balance of payments of the Malaysian economy.[117] Excessive corruption, collusion and nepotism were also endemic within its political and economic systems.[118]

The initial attempts of Malaysia to avoid the worst of the crisis by early measures to cool the economy[119] failed. International specu-lators were blamed for the country's troubles, 'guest workers' from other Asian countries were peremptorily expelled,[120] and political opposition at home was undermined by the arrest of Mahathir's critical former deputy, Anwar Ibrahim, on extraordinary charges of financial and sexual impropriety.[121] The crisis continued to afflict Malaysia, however. On 1 September 1998, the Malaysian govern-ment imposed a one-year foreign-exchange control regime,[122] and by October the Malaysian government was developing plans for the radical reconstruction of the national banking system.[123]

Other free-market East and South-East Asian economies   Thailand, Indonesia and South Korea were the three East and South-East Asian economies to be most directly entangled in the financial and currency crisis of the region during 1997 and early 1998. The other regional free-market economies were less affected initially, but ultimately involved in the general financial and economic dislocations that came in the wake of the initial financial crisis. Despite determined efforts by its government to clamp down on the activities of speculators,[124] the Taiwanese[125] currency was forced down to an eleven-year low by June 1998 and ended the year some 15 per cent lower in value in terms of US dollars than at the start of the year, as is indicated by Table 10.3. Growth of industrial production and GDP was, however, sustained in Taiwan during 1998, in marked contrast to the economies elsewhere within the region, as Figure 10.3 and Tables 10.4 and 10.5 indicate.

Table 10.4   East and South-East Asia – industrial production (% change from previous year)

Country	mid-December 1997	mid-December 1998
Hong Kong	−0.8	−4.5
Indonesia	15.6	−3.0
Malaysia	9.8	−10.4
Philippines	1.0	−16.4
Singapore	6.4	−7.9
South Korea	12.2	−8.0
Taiwan	10.8	1.6
Thailand	6.1	−6.1

Table 10.5   East and South-East Asia – growth (% change of Gross Domestic Product from previous year)

Country	mid-December 1997	mid-December 1998
Hong Kong	6.4	−5.2
Indonesia	8.0	−17.4
Malaysia	7.4	−8.6
Philippines	4.9	−0.1
Singapore	10.1	−0.7
South Korea	6.3	−6.8
Taiwan	6.9	4.7
Thailand	6.7	−0.4

The government of Singapore[126] relied upon the distinctive features of its socio-economic compact with its population to weather the economic and financial storm. The city-state's currency depreciated in line with that of Taiwan, but growth of industrial output and GDP was damaged by the crisis, as is indicated in Figures 10.2 and 10.3. In November 1998, the government's response to the crisis was to impose a 15 per cent cut in the wages paid from public funds and to ask private industry to follow suit, in an attempt to cut the public deficit and enhance international price competitiveness.[127]

Hong Kong[128] had been returned to China before the onset of the Asian economic and financial crisis. Its new connection with such a large and relatively protected economy provided the Hong Kong economy with a degree of cushioning against the worst of the storms that were besetting the region. However, the crisis exposed the role of property speculation within the Hong Kong economy; declining property values calling into question the security of the extensive loans that had previously been directed into the property market,[129] necessitating firm action by both Hong Kong's own government and that of mainland China.

In the Philippines,[130] the onset of the Asian economic and financial crisis exposed extensive institutional weaknesses in the social, economic and political systems. During 1998 the currency was devalued by just over 34 per cent (see Table 10.3) and the economy contracted by more than 15 per cent (see Figures 10.2 and 10.3). The Philippines government, never strong in infrastructural terms, struggled, more or less in vain, to formulate effective policies in the face of such serious economic dislocations.

Japan   The onset of the Asian economic and financial crisis was worrying enough for the world economy and its financial system. Japan, with its highly developed industrial economy and its orderly political system appeared, initially, to be relatively well insulated from the economic crisis afflicting the region within which it was located. There were, however, connections and parallels that were to undermine this initial confidence.

Japan's investments in the rest of East and South-East Asia and its level of intra-regional trade had risen to significant levels by the 1990s. Between 1998 and 1999 Japan's exports to other countries within the region had risen from 23.8 per cent to 28.8 per cent of her total exports,[131] and investments by her major companies were extensive throughout the region.

However, growth remained reasonable for 1997, as a whole, with buoyant exports to the United States of America.[132] A significant downturn was experienced during 1998, however, and signs of difficulties to come had already become apparent within the Japanese economy and financial system earlier in 1997, with the Japanese stock market in more or less continuous decline during the first half of the year,[133] and a full-blown 'crash' in mid-August 1997.[134]

The prospects of adverse developments within the Japanese economy were such as to induce real alarm across the world economy. Japan, by the early 1990s had become the world's second largest free-market economy, responsible for some 18.23 per cent of the world's annual production of wealth by 1993.[135] Significant economic problems in such a major actor upon the world economic stage were clearly a prospect to be approached with the greatest seriousness.

Structural weaknesses within the Japanese economy, and in its financial system, were thus beginning to become clear by late 1997. Growing fiscal deficits had prompted the government to increase the level of the sales tax in April 1997, adding deflationary effects to a recessionary international situation, and compounding a general decline in domestic property values. By October 1997, therefore, profit forecasts of Japanese businesses were becoming consistently gloomy.[136] Two unprecedented developments then followed before the end of the year. First, the Japanese government reversed its previous principles by allowing the Hokkaido Takushoku bank to fail on 17 November 1997.[137] Second, the leading Japanese securities broker – Yamaichi – failed on 24 November, following the failures of a handful of significant but smaller securities firms earlier in the month.[138] Such shocks to Japan's financial and economic system reflected, and then compounded, profound uncertainties about the proper course of policy that had seized the country's government as it was confronted by the nature and scale of the emerging crisis.[139]

The Japanese government was subsequently confronted by the classic dilemmas of policy-making in a severe recession: to cut expenditure in the face of declining tax revenues, or to engage in additional spending to restimulate the economy; to allow the failure of financial institutions to encourage financial restructuring, or to provide support against the danger of proliferating financial collapse.

Plans for a new Deposit Insurance Corporation, financed by premiums from banks and credit associations and the issuance of new bonds, were launched in December 1997 to stabilize the financial sector.[140] Larger than expected tax cuts were announced, and the Bank of Japan was authorized to act to support the international value of the yen.[141]

However, the clear wish of the government to seek the economic salvation of Japan through new measures to revive domestic demand, to preserve the financial system from any more catastrophic failures[142] and to support exports with new or enhanced measures of export credits and guarantees[143] did not generate the desired recovery during the first half of 1998. Japan's banks continued to suffer from inadequate capital bases and to seek public support,[144] her car manufacturers continued, with the exception of Toyota and Honda, to make serious losses,[145] and the profits of electronics firms fell dramatically.[146]

Persistent recession continued to confront the Japanese government with profound policy dilemmas,[147] prompting calls for an inflationary policy to revive the country's economy. However, bad debts and a failure to undertake industrial restructuring and a general collapse of consumer demand all continued to depress Japan's economic prospects and encourage proposals for inflationary policies to promote recovery.[148]

The bad debts of Japan's banking system now rose to an estimated £152 billion, however;[149] manufacturing industry proved slow to undertake timely restructuring;[150] Japan's consumers remained reluctant to return to high levels of consumption; and the dire financial condition of the country's local authorities continued to act as a serious constraint upon the government's ability to boost the economy.[151] Such conditions prompted desperate schemes to give £130 gift vouchers to every Japanese citizen and to increase the number of Monday holidays,[152] and to introduce legislation to inject public funds into the ailing financial system.[153] Some signs of possible recovery were evident by the end of 1998, with a recovery in banking shares[154] and a 2.5 per cent revival of industrial production.

External agencies and the East and South-East Asian economic and financial crisis

Crises like the Asian economic and financial crisis of 1997–98 stimulate a dense network of bilateral contacts amongst governments, few of which enter the public consciousness or record. The activities of multilateral agencies are, however, far more evident and, hence, amenable to record and reflection.

The International Monetary Fund was the prime intergovernmental actor within the Asian economic and financial crisis of 1997–98, with mixed effects and much controversy.[155] The questions raised by the policies adopted by the IMF towards the crisis turned on whether its 'orthodox' prescriptions were suited to the conditions being experienced by the East and South-East Asian economies or were actually promoting their further deterioration; whether the IMF's real concerns were for the well-being of creditor institutions, and their parent economies, particularly the United States of America, rather than with the economic health of the troubled societies;[156] and, finally, whether the IMF was motivated primarily by the defence of its own role within the international financial system rather than by the needs of the situation.[157] There was, moreover, the suspicion that prescriptions of devaluation, economic liberalization, and industrial privatization might be merely providing opportunities for Western transnational corporations to acquire new assets within East and South-East Asia at bargain-basement prices.[158]

Austerity packages, and increased interest rates, were imposed upon many of the afflicted East and South-East Asian economies as a condition of financial support. Recipients were also urged to liberalize their financial systems and, where pertinent, their wider economies; signalling to the wider world economy that there might be serious structural weaknesses within the economies of East and South-East Asia.[159] However, such prescriptions had recessionary, and even deflationary, implications in economies with relatively high levels of domestic savings that had been recycled through the economy by relatively weak financial institutions that were now coming under intense pressure.[160]

Such prescriptions also evoked local criticism. Malaysia's Mahathir Mohamad's attack upon the external sources of his country's economic woes were directed, in part, against the IMF and its policy prescriptions.[161] Relations with Indonesia remained troubled throughout the first year of the crisis. South Korea initially did all that it could to avoid having to turn to the IMF for support,[162] but was forced to resort to a $57 billion support package from that agency by 4 December 1997.[163] Criticisms of the IMF package within South Korea were exacerbated by its coincidence with a general election[164] that was to see the established government replaced by the opposition led by Kim Dae-jung.

The IMF's support package was eventually secured, in the face of the imminent danger of a default on the $30 billion of South Korea's overseas debt payments, at the end of January 1998. The IMF also joined the governments of its leading contributing states in persuading banks and other private financial institutions to reschedule debts,[165] on condition of further liberalization of the country's financial system, labour market reforms and increased interest rates.[166]

The South Korean rescue did, however, reveal some slightly unorthodox features. The additional $10 billion of financial support seemed to contradict earlier declarations that South Korea had no need of further finance, which the IMF thus had no intention of supplying.[167] Banks and private financial institutions also appeared to be reversing their earlier unwillingness to roll over loans to S. Korea or to extend new credit.[168] Sceptical observers, however, concluded that, when faced with an impending default of the scale and potential impact of that of South Korea, the IMF, the governments of the major industrial economies and the international banks had all abandoned prior principle in favour of any measures that promised some relief from the immediate crisis.[169]

Such possibilities provided the backdrop to the 'cat and mouse' game that often developed between the IMF and its client governments in East and South-East Asia. By the summer of 1998, the depth and persistence of the Asian economic and financial crisis was such as to prompt growing doubts about the wisdom of the IMF's standard conditions for financial support and to encourage wider acceptance of the notion that intentional reflation might now offer the only local path to recovery for many of the affected economies.[170]

Conclusions: states, globalization and the East and South-East Asian economic and financial crisis

The East and South-East Asian economic and financial crisis, its origins, course and 'management', are open to diverse interpretations, which reflect much uncertainty about the extent and implications of a world of increasing internationalization and/or globalization and its connections with the role of states in the evolving international order.

At one level, many features of the economic and financial crisis seem to demonstrate the extent and impact of globalization. The crisis crystallized with speed and ferocity as mobile short-term funds were withdrawn, in massive amounts, from the more exposed of the East and South-East Asian economies. The crisis was then transmitted to other regional economies, rapidly in some cases; more slowly and more indirectly in the case of others. By 1998, the global impact of the economic and financial crisis was becoming ever more clear: a fragile Russia was plunged into renewed crisis, with a forced devaluation and bond default in August 1998,[171] by the rapid decline in world prices for a range of primary commodities, including oil. The weaknesses of the Brazilian economy,[172] with large domestic budget deficits and an overvalued currency,[173] also came under closer, more critical international inspection and increasing financial pressure. Such experiences seemed to reinforce the 'strong globalization' view that states were now compelled to accede to the imperatives of the new global economy; that discretion, even for such multilateral agencies as the IMF, was now reduced to fine-tuning policy within the constraints to which all were now subjected; and that the future would be one of the continued retreat of the state from any attempts to direct domestic economies unilaterally.

The background, course and consequences of the crisis, however, reveal a far more complex picture of the contemporary international order. The rapid expansion of mobile short-term capital was, as has been seen earlier, a function of the combined effects of policy decisions and non-decisions by the governments of leading economies during the late 1960s, the 1970s and the 1980s and the new information technologies. Most significantly, the volatility of such short-term financial capital was encouraged by the general weakening of regulation by the authorities of the rich countries, individually and collectively, from which such funds were emanating. The availability of such short-term finance was not sufficient alone, however, to create the critical exposure of many of the East and South-East Asian economies by 1997. Weak regulation and monitoring of domestic financial systems by their own governments was also a condition for excessive borrowing of short-term international funds by local banks and businesses.

The onset of the acute phase of the Asian economic and financial crisis in 1997 did expose the weakness of the short-term measures that were available to many of the region's governments. Malaysia's reimposition of foreign-exchange controls on 1 September 1998[174] was rather too little and too late to avert the worst of the financial and currency crisis that had already overwhelmed it. However, those economies that had been protected from excessive inflows of short-term capital, prior to the crystallization of the crisis, were preserved from the worst effects of the capital flight that marked the first phase of the economic and financial crisis in 1997. Thus, Taiwan's prior accumulation of substantial reserves and preservation of some currency controls[175] protected it from much of the first phase of the crisis. China's preservation of wide-ranging currency and capital controls[176] did much to insulate it from the initial phase of financial turmoil, but not from the longer-term effects of the crisis upon real economic activity.[177]

Enhanced institutions for the support of troubled economies were also considered at various stages of the crisis. Plans for a new regional monetary fund for East and South-East Asia were floated during the latter part of 1997.[178] An enhanced role for the IMF was being proposed by end of 1998, and increased financial resources were granted to it at stages during 1998.[179]

The impact of the East and South-East Asian economic and financial crisis was also such as to prompt some reconsideration of the general wisdom of relatively unregulated international financial transactions. Early proposals for the taxation of all international financial transfers – the Tobin tax – remained in the background. By late 1998, however, the severity of recent experiences had prompted numerous proposals for the construction of a 'new architecture' for the regulation of the international financial system. In November 1998, the meeting of the influential Group of Seven declared itself in favour of new principles for the regulation of international finance, with particular emphasis upon an enhanced transparency of the books of lenders and borrowers and greater disclosure by all those engaged in international financial transactions.[180] However, apart from a specific commitment to a new IMF lending facility to assist troubled emerging economies, the details and import of these principles remained vague and unclear.[181]

The idea of a global 'lender of last resort', however, raised troubling questions about 'moral hazard', and the sense of freedom from responsibility among lenders that might follow. Indeed, voices were still being raised in favour of new patterns of self-regulation within the financial services industries, in which greater transparency, alone, would supposedly ensure sufficient restraint and discipline.[182] The virtues of purely market-based regulation had, however, been thrown into serious doubt by the generally poor record of the authoritative risk-rating agencies – Moody's, Standard and Poor's, Duff and Phelps and IBCA – in anticipating, and providing advance warning of, the impending crisis within East and South-East Asia.[183]

In practice, however, the actions of both the International Monetary Fund and the governments of individual Advanced Industrial Countries suggested that remedial action by public authorities continued to be both likely and often critical, even in a world of free-market rhetoric. The IMF's support for both Brazil and Russia during the middle and latter part of 1998 demonstrated a clear relaxation of conditions that had previously been emphasized. However, the further adverse development of the financial crises of these two countries during late 1998 and early 1999 also indicated the limitations of effective IMF support in the face of serious domestic weaknesses.[184] The extensive financial support provided by the Federal Reserve in the aftermath of the collapse of the hedge fund, Long Term Capital Management, in late September and early October 1998 demonstrated a willingness to rescue financial institutions from the folly of their own ways that was at clear variance with neo-liberal principles and practices.[185] The regulation of hedge-funds, new rules to separate retail banking from investment banking, the general tightening of bank supervision and bank capital adequacy standards, and a reconsideration of the virtues of capital controls all resurfaced as possibilities in the aftermath of the shocks of 1997 and 1998.[186]

The critical political responses to the Asian economic and financial crisis of 1997–98 lay with the individual governments of the afflicted region and those of a handful of Advanced Industrial Countries. New measures to constrain the inward flow of short-term finance by the governments of emerging economies could do much to reduce the risk of a repetition of the crisis in the form in which it surfaced in 1997 and 1998. The acceptability of such new constraints to the governments of the world's leading economies and the multilateral agencies that they dominate, such as the IMF, would reinforce the likelihood of such measures. New unilateral and multilateral measures to regulate the behaviour of lending institutions by the governments of the world's leading economies would further limit future repetitions of the crisis.

Whatever the diagnoses of and prescriptions for the Asian crisis, the turn of 1998/9 saw as many uncertainties as had been evident at the end of 1997. While signs of muted optimism began to emerge in Japan,[187] and, to a lesser extent, Thailand,[188] pessimistic views were also in evidence[189] – pessimism that also extended to the prospects of East and South-East Asia as a whole. [190] Moreover, the probable spread of the effects of the financial and economic crash to the rest of the world economy was seen to carry with it the danger of an economic downturn within both the United States of America and the European Union, despite mixed evidence from the financial[191] and industrial[192] sectors. The onset of economic difficulties within the major Advanced Industrial Countries was, however, prompting renewed fears of spreading protectionism.[193]

Analytical puzzles also continue to accompany uncertainties about the future course of events, however. Job losses in economies like that of the United Kingdom during the latter part of 1998 may owe as much to technological innovations as to the general effects of the East and South-East Asian economic and financial crisis. Such uncertainties, however, do not fully condition the pattern of political response to such increases in unemployment, as varying interpretations may evoke different popular responses and, hence, pressures upon political authorities.

The impact of the East and South-East Asian economic and financial crisis may also have dynamic implications for the future role and capability of states, particularly the richer and more economically advanced states. It is possible that the shock of the crisis will provoke a serious reassessment of the virtues of increasing internationalization and/or globalization and the neo-liberal philosophy upon which it has rested. Paradoxically, then, a phenomenon that reflects the degree of globalization in the international financial system might actually prompt responses that serve to constrain further internationalization and/or globalization in the future, at least in some areas of international and transnational economic transactions.

Notes

1 'Economic miracle or myth?', *The Economist*, 2 October 1993, pp. 73–4.

2 See the seminal study of Robert Wade, *Governing the Market: Economic Theory and the Role of Government in East Asian Industrialization* (Princeton, NJ: Princeton University Press, 1990); also Linda Weiss and John M. Hobson, *States and Economic Development: A Comparative Historical Analysis* (Cambridge: Polity Press, 1995).

3 For a sceptical discussion of this view see the report: 'Assembling the new economy', *The Economist*, 13 September 1997, pp. 105–11.

4 'Dollar next up for a roller coaster ride', *Guardian Weekly*, 13 December 1998, p. 14.

5 For a summary of Krugman's views, see: 'The miracle of the sausage-makers', *The Economist*, 9 December 1995, pp. 71–2.

6 'Indonesia's national car drives into controversy', *Financial Times*, 30 August 1996, p. 6; and 'Malaysia plans car export drive in Europe', *Financial Times*, 18 November 1996, p. 1.

7 'Asia's currency headache', *The Economist*, 19 August 1995, pp. 71–2.

8 'Web site', *The Economist*, 13 December 1997, p. 79.

9 See the survey: 'The house that Park built', *The Economist*, 3 June 1995, after p. 66.

10 'Those lovely chaebols and their little local difficulty', *The Economist*, 11 November 1995, pp. 101–2.

11 United Nations Conference on Trade and Development, *Handbook of International Trade and Development Statistics*, 1991 (New York: United Nations, 1992), Table 3.2, page 90.

12 *Ibid.*

13 See the report: 'Coping with capital', *The Economist*, 29 October 1994, p. 118.

14 'World trade slumps as Tigers flag', *The Guardian Weekly*, 20 April 1997, p. 5.

15 'Debt surge raises fears over Korea', *Financial Times*, 7 May 1997, p. 5.

16 'The baht spills over', *The Economist*, 24 May 1997, pp. 112–16.

17 'Scraply Islands', *The Economist*, 24 May 1997, pp. 85–6.

18 'Why is North Korea starving?', *The Economist*, 7 June 1997, pp. 75–6.

19 'Nightmare', *The Economist*, 21 June 1997, p. 75.

20 'Bailing and failing', *The Economist*, 28 June 1997, p. 88.

21 'Thawed up in knots', *The Economist*, 5 July 1997, pp. 97–8.

22 'What the doctor ordered', *The Economist*, 9 August 1997, pp. 52–3.

23 See: 'Lifebelts on', *The Economist*, 12 July 1997, pp. 82–5; and 'Unpegged', *The Economist*, 19 July 1997, pp. 58–9.

24 'More turbulence ahead', *The Economist*, 23 August 1997, pp. 62–3; and 'Too late for a gentle landing', *The Economist*, 6 September 1997, pp. 93–4.

25 'Asia's endangered tigers', *Financial Times*, 30/31 August, 1997, p. 6.

26 'Kia keels over', *The Economist*, 19 July 1997, pp. 67–8.

27 See the reports: 'An Asian pea-souper', *The Economist*, 27 September 1997, p. 82.

28 'When the smoke clears in Asia', *The Economist*, 4 October 1997, p. 85.

29 'Drought and smog hit SE Asian growth', *Financial Times*, 30 September 1997, p. 6; and 'A smouldering catastrophe', *Guardian Weekly*, 23 November 1997, p. 30.

30 'South Korea to nationalise carmarker Kia', *Financial Times*, 23 October 1997, p. 19.

31 'The giants stumble', *The Economist*, 18 October 1997, pp. 113–14.

32 'Safe harbour no more', *The Economist*, 25 October 1997, pp. 119–20.

33 'Asia's stock market nightmare', *The Economist*, 20 December 1997, pp. 127–8.

34 'No thanks IMF', *The Economist*, 1 November 197, pp. 81–2.

35 'S Korea pays for breaking cardinal rule', *Financial Times*, 30 December 1997, p. 11; and 'South Korea's meltdown', *The Economist*, 13 December 1997, p. 67.

36 'Kim fuels fears of debt default', *Financial Times*, 24 December 1997, p. 1.

37 See the report: 'Tokyo is the real problem', *Financial Times*, 17 November 1997, p. 16.

38 'Japan lets bank go to wall, gently', *Financial Times*, 18 November 1997, p. 8.

39 'And finally it came to tears', *The Economist*, 29 November 1997, pp. 109–11.

40 'Tokyo markets face a "death spiral"', *Financial Times*, 23 December 1997, p. 3.

41 On Taiwan see: 'The flexible tiger', *The Economist*, 3 January 1998, p. 73; and 'Chips on their shoulders', *The Economist*, 1 November 1997, pp. 86–9.

42 'Asian tigers catch a virus', *Financial Times*, 17 July 1997, p. 23.

43 See the reports: 'Dow posts largest ever one-day gain', 'Amsterdam and Paris surge more than 4%' and 'Nikkei rebounds, recapturing 18,000 point level', *Financial Times*, 3 September 1997.

44 'Amsterdam and Paris surge more than 4%', *Financial Times*, 3 September 1997.

45 'Nikkei rebounds, recapturing 18,000 point level', *Financial Times*, 3 September 1997.

46 'Hong Kong leads eastern rebound', *Financial Times*, 4 September 1997.

47 'Economic signals send Dow lower', *Financial Times*, 5 September, p. 35.

48 'Kuala Lumpur's 10-day fall reaches 21%', *Financial Times*, 5 September 1997, p. 35.

49 ' "Bloodbath" over HK$', *Financial Times*, 24 October 1997.

50 See the reports: 'World bourses slide on Hang Seng's woes', and 'Asian crisis sends Dow plummeting', *Financial Times*, 24 October 1997.

51 'Korean currency slide shakes economy', *Financial Times*, 12 November 1998.

52 See: 'Global markets can see a lot to worry about', *Financial Times*, 12 November 1998.

53 'Pick-up in Tokyo provides a tonic', *Financial Times*, 21 November 1998.

54 'Bulls propel Dow back above 7,800', *Financial Times*, 21 November 1998.

55 'Kuala Lumpur tumbles to five-year low', *Financial Times*, 21 November 1998.

56 'Banks "face years of losses and cuts" ', *Financial Times*, 25 November 1997, p. 10; and 'S. Korean shipbuilder in mass sackings', and 'Seoul warned on union anger', *Financial Times*, 27 November 1997, p. 6; and the survey article – 'Might Asia lose a decade?', *Financial Times*, 27 November 1998, p. 19.

57 'Bulls may keep the bears at bay again', *Financial Times*, 2 January 1998, p. 30.

58 'Asia picks up the pieces', *The Economist*, 3 January 1998, pp. 69–70.

59 'Asian crisis gains fresh impetus', *Financial Times*, 8 January 1998, p. 1.

60 'HK bank collapse hits markets', *Financial Times*, 13 January 1998, p. 1.

61 See: 'Export boom eludes "tiger" economies', *Financial Times*, 30 January 1998, p. 6.

62 'Crisis leaves carmakers running on empty', *Financial Times*, 4 February 1998, p. 26.

63 'Export boom eludes "tiger" economies'.

64 'Off the peg?', *The Economist*, 14 February 1998, p. 99.

65 'A fresh gale blowing east', *Financial Times*, 11 May 1998, p. 19.

66 'Indonesia shudders', *The Economist*, 9 May 1998, p. 79.

67 'Gone at last', *The Economist*, 23 May 1998, pp. 17–18.

68 'Economic turmoil in Asia halves exports', *Financial Times*, 30/31 May 1998, p. 5.

69 See the reports: 'The darkest hour comes just before the dawn', *The Economist*, 17 October 1998, pp. 117–19.

70 'Honeymoon turns sour in South Korea', *Guardian Weekly*, 18 October 1998, p. 18 – report reprinted from the *Washington Post*.

71 'Asia still haunted by weak fundamentals', *Financial Times*, 19 October 1998, p. 29.

72 'The bakers take cover', *The Economist*, 19 September 1998, pp. 109–13.

73 'Korean rebound may be short-lived', *Financial Times*, 26 October 1998.

74 See the reports: 'Worst of Asia's crisis may be over', and 'Hong Kong data deflate optimism', *Financial Times*, 24 November 1998, p. 6; 'Malaysia slips deeper into recession', *Financial Times*, 30 November 1998, p. 6; and 'Doubts cast a shadow over chaebol restructuring plans', *Financial Times*, 18 December 1998, p. 30.

75 On the 'contagion' see: R.K. McLeod and R. Garnaut (eds), *East Asia in Crisis: From Being a Miracle to Needing One?* (London: Routledge, 1998), esp. pp. 14–16, 271–7 and 362–4.

76 See the arguments of Michael Bordo, reviewed in: 'Is contagion a myth?', *The Economist*, 31 October 1998, p. 110.

77 See the report: 'A deal at last', *The Economist*, 17 October 1998, p. 127.

78 'A detour or derailment', *The Economist*, 22 August 1998, pp. 61–2.

79 'Emerging-market measles', *The Economist*, 22 August 1998, pp. 62–3; and the survey report: 'Asia's ripple effect', *Financial Times*, 2 July 1998, p. 25.

80 See: the reports in the *Financial Times* of 27 January 1998, p. 26.

81 *Ibid.*

82 'A boom ends?', *The Economist*, 17 January 1998, p. 72.

83 'ECGD expects a rise in claims from exporters hit by turmoil', *Financial Times*, 18 December 1998, p. 10.

84 'Banks' exposure starts coming into focus', *Financial Times*, 20 February 1998, p. 27.

85 'Long-term sickness?', *The Economist*, 3 October 1998, pp. 127–8.

86 On which see: 'Reform in the air', *The Economist*, 19 July 1997, pp. 59–60; and 'The long march to capitalism', *The Economist*, 13 September 1997, pp. 23–6.

87 See the Survey 'In praise of paranoia', *The Economist*, 7 November 1997, after p. 88.

88 See: Peter G. Warr, 'Thailand', in McLeod and Garnaut, *East Asia in Crisis*, pp. 49–65.

89 'What the doctor ordered', *The Economist*, 9 August 1997, pp. 52–3.

90 'First in, first out?', *Financial Times*, 25 February 1998, p. 14.

91 'Thailand to relax monetary policy', *Financial Times*, 28 May 1998, p. 4.

92 *Ibid.*

93 See: R.H. McLeod, 'Indonesia', in McLeod and Garnaut, *East Asia in Crisis*, pp. 31–48.

94 'No thanks, IMF', *The Economist*, 1 November 1997, pp. 81–2.

95 *Ibid.*

96 'Move on banks gets a mixed reception', *Financial Times*, 3 November 1997, p. 4.

97 'Jakarta pledge steadies markets', *Financial Times*, 13 January 1998, p. 5.

98 See the reports: 'Indonesia calls for "pause" over debt', *Financial Times*, 28 January 1998, p. 22; and 'Debt relief', *The Economist*, 31 January 1998, p. 74.

99 'Indonesian Chinese made scapegoat of crisis', *Guardian Weekly*, 1 February 1998, p. 5.

100 An idea that was considered in the case of Russia and its currency crisis later in 1998, see: 'By the board', *The Economist*, 5 September 1998, p. 94.

101 'Going by the board', *The Economist*, 14 February 1998, pp. 96–9; and 'The price of the prize', *Financial Times*, 12 February 1998, p. 13.

102 'Suharto's family values', *The Economist*, 14 March 1998, pp. 79–80.

103 'No credit', *The Economist*, 11 April 1998, p. 87.

104 'Java's uneasy riders', *The Economist*, 11 April 1998, p. 59.

105 'Fire sale brigade – Indonesia', *The Economist*, 14 November 1998, pp. 137–40.
106 See: Heather Smith, 'Korea', in McLeod and Garnaut, *East Asia in Crisis*, pp. 66–84.
107 'A fatal resolve not to budge', *The Economist*, 22 November 1997, pp. 119–20.
108 'A year of reckoning', *Financial Times*, 1 July 1998, p. 23.
109 'The chaebol in denial', *The Economist*, 24 January 1998, p. 80.
110 'A year of reckoning'.
111 'A last chance for Korea', *Financial Times*, 27 May 1998, p. 19.
112 *Ibid.*
113 *Ibid.*
114 'Chaebol fined for aiding weaker units', *Financial Times*, 30 July 1998, p. 6.
115 'Thinking small', *The Economist*, 14 November 1998, p. 108.
116 See: Prema-chandra Athukorala, 'Malaysia', in McLeod and Garnaut, *East Asia in Crisis*, pp. 85–101.
117 'Grand plans', *The Economist*, 11 May 1996, p. 76.
118 'Just do as the doctor says', *The Economist*, 27 June 1998, p. 77.
119 'Malaysia moves to cool economy', *Financial Times*, 18/19 October 1997, p. 3.
120 'The unwanted', *The Economist*, 28 March 1998, p. 75.
121 'No room for rivals in Mahathir's Malaysia', *The Economist*, 26 September 1998, pp. 81–2.
122 'Under control?', *The Economist*, 21 November 1998, p. 103.
123 'Malaysia prepares bank revamp', *Financial Times*, 19 October 1998, p. 28.
124 'Wrong lessons in Taiwan', *The Economist*, 25 April 1998, p. 102.
125 On Taiwan, see: Shirley W.Y. Kuo and Christina Y. Liu, 'Taiwan', in McLeod and Garnaut, *East Asia in Crisis*, pp. 179–88.
126 Yuk-shing Cheng, Wong Marn-beong and Chrisopher Findlay, 'Singapore and Hong-Kong', in McLeod and Garnaut, *East Asia in Crisis*, pp. 162–78.
127 'Singaporeans stick with government's social contact', *The Economist*, 27 November 1998, p. 7.
128 Cheng, Marn-beong and Findlay, 'Singapore and Hong-Kong'.
129 'A high-rise bust', *The Economist*, 27 June 1998, pp. 74–7.
130 See: Ponciano Intal Jr., Melanie Milo, Celia Reyes and Leilanie Basilio, 'The Philippines', in McLeod and Garnaut, *East Asia in Crisis*, pp. 145–61.

131 United Nations Conference on Trade and Development, *Handbook of International Trade and Development Statistics 1991* (New York: United Nations, 1992), Table 3.4.

132 'Waiting for Japan's typhoon to pass by', *The Economist*, 29 November 1997, p. 110.

133 'On the edge of the abyss again', *The Economist*, 11 January 1997, pp. 81–4.

134 See the report: 'Thud', *The Economist*, 16 August 1997, pp. 72–4.

135 See: World Bank, *World Development Report, 1995* (New York: Oxford University Press for the World Bank, 1995), Table 3, p. 167.

136 'On the brink of recession', *Financial Times*, 7 October 1997, p. 19.

137 'Japan lets bank go to wall, gently', *Financial Times*, 18 November 1997.

138 'Japan's bombshell explodes', *Financial Times*, 27 November 1998, p. 23.

139 See, for example, the report: 'Tokyo at odds over economic remedies', *Financial Times*, 15 October 1997.

140 'Bond issue at heart of effort to bolster financial system', *Financial Times*, 17 December 1997, p. 3.

141 'Japan gives the world a double surprise', *Financial Times*, 18 December 1997, p. 37.

142 'A man with yen', *The Economist*, 21 February 1998, pp. 78–9.

143 'Japan may urge common currency system for Asia', *Financial Times*, 21/22 February 1998, p. 4.

144 'Japan's top banks seek public funds', *Financial Times*, 5 March 1998, p. 34.

145 'Japan's car makers stall', *The Economist*, 21 March 1998, pp. 91–2.

146 'Triple blow hits Japanese electronics', *Financial Times*, 29 May 1998, p. 23.

147 'Total restructuring – without winners', and 'Pressure on Hashimoto to act', *Financial Times*, 19 June 1998, p. 2.

148 'Messing with money', *The Economist*, 25 July 1998, p. 96.

149 'Japanese bank bad debt burden soars', *Financial Times*, 18/19 July 1998, p. 4.

150 'Corporate Japan goes to waste', *The Economist*, 29 August 1998, pp. 63–4.

151 'Spend dammit!', *The Economist*, 10 October 1998, pp. 115–16.

152 'Happy Mondays: Japan's antidote to depression', *The Economist*, 6 October 1998, p. 1.

153 'Japan bank shares surge by 8.7%', *Financial Times*, 8 October 1998, p. 7.

154 *Ibid.*

155 See the interview with Michael Camdessus: 'Defending the Fund', *Financial Times*, 9 February, 1998, p. 17; and Stanley Fisher: 'IMF – the right stuff', *Financial Times*, 17 December 1997, p. 20; and 'Lessons from a crisis', *The Economist*, 3 October 1998, pp. 27–9.

156 On which see: 'No bargains for Korea this sale', *Guardian Weekly*, 11 January 1998, p. 12; and 'Washington shatters Asia's dreams', *Guardian Weekly*, 25 January 1998, p. 1; and George Soros, 'To avert the next crisis', *Financial Times*, 4 January 1999, p. 20.

157 'After Indonesia', *Financial Times*, 6 November 1997, p. 24.

158 'Bargains galore', *The Economist*, 7 February 1998, pp. 89–92.

159 'Asian water torture', *Financial Times*, 23 June 1998, p. 24.

160 See the discussion in: 'The IMF: one size doesn't fit all', *Guardian Weekly*, 12 July 1998, p. 14.

161 'Malaysian PM attacks the IMF and speculators', *Financial Times*, 1 September 1997, p. 20.

162 See: 'Seoul tries to avoid seeking IMF aid', *Financial Times*, 19 November 1997, p. 6.

163 'This is an unusual situation', *Financial Times*, 12 December 1997, p. 19.

164 'IMF shadow over South Korean poll', *Financial Times*, 18 December 1997, p. 6.

165 'Reform schedule in price of Korean Christmas rescue', and 'Banks start to roll over loans', *Financial Times*, 27/28 December 1997, p. 3.

166 'Strict conditions imposed on bail-out', *Financial Times*, 27/28 December 1997, p. 3.

167 'S. Korea rescue raises uncomfortable questions', *Financial Times*, 2 January 1998, p. 3.

168 *Ibid.*

169 *Ibid.*; and see also: 'Averting a global financial catastrophe was no holiday', *Financial Times*, 7 January 1998, p. 8.

170 'Still sick and gloomy, now rebellious', *The Economist*, 11 July 1998, pp. 71–2.

171 'A detour or derailment?', *The Economist*, 22 August 1998, pp. 61–2.

172 'Brazil heads for recession', *The Economist*, 15 November 1998, pp. 69–70.

173 'Brazil on borrowed time', *The Economist*, 8 November 1998, pp. 69–70.

174 'Under control', *The Economist*, 21 November 1998, p. 103.
175 See the Survey: 'Taiwan: in praise of paranoia', *The Economist*, 7 November 1998, after p. 88.
176 See the Survey: 'Ready to face the world?', *The Economist*, 8 March 1997, p. 70.
177 'China's coming recession', *The Economist*, 2 May 1998, p. 15.
178 'Beggars and choosers', *The Economist*, 6 December 1997, pp. 87–90.
179 $3.4 billion of emergency credit and $14.5 billion of additional core capital being granted in October 1998: 'A deal at last', *The Economist*, 17 October 1998, p. 127.
180 'Transparent hype', *The Economist*, 7 November 1998, p. 142.
181 *Ibid.*
182 'Could banks police each other?', *The Economist*, 17 October 1998, p. 128.
183 'Risky beyond measure', *The Economist*, 13 December 1997, pp. 98–101.
184 'IMF limitation thrown into relief', *Financial Times*, 18 January 1999, p. 4.
185 'Long-term sickness?', *The Economist*, 3 October 1998, pp. 127–31.
186 See, for instance, the article: 'Don't wait up', *The Economist*, 3 October 1998, pp. 131–4.
187 See: 'Upturn is likely in Japan next year, says top official', *Financial Times*, 28 December 1998, p. 16.
188 'The faltering front-runner', *The Economist*, 12 December 1998, p. 77.
189 'LDP brings Liberals on board', *Financial Times*, 21 December 1998, p. 3.
190 'Sustained recovery in Asia may have to wait', *Financial Times*, 28 December 1998, p. 32.
191 'Europe flies higher in face of low volumes', *Financial Times*, 22 December 1998, p. 38.
192 'Industry captains see economic gloom as key concern', *Financial Times*, 22 December 1998, p. 8.
193 'Cauldron bubble', *Financial Times*, 23 December 1998, p. 13.

11

Conclusions

This book has addressed a number of central questions about contemporary developments in the global system. The first set of questions concerned the issue of whether a general, and often loosely defined, term like 'globalization' is definitive of contemporary developments: an issue that opened up further questions about whether the world is witnessing a period of increasing internationalization, in a number of important areas of activity, rather than a qualitatively distinct experience of globalization; and the loosely related question of the actual extent of those conditions and developments that are, to some observers at least, definitive of globalization.

The second major set of questions then concerned the novelty and possible reversibility of the conditions and developments commonly associated with globalization. Such questions invited comparisons between contemporary developments and those that characterized earlier periods of development within the international political economy – particularly that around the end of the nineteenth century and the start of the twentieth. They also required consideration of the conditions that might lead to the reversal of the contemporary path towards increasing internationalization and/ or globalization.

Methodologically, such core questions about globalization, its reality, extent and prospects, encounter fundamental issues of quantity versus quality; of whether a range of developments, which can be represented as discrete quantitative data, justify claims about the emergence of qualitatively novel conditions. Such issues, in turn, shade into methodological disputes between atomists and holists.[1]

Substantively, the core questions about globalization impact directly upon the issue of the state in the contemporary global political economy. Many vocal observers of contemporary developments have seen in the coming of globalization the effective demise of the state. Should globalization mark the coming of an age in which the unconstrained world market ushered in an era of benign interdependence, then much of the traditional role of the state as a defence against external aggression would dissolve in the new world of peace and harmony. Should globalization undermine the state's capacity for effective economic and industrial policy, then the state's more recent role within the domestic economy would also decline and ultimately dissolve. Should, moreover, populations turn to the market for an increasing range of provisions – in health, general care, personal security and education – as some free-market enthusiasts would recommend, then many of the non-economic functions of the state would also be minimized.

The more extreme visions of a globalized world, and its effects upon the 'traditional' state, turn, however, upon interpretations of the nature of globalization, the character of contemporary developments and the continuing role of the state. These arguments warrant a further brief summary.

The nature of globalization

The basic question confronting the idea of globalization is whether it can be differentiated from the mere increase of internationalization within the international system. The answer to this question involves quantitative evidence and qualitative judgements about the distinctive character of developments during the latter part of the twentieth century: particularly the arrival of the new information technology, improvements in long-distance transport and communication and structural changes in the economic and financial system. Such developments combine, in the eyes of 'strong globalization' theorists to introduce a world, not necessarily of universal homogeneity, but of unprecedented 'space and time compression'. Such a new world, moreover, is one that fundamentally challenges the role and capabilities of states.

Supporters of the 'weak globalization' view accept the salience of many of the developments emphasized by 'strong globalization' theorists and acknowledge their significant implications for contemporary economics and politics, particularly the weakening of effect of many of the 'traditional' instruments of economic policy.

'Weak globalizationists' are less sure, however, of a qualitative change in human affairs, are impressed by historical parallels, particularly from the end of the nineteenth century and the start of the twentieth, and are convinced, therefore, that recent developments are far from irreversible. The state may, moreover, be challenged in a number of important respects by recent developments, but remains central to the well-being of its citizens and to the proper management of economic developments, and is, paradoxically, essential to many of the conditions upon which increasing internationalization and/or globalization has depended and continues to depend.

Globalization and the future of the state

Increasing internationalization and/or globalization does confront established states with serious challenges. Global financial integration without corresponding structures of effective public governance threatens the kind of instability and general damage witnessed in the East and South-East Asian financial and economic crisis of the late 1990s. The activities of transnational corporations can also threaten economic and social stability where they are not subject to sufficient controls upon their investment decisions, their production and marketing strategies and their financial manipulations. A poorly regulated global system is also prey to the activities of a wide range of criminal organizations, terroristic organizations and associations of zealous enthusiasts for a myriad of causes.

The general problem remains that of maintaining effective structures of public governance in a world in which the traditional state is placed under increasing pressure. However, the need to supply collective goods, to manage significant externalities and to provide for minority needs will persist even in a world of increased internationalization and/or globalization. If established states falter and no new global institutions of effective public governance emerge, then such functions of government will either fail to be fulfilled or will be undertaken by private organizations and associations. Unfortunately, such private arrangements are generally compromised by partiality of interest, insufficiency of resources and a general lack of legitimacy. Democracy will, in particular, be a major victim of any privatization of public governance.

The privatization of public governance would, however, be compatible with a number of the more dystopian visions of the future that have become popular during the late twentieth century. Growing divisions between the rich 'North' and the ever-poorer 'South' reflect one face of a world of growing partiality of perspective and self-interest in public governance. The emergence of 'world cities' might amplify such a prospect and compound it by adding more local patterns of stratification – between city and countryside, between elite groups and marginal dwellers, and between the technologically attuned and the technologically deprived – to the growing world division of well-being. The antagonistic world associated with such prospects approaches a malign version of a 'new medievalism' or, at its extreme, a descent into acute fragmentation, disorder and anarchy, more reminiscent of the 'Dark Ages'.

The possibility persists, however, of the reinvigoration of the state in the face of the problems and pressures generated by increasing internationalization and/or globalization. Such reinvigoration might assume a simple form, as the citizens of the more robust states demand the restoration of control over worrying aspects of economic and social life. Such reinvigoration might also take a dramatic course if the effects of increasing internationalization and/or globalization prove to be such as to precipitate the effective breakdown of cohesion in societies that then generate authoritarian, and possibly aggressive, movements and leaders, as the possibilities in Russia continue to warn.

Reinvigoration might also assume a more complex form in the enhanced role of states in the creation and maintenance of a multi-layered structure of governance, local, regional and global. New regional entities like the European Union might form a critical component of such a new structure or might, in contrast, form the basis of new, geographically defined, alternatives to the state. Whatever the pattern, simple notions of sovereignty that informed the state during its ascendancy over the last two to three centuries might be complicated and compromised by such developments, but exchanged willingly for the peaceful re-establishment of suitable levels of control over critical aspects of the world's financial, economic, and criminal systems. Enhanced roles for agencies like the International Monetary Fund, the Bank for International Settlements and the Basle Committee on Bank Supervision, in addition to a range of rather less visible intergovernmental agencies in the areas of security and transnational policing, might mark a first step towards the emergence of such a complex, multi-layered structure of public global governance.

The onset of the Asian financial and economic crisis in 1997 demonstrated many of the consequences and dangers of a world of increasing internationalization and/or globalization. The spread of the crisis reflected the impact of modern technologies, and its scale reflected the extent and scale of financial integration within the international system. Serious crises have, however, afflicted the world economy many times before and spread widely at an unsettling speed. The crisis has not, therefore, entirely resolved the debate between 'strong' and 'weak' globalizationists. Future responses to the crisis will, however, prove particularly interesting for those engaged in this debate. The emergence of new structures of global financial governance might support 'strong globalizationists'. If the activities of a small number of critical states prove to be central to the future management of the international financial system, this will, however, lend credence to the views of 'weak globalizationists' (or even rejectionists). A failure to bring the global financial system under control and any recurrence of world-wide financial and economic crises will leave the question unresolved and the future open to many of the more malign developments so favoured by dystopian visionaries. Indeed it is also difficult to envisage any agency other than the state, or its functional equivalent, acting individually or in concert with others, capable of confronting the growing danger of cyber-warfare.

The possible 'withering away of the state' in the face of a world of increasing internationalization and/or globalization is not, therefore, a matter to be assumed *a priori* or to be taken lightly if it comes to pass. Developments, both past and present, are far more complicated than they are often presented as being in some of the less critical literature on globalization. The state has played a central role in most of the major developments that have shaped the lives of those living at the end of the twentieth century and the start of the twenty-first. The state also remains the major agency of public governance and the major guarantor of a range of vital requirements for its citizens. Equanimity in the face of its possible dissolution would be warranted, therefore, only in the presence of robust alternatives or considerable confidence in their imminent emergence.

Note

1 For a further discussion of which see: R.J. Barry Jones and Peter Willetts, 'Introduction', in R.J. Barry Jones and Peter Willetts, *Interdependence on Trial: Studies in the Theory and Reality of Contemporary Interdependence* (London: Frances Pinter, 1984), pp. 1–16; and R.J. Barry Jones 'The definition and identification of interdependence', in Jones and Willetts, *Interdependence on Trial*, pp. 17–63, esp. pp. 30–3.

Select bibliography

Agnew, J.A. and S. Corbridge (1995) *Mastering Space: Hegemony, Territory and International Political Economy*, London: Routledge.

Albrow, Martin (1996) *The Global Age*, Cambridge: Polity Press.

Altvater, Elmar and Birgit Mahnkopf (1997) 'The world market unbound', *Review of International Political Economy*, vol. 4, no. 3 (Autumn), pp. 448–71.

Anderson, Malcolm (1996) *Frontiers: Territory and State Formation in the Modern World*, Cambridge: Polity Press.

Angell, N. (1909) *The Great Illusion: A Study in the Relation of Military Power in Nations to their Economic and Social Advantage*, London: Weidenfeld and Nicolson and New York: Putnam.

Armstrong, David (1998) 'Globalisation and the Social State', *Review of International Studies*, vol. 24, no. 4 (October), pp. 461–78.

Ashley, Richard K. (1984) 'The Poverty of Neorealism', *International Organization*, vol. 38, no. 2 (Spring), pp. 225–61.

Axford, Barrie (1995) *The Global System: Economics, Politics and Culture*, Cambridge: Polity Press.

Axtmann, Roland (1998) *Globalization and Europe: Theoretical and Empirical Investigations*, London: Pinter.

Bailey, P., A. Parisotto and G. Renshaw (eds) (1993) *Multinationals and Employment: The Global Economy of the 1990s*, Geneva: International Labour Office.

Baldwin, David (1980) 'Interdependence and power: a conceptual analysis', *International Organization*, vol. 34, no. 3 (Summer), pp. 471–506.

Baran, P. (1957) *The Political Economy of Growth*, New York: Monthly Review Press.

Berger, Suzanne and Ronald Dore (eds) (1996) *National Diversity and Global Capitalism*, Ithaca, NY: Cornell University Press.

Boyer, R. and D. Drache (eds) (1996) *States Against Markets: The Limits of Globalization*, London: Routledge.

Bramstead, E.K. and K.J. Melhuish (1978) *Western Liberalism: A History in Documents from Locke to Croce*, London: Longman.

Brenner, Neil (1998) 'Global cities, glocal states: global city formation and state territorial restructuring in contemporary Europe', *Review of International Political Economy*, vol. 5, no. 1 (Spring), pp. 1–37.

Briggs, Asa and Daniel Snowman (1996) *Fins De Siècle: How Centuries End 1400–2000*, New Haven, CT and London: Yale University Press.

Bryan, L. and D. Farrell (1996) *Market Unbound: Unleashing Global Capitalism*, New York: John Wiley and Sons.

Bull, Hedley (1977) *The Anarchical Society: A Study of Order in World Politics*, London: Macmillan.

Bull, H. and A. Watson (eds) (1984) *The Expansion of International Society*, Oxford: Clarendon Press.

Buzan, Barry (1993) 'From international system to international society: structural realism and regime theory meet the English School', *International Organization*, vol. 47, no. 3, pp. 327–52.

Cable, Vincent (1994) *The World's New Fissures: Identities in Crisis*, London: Demos.

Cairncross, Frances (1997) *The Death of Distance: How the Communications Revolution Will Change Our Lives*, London: Orion Business Books.

Carter, April (1971) *The Political Theory of Anarchism*, London: Routledge and Kegan Paul.

Casson, Mark (1983) *The Growth of International Business*, London: George Allen and Unwin.

Casson, Mark (ed.) (1992) *International Business and Global Integration: Empirical Studies*, Houndmills: Macmillan.

Castells, Manuel (1989) *The Informational City: Information Technology, Economic Restructuring and the Urban-Regional Process*, Oxford: Basil Blackwell.

Castells, Manuel (1996) *The Rise of the Network Society*, Malden, MA and Oxford: Blackwell Publishers.

Cerny, P.G. (ed.) (1993) *Finance and World Politics: Markets, Regimes and States in the Post-hegemonic Era*, Aldershot: Edward Elgar.

Chin, Christine B.N. and James H. Mittelman (1997) 'Conceptualising resistance to globalization', *New Political Economy*, vol. 2, no. 1 (March), pp. 25–37.

Cho, George (1995) *Trade, Aid and Global Interdependence*, London: Routledge.

Clark, Ian (1997) *Globalization and Fragmentation: International Relations in the Twentieth Century*, Oxford: Oxford University Press.

Clark, Ian (1998) 'Beyond the Great Divide: globalization and the theory of international relations', *Review of International Studies*, vol. 24, no. 4 (October), pp. 479–98.

Coleman, D.C. (ed.) (1969) *Revision in Mercantilism*, London: Methuen.

Coleman, William D. and Geoffrey R.D. Underhill (1998) *Regionalism and Global Economic Integration*, London: Routledge.

Commission on Global Governance (1995) *Our Global Neighbourhood*, Oxford: Oxford University Press.

Connors, Michael (1997) *The Race to the Intelligent State*, Oxford: Capstone.

Cooper, Richard N. (1968) *The Economics of Interdependence*, New York: McGraw-Hill.

Cooper, Richard N. (1986) *Economic Policy in an Interdependent World*, Cambridge, MA: The MIT Press.

Courchene, Thomas J. (ed.), *The Nation State in a Global/Information Era: Policy Challenges*, Kingston, Ontario: John Deutsch Institute for the Study of Economic Policy.

Cox, Kevin R. (ed.) (1997) *Spaces of Globalization: Reasserting the Power of the Local*, New York: The Guildford Press.

Cox, R.W. (1978) *Production, Power and World Order: Social Forces in the Making of History*, New York: Columbia University Press.

Cox, R.W., with T.J. Sinclair (1996) *Approaches to World Order*, Cambridge: Cambridge University Press.

Cutler, Claire A. (1995) 'Global capitalism and liberal myths: dispute settlement in private international trade relations', *Millennium – Journal of International Studies*, vol. 24, no. 3 (Winter), pp. 377–97.

Desai, Meghnad and Paul Redfern (1995) *Global Governance: Ethics and Economics of World Order*, London: Pinter.

Deutsch, Karl W., *et al.* (1957) *Political Community and the North Atlantic Area*, Princeton, NJ: Princeton University Press.

Dombrowski, Peter (1998) 'Haute finance and high theory: recent scholarship on global financial relations', *Mershon International Studies Review*, vol. 42 supplement 1 (May), pp. 1–28.

Dunning, J.H. (1981) *International Production and the Multinational Enterprise*, London: George Allen and Unwin.

Dunning, J.H. (1993) *The Globalization of Business: The Challenges of the 1990s*, London: Routledge.

Dunning, J.H. (ed.) (1997) *Governments, Globalization and International Business*, Oxford: Oxford University Press.

Edwards, G. and E. Regelsberger (1990) *Europe's Global Links: The European Community and Inter-Regional Cooperation*, London: Pinter Publishers.

Environment and Planning A, special section *On the nation-state, the global and social science* (1996), vol. 28, pp. 1917–28, with contributions by: P.J. Taylor, J. Agnew, A. Gamble, U. Hannerz, G.M. Hodgson, R.J. Johnston, R.J. Barry Jones, A.D. King, A.D. Mann, J.A. Scholte, L. Sklair, J. Tomlinson and J. Urry.

Evans, Peter (1995) *Embedded Autonomy: States and Industrial Transformation*, Princeton, NJ: Princeton University Press.

Fawcett, Louise and Andrew Hurrell (eds) (1995) *Regionalism in World Politics*, Oxford: Oxford University Press.

Ferguson, Niall (1998) *The World's Banker, The History of the House of Rothschild*, London: Weidenfeld and Nicolson.

Ferguson, Yale H. and Richard W. Mansbach (1989) *The State, Conceptual Chaos, and the Future of International Relations Theory*, Boulder, CO: Lynne Rienner.

Ferguson, Yale H. and Richard W. Mansbach (1996) *Polities: Authority, Identities and Change*, Columbia, SC: University of South Carolina Press.

Fieldhouse, D.K. (1965) *The Colonial Empires: A Comparative Survey from the Eighteenth Century*, London: Weidenfeld and Nicolson.

Financial Times, Surveys of the World Economy and Finance, 27 September 1996; 19 September 1997; and 2 October 1998.

Foreman-Peck, James (ed.) (1998) *Historical Foundations of Globalization*, Cheltenham, Glos.: Edward Elgar.

Frank, Andre Gunder (1975) *On Capitalist Underdevelopment*, Bombay: Oxford University Press.

Frank, Andre Gunder (1978) *Dependent Accumulation and Underdevelopment*, London: Macmillan.

Frohlich, N. and J.A. Oppenheimer (1978) *Modern Political Economy*, Englewood Cliffs, NJ: Prentice-Hall.

Frohlich, N., J.A. Oppenheimer and O.R. Young (1971) *Political Leadership and Collective Goods*, Princeton, NJ: Princeton University Press.

Fukuyama, Francis (1992) *The End of History and the Last Man*, London: Hamish Hamilton.

Galbraith, J.K. (1977) *The Age of Uncertainty*, London: BBC/Andre Deutsch.

Gamble, A. and A. Payne (1996) *Regionalism and World Order*, London: Macmillan.

Germain, R. (1997) *The International Organization of Credit: States and Global Finance in the World Economy*, Cambridge: Cambridge University Press.

Germain, R. (2000) *Globalisation and its Critics: Perspectives from International Political Economy*, London: Macmillan.

Giddens, Anthony (1984) *The Constitution of Society: Outline of the Theory of Structuration*, Cambridge: Polity Press.

Gill, Stephen (1991) *American Hegemony and the Trilateral Commission*, Cambridge: Cambridge University Press.

Gill, Stephen (1995) 'Globalisation, market civilisation, and disciplinary neoliberalism', *Millennium: Journal of International Studies*, vol. 24, no. 3 (Winter), pp. 399–423.

Gill, Stephen and D. Law (1988) *The Global Political Economy: Perspectives, Problems and Policies*, London: Harvester/Wheatsheaf.

Gills, Barry K. (ed.) (1997) *Globalisation and the Politics of Resistance*, special edition of *New Political Economy*, vol. 2, no. 1 (March).

Gilpin, R. (1975) *US Power and the Multinational Corporation: The Political Economy of Direct Investment*, New York: Macmillan.

Gilpin, R. (1987) *The Political Economy of International Relations*, Princeton, NJ: Princeton University Press.

Goldsmith, James (1994) *The Trap*, London: Macmillan.

Goldsmith, James (1995) *The Response: GATT and Global Free Trade*, London: Macmillan.

Gray, John (1998) *False Dawn: The Delusions of Global Capitalism*, London: Granta Books.

Greedier, William (1997) *One World Ready or Not: The Manic Logic of Global Capitalism*, Harmondsworth: Allen Lane, The Penguin Press.

Groom, A.J.R. and P. Taylor (eds) (1975) *Functionalism: Theory and Practice in International Relations*, London: University of London Press.

Hampden-Turner, C. and F. Trompenaars (1993) *The Seven Cultures of Capitalism: Value Systems for Creating Wealth in the United States, Britain, Japan, Germany, France, Sweden and the Netherlands*, New York: Doubleday.

Harvey, David (1989) *The Condition of Postmodernity*, Oxford: Basil Blackwell.

Held, D. (1995) *Global Democracy*, Cambridge: Polity Press.

Held, D. (1995) *Democracy and the Global Order: From the Modern State to Cosmopolitan Governance*, Cambridge: Polity Press.

Held, D. (1996) *Models of Democracy*, 2nd edn, Cambridge: Polity Press.

Held, D., A. McGrew, D. Goldblatt and J. Perraton (1999) *Global Transformations*, Cambridge: Polity Press.

Herman, Edward S. and Robert W. McChesney (1997) *The Global Media: The New Missionaries of Corporate Capitalism*, London: Cassell.

Hirst, Paul (1997) 'The global economy – myths and realities', *International Affairs*, vol. 73, no. 3 (July), pp. 409–25.

Hirst, P. and G. Thomson (1996) *Globalization in Question: The International Economy and the Possibilities of Governance*, Cambridge: Polity Press.

Hoekman, Bernard and Michel Kostecki (1995) *The Political Economy of the World Trading System: From GATT to WTO*, Oxford: Oxford University Press.

Holton, Robert J. (1998) *Globalization and the Nation-State*, Houndmills: Macmillan.

Hoogvelt, Ankie (1997) *Globalisation and the Post-colonial World: The New Political Economy of Development*, Houndmills: Macmillan.

Howard, F.M.C. and J.E. King (1975) *The Political Economy of Marx*, Harlow: Longman.

Huntingdon, Samuel P. (1993) 'The clash of civilizations?', *Foreign Affairs*, vol. 72, no. 3 (Summer), pp. 22–49.

Huntington, Samuel P. (1996) *The Clash of Civilizations and the Remaking of the World Order*, New York: Simon and Schuster.

Hurrell, Andrew (1994) 'A crisis of ecological viability? Global environmental change and the nation state', *Political Studies*, special issue 1994: *Contemporary Crisis of the Nation State?* vol. 42, pp. 146–65.

Hurrell, A. and N. Woods (1995) 'Globalisation and inequality', *Millennium: Journal of International Studies*, vol. 24, no. 3 (Winter), pp. 447–70.

Hutton, Will (1995) *The State We're In*, London: Jonathan Cape.

Hutton, Will (1997) *The State To Come*, London: Vintage Books.

Johnson, H.G. (ed.) (1974) *The New Mercantilism: Some Problems in International Trade Money and Investment*, Oxford: Basil Blackwell.

Johnson, H.J. (1975) *Technology and Economic Interdependence*, London: Macmillan.

Jones, R.J. Barry (1984) The definition and identification of interdependence, in R.J. Barry Jones and Peter Willetts (eds), *Interdependence on Trial: Studies in the Theory and Reality of Contemporary Interdependence*, London: Frances Pinter.

Jones, R.J. Barry (1986) *Conflict and Control in the World Economy: Contemporary Economic Realism and Neo-Mercantilism*, Brighton: Harvester/Wheatsheaf.

Jones, R.J. Barry (1991) *Anti-Statism as a Critical Disposition in International Relations*, Reading: Reading Papers in Politics.

Jones, R.J. Barry (1995) *Globalisation and Interdependence in the International Political Economy: Rhetoric and Reality*, London: Pinter Publishers.

Jones, R.J. Barry (1996) 'Social Science, globalisation and the problem of the state', *Environment and Planning A*, vol. 28, no. 11 (November), pp. 1948–53.

Jones, R.J. Barry (1999) 'Globalization and change in the international political economy', *International Affairs*, vol. 75, no. 2, pp. 357–67.

Jones, R.J. Barry and Peter Willetts (1984) *Interdependence on Trial: Studies in the Theory and Reality of Contemporary Interdependence*, London: Frances Pinter.

Kapstein, Ethen B. (1994) *Governing the Global Economy: International Finance and the State*, Cambridge, MA: Harvard University Press.

Kegley jr., C.W. (ed.) (1995) *Controversies in International Relations Theory: Realism and the Neoliberal Challenge*, New York: St Martin's Press.

Keil, Roger (1998) 'Globalization makes states: perspectives of local governance in the age of the world city', *Review of International Political Economy*, vol. 5, no. 4 (Winter), pp. 616–46.

Kenen, Peter B. (ed.) (1994) *Managing the World Economy: Fifty Years After Bretton Woods*, Washington DC: Institute for International Economics.

Kennedy, Paul (1988) *The Rise and Fall of the Great Powers: Economic Change and Military Conflict from 1500 to 2000*, New York: Random House.

Kennedy, Paul (1989) *The Rise and Fall of the Great Powers*, London: Fontana Papertacks.

Keohane, Robert O. (1984) *After Hegemony: Cooperation and Discord in the World Political Economy*, Princeton, NJ: Princeton University Press.

Keohane, Robert O. and Helen V. Milner (1996) *Internationalization and Domestic Politics*, Cambridge: Cambridge University Press.

Keohane, Robert O. and Joseph S. Nye (1971) *Transnational Relations and World Politics*, Cambridge, MA: Harvard University Press. (Reprint of a special edition of *International Organization*, vol. 25, no. 3 (Summer 1971).)

Keohane, Robert O. and Joseph S. Nye (1987) '*Power and Interdependence* revisited', *International Organisation*, vol. 41, no. 4 (Autumn).

Keohane, Robert O. and Joseph S. Nye (1977) *Power and Interdependence: World Politics in Transition*, Boston: Little, Brown.

Kidron, M. (1968) *Western Capitalism since the War*, London: Weidenfeld and Nicolson.

Kindleberger, C.P. (1996) *Manias, Panics and Crashes: A History of Financial Crises*, 3rd edn, New York: Wiley.

Knox, Paul L. and Peter J. Taylor (1995) *World Cities in a World System*, Cambridge: Cambridge University Press.

Kofman, Eleonore and Gillian Youngs (1996) *Globalization: Theory and Practice*, London: Pinter.

Krasner, S. (1983) *International Regimes*, Ithaca, NY: Cornell University Press.

Krasner, S. (1985) *Structural Conflict: The Third World Against Global Liberalism*, Berkeley, CA: University of California Press.

Lawrence, Robert Z., Albert Bressand and Ito Takatoshi (1996) *A Vision for the World Economy: Openness, Diversity and Cohesion*, Washington DC: The Brookings Institute.

Lenin, V.I. (1916) *Imperialism: The Highest Stage of Capitalism*, Petrograd – various editions.

Lens, S. (1971) *The Military–Industrial Complex*, London: Stanmore Press.

Lever, H. and C. Huhne (1985) *Debt and Danger: The World Financial Crisis*, Harmondsworth: Penguin Books.

Loxley, John (1998) *Interdependence, Disequilibrium and Growth: Reflections on the Political Economy of North–South Relations at the Turn of the Century*, Basingstoke: Macmillan.

McLeod, R.K. and R. Garnaut (eds) (1998) *East Asia in Crisis: From Being a Miracle to Needing One?*, London: Routledge.

Mann, Michael (1986) *The Sources of Social Power, Vol. 1, A History of Power from the Beginning to A.D. 1760*, Cambridge: Cambridge University Press.

Mann, Michael (1997) Has globalization ended the rise of the nation-state? Review of *International Political Economy*, vol. 4, no. 3 (Autumn), pp. 472–96.

Mansbach, R.W., Y.H. Ferguson and D.E. Lampert (1976) *The Web of World Politics: Nonstate Actors in the Global System*, Englewood Cliffs, NJ: Prentice-Hall.

Milivojevic, Marko (1985) *The Debt Rescheduling Process*, London: Frances Pinter.

Mitchell, B.R. (1973) Statistical appendix, in C.M. Cipolla (ed.), *The Fontana Economic History of Europe: The Emergence of Industrial Societies – Part 2*, London: Fontana Books.

Mitrany, David (1966) *A Working Peace System*, Chicago, IL: Quadrangle Bolos.

Mitrany, David (1994) *The Road to Security*, London: National Peace Council.

Mittelman, James H. (ed.) (1997) *Globalization: Critical Reflections*, Boulder, CO: Lynne Rienner.

Modelski, George and William R. Thompson (1996) *Leading Sectors and World Powers: The Coevolution of Global Economics and Politics*, Columbia, SC: University of South Carolina Press.

Moravcsik, Andrew (1991) 'Negotiating the Single European Act', *International Organization*, vol. 45, no. 1, pp. 19–56.

Moravcsik, Andrew (1993) 'Preferences and power in the European Community: a liberal intergovernmentalist approach', *Journal of Common Market Studies*, vol. 31, no. 4 (December), pp. 473–524.

Morgenthau, Hans J. (1946) *Politics among Nation: The Struggle for Power and Peace*, New York: Alfred Knopf.

Murray, Robin (1981) *Multinationals Beyond the Market*, Brighton: Harvester.

Nkrumah, K. (1965) *Neo-Colonialism: The Last Stage of Imperialism*, London: Heinemann.

O'Brien, Richard (1992) *Global Financial Integration: The End of Geography*, London: RIIA/Pinter Publishers.

Odell, Peter (1974) *Oil and World Power: Background to the Oil Crisis*, 3rd edn, Harmondsworth: Penguin Books.

Ohmae, Kenichi (ed.) (1985) *The Evolving Global Economy: Making Sense of the New World Order*, Boston, MA: Harvard Business School.

Ohmae, Kenichi (1995) *The End of the Nation State: The Rise of Regional Economies*, New York: Free Press.

Palan, Ronen (1998) 'Trying to have your cake and eat it: how the state system created Offshore', *International Studies Quarterly*, vol. 42, no. 4 (December), pp. 625–43.

Palan, Robert and Jason Abbot, with Phil Deans (1996) *State Strategies in the Global Political Economy,* London: Pinter Publishers.

Parry, Geraint (ed.) (1994) *Politics in an Interdependent World*, Aldershot: Edward Elgar.

Porter, Michael (1990) *The Competitive Advantages of Nations*, Houndmills: Macmillan.

Przeworski, Adam, *et al.* (1995) *Sustainable Democracy*, Cambridge: Cambridge University Press.

Rhodes, R.A.W. (1996) 'The new governance: governing without government', *Political Studies*, vol. 44, pp. 652–67.

Richards, J.H. (1970) *International Economic Institutions*, London and New York: Holt Rinehart and Winston.

Rittberger, V. (ed.) (1993) *Regime Theory and International Relations*, Oxford: Oxford University Press.

Roberson, Barbara (ed.) (1998) *International Society and the Development of International Relations Theory*, London: Pinter.

Rosenau, James N. (1990) *Turbulence in World Politics: A Theory of Change and Continuity*, Hemel Hempstead: Harvester Wheatsheaf.

Rosenau, J.N. and E.O. Czempiel (1992) *Governance without Government: Order and Change in World Politics*, Cambridge: Cambridge University Press.

Ruggie, John Gerrard (1998) *Constructing the World Polity: Essays on International Institutionalization*, London: Routledge.

Ruigrok, W. and R. Van Tulder (1995) *The Logic of International Restructuring*, London: Routledge.

Sassen, Saskia (1991) *The Global City*, Princeton, NJ: Princeton University Press.

Sen, Gautam (1984) *The Military Origins of Industrialisation and International Trade Rivalry*, London: Frances Pinter.

Scholte, Jan Aart (1997) 'Global Capitalism and the State', *International Affairs*, vol. 73, no. 3 (July), pp. 427–52.

Schumpeter, J.A. (1976) *Capitalism, Socialism, and Democracy*, 5th edn, London: George Allen and Unwin.

Shatz, Marshall S. (ed.) (1971) *The Essential Works of Anarchism*, New York: Bantam Books.

Shaw, Martin (1994) *Global Society and International Relations: Sociological Concepts and Political Perspectives*, Cambridge: Polity Press.

Sklair, Leslie (1997) 'Social movements for global capitalism: the transnational capitalist class in action', *Review of International Political Economy*, vol. 4, no. 3 (Autumn), pp. 514–38.

Soros, George (1998) *The Crisis of Global Capitalism: Open Society Endangered*, London: Little, Brown and Company (UK).

Spero, J.E. and J.A. Hart (1997) *The Politics of International Economic Relations*, 5th edn, London: Routledge.

Sprout, H. and M. (1965) *The Ecological Perspective on Human Affairs, with Special Reference to International Politics*, Princeton, NJ: Princeton University Press.

Stallings, Barbara (ed.) (1995) *Global Change, Regional Response: The New International Context of Development*, Cambridge: Cambridge University Press.

Stone, N. (1983) *Europe Transformed 1878–1919*, London: Fontana.

Strange, Susan (1986) *Casino Capitalism*, Oxford: Basil Blackwell; republished by Manchester University Press (Manchester, 1997).

Strange, Susan (1988) *States and Markets: An Introduction to International Political Economy*, London: Pinter Publishers.

Strange, Susan (1996) *The Retreat of the State*, Cambridge: Cambridge University Press.

Strange, Susan (1998) *Mad Money*, Manchester: Manchester University Press.

Swank, Duane (1998) 'Funding the welfare state: globalization and the taxation of business in advanced market economies', *Political Studies*, vol. 46, no. 4 (September), pp. 671–92.

Tetreault, Mary Ann (1980) 'Measuring interdependence', *International Organization*, vol. 34, no. 3 (Summer), pp. 429–516.

Thurow, Lester (1997) *The Future of Capitalism*, London: Nicholas Brealey.

Trebilcock, M.J. and R. Howse (1995) *The Regulation of International Trade*, London: Routledge.

Tucker, Robert W. (1977) *The Inequality of Nations*, New York: Basic Books.

United Nations Conference on Trade and Development Report (1996) *Globalization and Liberalization: Development in the Face of Two Powerful Currents*, New York and Geneva: United Nations.

Vernon, Raymond (1971) *Sovereignty at Bay*, New York: Basic Books.

Vogler, J. and M.F. Imber (1996) *The Environment and International Relations*, London: Routledge.

Wade, Robert (1990) *Governing the Market: Economic Theory and the Role of Government in East Asian Industrialization*, Princeton, NJ: Princeton University Press.

Wallerstein, Immanuel (1979) *The Capitalist World-Economy*, Cambridge: Cambridge University Press.

Walter A. (1991) *World Power and World Money: The Role of Hegemony and International Monetary Order*, Hemel Hempstead: Harvester/Wheatsheaf.

Walzer, Michael (ed.) (1995) *Toward a Global Civil Society*, Providence, RI and Oxford: Berghahn Books.

Waters, Malcolm (1995) *Globalization*, London: Routledge.

Weiss, Linda (1998) *The Myth of the Powerless State: Governing the Economy in a Global Era*, Cambridge: Polity Press.

Weiss, Linda and John M. Hobson (1995) *States and Economic Development: A Comparative Historical Analysis*, Cambridge: Polity Press.

Woodcock, George (1962) *Anarchism*, Harmondsworth: Penguin Books.

Woodis, Jack (1967) *An Introduction to Neo-Colonialism*, London: Lawrence and Wishart.

Woodruff, William (1971) The emergence of an international economy, 1700–1914, in C.M. Cipolla (ed.), *The Fontana Economic History of Europe*, vol. 4, London: Fontana Books.

World Bank (1997) *World Development Report 1997*, New York: Oxford University Press for the World Bank.

Yergin, Daniel (1991) *The Prize: The Epic Quest for Oil, Money and Power*, New York: Simon and Schuster.

Yergin, Daniel and Joseph Stanislaw (1998) *The Commanding Heights: The Battle Between Government and the Marketplace That Is Remaking the Modern World*, New York: Simon and Schuster.

Zacher, Mark W., with Brent A. Sutton (1996) *Governing Global Networks: International Regimes for Transportation and Communications*, Cambridge: Cambridge University Press.

Index